THE PERFECT SOLDIER

THE
PERFECT
SOLDIER

SPECIAL OPERATIONS, COMMANDOS,
AND THE FUTURE OF U.S. WARFARE

James F. Dunnigan

CITADEL PRESS
Kensington Publishing Corp.
www.kensingtonbooks.com

To the men who fight on the ground, be they infantry,
marines, or commandos. While you can win a battle
without fighting, you can't win without these guys.

CITADEL PRESS BOOKS are published by

Kensington Publishing Corp.
850 Third Avenue
New York, NY 10022

All Kensington titles, imprints, and distributed lines are available at special quantity
discounts for bulk purchases for sales promotions, premiums, fund-raising,
educational, or institutional use. Special book excerpts or customized printings can
also be created to fit specific needs. For details, write or phone the office of the
Kensington special sales manager: Kensington Publishing Corp., 850 Third Avenue,
New York, NY 10022, attn: Special Sales Department, phone 1-800-221-2647.

CITADEL PRESS and the Citadel logo are Reg. U.S. Pat. & TM Off.

All photos have been provided courtesy of the U.S. Department of Defense.

First printing: June 2003
10 9 8 7 6 5 4 3 2 1
Printed in the United States of America

Library of Congress Control Number: 2002116578
ISBN 0-8065-2415-4

AUTHOR'S NOTE

Operation Iraqi Freedom was a record-breaking operation in ways most people don't realize. Most startling was the low number of friendly casualties. Never had there been so few friendly losses in a campaign like this. The four U.S. and British divisions who did most of the work in the crucial first 21 days of the operation took seven combat casualties (dead, wounded, missing) per division per day. That's about one casualty per day for every 3,000 troops involved. The 1991 war, which involved more troops, ended with twelve casualties per division per day. That war lasted only five days—officially 100 hours. (The actual ground combat began nearly a day before the official start time, and there was some combat after the official end.)

What happened? It's called professional soldiers versus amateurs. The Afghanistan war was the same. With 8,000 coalition troops out in the field (not counting the peacekeepers in Kabul) for 17 months, the total combat casualties have yet to reach a hundred, with only 26 dead. That's one third the rate suffered in Iraq—mainly because a higher proportion of the troops in Afghanistan are commandos and the tempo of combat is lower.

One characteristic of commando operations is that if the plan is well executed, there will be few, if any, friendly casualties. Since many commando operations involve less than a dozen troops, and most involve less than a few dozen, any friendly casualties are going to take someone important out of the lineup. One man killed or wounded out of a dozen is an 8 percent casualty rate. An exception that proves the rule, the 1993 battle in Mogadishu, Somalia, was a commando operation gone wrong, and the casualties (102 out of 400 troops involved) were high. The U.S. forces were outnumbered about ten to one yet inflicted about ten casualties for every one they took. But the lesson of Somalia was that you don't go trying to be a peacekeeper when the other side wants to make war. What is generally forgotten about Mogadishu was that the Rangers wanted to go back in and finish off the Somali force that had mauled them, and the Somalis expected that with considerable dread. But President Clinton, not wanting a war, called the Rangers off and pulled them out.

In Afghanistan and Iraq, professional troops went in to win a war. And in both cases the American troops had all the advantages. But the biggest advantage was that the Americans were better trained, not just the soldiers manning the guns, but the officers planning and leading the operation and the far larger number of troops providing all manner of support. What happens when you go to war like that? Quick victory and low casualties. And it's not unique to America in the twenty-first century. Thousands of years of military history show the same thing happening over and over again. Yes, if you run up against a really tough opponent, you will take higher casualties. Still, the Afghans were tough—they drove the invading Russians out during the 1980s. This is where planning and leadership comes in (as well as the ability to pick fights carefully). The low losses against the formidable Afghans were largely a result of American tactics that made it difficult for the Afghans to use their advantages. Studying the Russian experience in the 1980s, American planners noted that the Afghans had the hardest time with Russian commandos (Spetsnaz) operating with lots of helicopters. In Afghanistan, they avoided letting the hostile Afghans fight on faborable terms.

The same approach was used with the Iraqis in 1991 and 2003. U.S. planners studied how the Iraqis operated and figured out what they would do if invaded. Actually, the Iraqi use of guerilla warfare in 2003 was not unanticipated. Unlike some others in the media, when I did my daily punditry in front of the camera, I simply pointed out that the guerilla attacks weren't working and explained why. Helicopter gunships or other aircraft were used to keep an eye on the route convoys were taking, as well as troops trained to deal with ambushes. If an area was too favorable for an ambush, the troops went around it. Other combat units went in and used better reconnaissance and fighting skills to methodically eliminate the irregulars. The bottom line was that the American casualty rate stayed low and U.S. troops got to Baghdad in less than three weeks. There were Iraqi guerillas, but they didn't matter.

There is so much you don't see in the media regarding military operations that is crucial to their success or failure. For example, behind-the-scenes reconnaissance (with aircraft, patrols, or electronic eavesdropping): It was inadequate in Mogadishu; in Afghanistan and Iraq, it wasn't. Working out plans that can deal with everything, including the unexpected, takes practice, training—and because of that, a massacre like the one in Mogadishu was prevented. Developing combat leaders, officers, and NCOs, however, takes decades. And you have to keep at it, for any screw-up in this training, even if only for a few years, will keep on hurting you ten years down the line with regard to troop training. Britain, the United States, and a few other nations have proved that they know this. It's no accident, however, and it's not a matter of luck. It's because it was decided, decades ago, to do things right.

CONTENTS

THE PERFECT SOLDIER

1 "SEND ME YOUR BEST MEN . . ."

Mention "commandos," "Special Operations," or "Special Forces" and most people will conjure up an image of musclebound supersoldiers blasting their way through hordes of inept enemy troops. That works in movies and novels, but the reality is quite different. And that's what this book is all about.

Perfect Soldiers are those who are trained, equipped, and led to a high standard. They are simply better than the opposition and tend to win quick victories, with fewer losses to themselves, even when outnumbered. Mention soldiers who fight like that and most people will think of commandos, those elite World War II troops whose real-life exploits provided generations of novelists with stunning story lines.

But commandos are nothing new. Historically, there have always been situations in which you needed exceptionally good troops for a special mission. That's what commandos are: the most capable troops sent to take care of the most difficult missions. Until a century ago, commandos were summoned with the phrase, "Send me your best men." The exploits of these exceptional warriors became part of many cultures, the warrior myths that were based on real exploits. These formidable warriors were seen as Perfect Soldiers, and often they were, even in the modern sense. This means well-trained and well-equipped fighters carrying out a carefully planned operation. The ancient sagas often include details making it clear that the hero was indeed well trained, well equipped, and quite thorough in his preparations.

1

Thus it's clear that the Perfect Soldier isn't a myth. For thousands of years, nations, tribes, and empires sought to create this perfect fighting machine. Few succeeded. Ancient Rome perfected the combination of selectiveness, training, good leadership, and long service to produce enough Perfect Soldiers to keep their empire going for a thousand years. The Romans were a major exception, though—most other armies then, and now, are unable to select and train troops to a consistently high standard. Why is it so hard to produce the Perfect Soldier? For one thing, these troops are expensive, and the training takes years to complete. As desirable as the Perfect Soldier is in wartime, he is often seen as an unnecessary expense in peacetime. And then there's the political angle. Kings and emperors often rest on very shaky thrones. They see enemies everywhere, and often it's not just paranoia. Most monarchs trace their power to an ambitious ancestor with a sharp sword. So creating a bunch of supersoldiers and keeping them handy ends up making a monarch nervous. Rome was a democracy, so the loyalty of the Perfect Soldiers was less of a problem.

When democracies became more common in the nineteenth century, the Perfect Soldier didn't become popular because there was still the expense problem. The alternative was the reserve system, in which nearly every young man was conscripted, given two or three years' training, and then put in the reserves for the next fifteen years or so. The reserve soldiers spent a few weeks each year keeping up on their military skills and were organized into units ready to go off to war on short notice. Nearly every major nation on the planet adopted the reserve system by the early twentieth century. After a century or so, it was realized that this system was more likely to get a lot of poorly trained soldiers killed faster than it was to ensure victory.

After World War II, nations began to notice that their best-trained professional soldiers were far more effective than their conscripts and reservists. By the end of the twentieth century, most industrialized nations had dropped conscription to rely on smaller, all-volunteer armed forces. Once politicians realized that the voters were willing to pay for a professional military, and were happy to see conscription disappear, the age of the Perfect Soldier became possible.

All professional military forces are not composed of Perfect Soldiers. What makes Perfect Soldiers happen is willingness to pay for the training—lots of training. And Perfect Soldiers have to be paid even more than your average volunteer soldier to keep them in uniform. It also helps if you equip your Perfect Soldiers with the best equipment. This is expensive. For a nation converting from a conscript (drafted) army to an all-volunteer force, it will cost three to four times as much per soldier. The difference is even more stark when you compare, say, the all-volunteer, high-tech U.S. armed forces to the Chinese conscript army. America spends (on average) seven hundred times more per soldier than does China. You get what you pay for.

In the early 1950s, the first two Perfect Soldier organizations appeared: the British SAS and the American Special Forces. Many nations also had airborne and marine units that were "nearly perfect" soldiers. The difference here was that the paratroopers and marines were composed mostly of young men who were only going to be in uniform three or four years. Although they were excellent at what they did, they could never catch up with commandos or Special Forces in the combat capabilities department.

During the 1980s, the U.S. military had enough money to undertake an intensive training program for the average combat soldier. No one knew how successful this was until the Gulf War came along. One of the little-heralded results of that war was the pleasant surprise officers and noncommissioned officers (NCOs) got when they saw how capable their well-trained young soldiers were in combat against the Iraqis. The public perception is that the Iraqis got blown away because they were a sad-sack bunch of second-rate fighters. There's something to that, but the main reason for the rapid Iraqi defeat was that the Americans were using an army of Perfect Soldiers.

Going into the twenty-first century, most professional military men are believers in the superiority of Perfect Soldiers. Even relatively poor nations such as China and Russia, which have long relied on large armies of less-than-perfect soldiers, are scraping together resources to produce more competent units. But most civilian leaders, and many voters, still don't get it. Politicians see the defense budget as peacetime pork, and money for training does not make good pork. Large weapons projects are what the porkmeisters are after, so we end up with a constant struggle between the generals (who want money to train the troops to higher standards) and the politicians (who want the money for pork-barrel projects that will help keep them in office).

While the skillful and effective use of U.S. Special Forces in Afghanistan impressed politicians, getting the money to train the rest of the armed forces to Special Forces standards is still a hard sell. The problems of getting Perfect Soldiers, and the examples of their superiority in combat, are ancient. Here we explain it all to you.

THINGS YOU NEED TO KNOW

For those who can't wait to read this entire book, don't have the time to, or are simply more comfortable with a headline version, here are some of its more useful points.

Special Operations Forces (SOF) is the term currently used to describe commandos, Raiders, Rangers, Spetsnaz, or Special Forces. They are Perfect Soldiers, as are many other troops who train to a standard that, a few decades ago, only commandos achieved.

- SOF are highly skilled infantry trained to operate quietly in small groups.
- In theory, small groups of well-prepared infantry should be much more efficient. In practice, many nations try to have it both ways and use these troops in large groups. Under such conditions they usually attract too much attention, and enemy firepower. These guys are good, but not bulletproof.
- SOF earn their keep when doing what they do best—raids, reconnaissance, and other special operations. These actions are expensive to support with the required aircraft, ships, and staging areas. Moreover, there are few of these tasks to be done compared to the more massive ground fighting found in a major war.
- As far back as the Vietnam War, small groups of commandos made themselves much more lethal by finding enemy positions and calling in air strikes and artillery. This tactic was repeated during the 2001 Afghanistan war. You can't win a war with this technique alone, though; you still need lots of infantry to go round up the enemy prisoners and occupy their territory.
- Special Operations troops are elite forces, small units of men carefully selected and intensively trained for the most difficult operations. Even among seemingly fit (physically and mentally) candidates, only 10 percent will make it through the one to three years of training required to produce a competent commando.

- The first commandos were exceptionally effective hunting bands (usually less than a dozen men, because more would scare the game away) who often exercised their skills on hostile humans.
- Special Operations troops are an ancient phenomenon. It's long been known that a few well-trained, well-led, and skillful troops can use a carefully planned attack to enormous effect.
- Every century for the past several thousand years has seen some commando-class units. But no one wrote down what it took to select and train commandos, so the process had to be constantly reinvented.
- What we think of as commandos were developed during World War I, the most memorable example being the German storm troopers.
- The need for commandos was seen early in World War II, first by the Germans and British. The United States formed six battalions of U.S. Army Rangers, as well as additional battalions of Marine Raiders, Navy Underwater Demolition Teams (UDTs), and such units as Merrill's Marauders in the Far East. The Germans formed their Brandenburg regiment, and the British basically wrote the book on commando operations while forming several different commando units: the Special Air Service (SAS), Special Boat Squadron (SBS), Long Range Desert Patrol, Popski's Private Army, and so on.
- After World War II, all commando units were disbanded, except for three battalions of British Royal Marine Commandos. But as the Cold War turned hot in 1950 (Korea, Malaya, elsewhere), the World War II SOF veterans were recalled, the SAS and Rangers reappeared, and the U.S. Special Forces were created. Some of the Navy UDT members were converted to Sea-Air-Land teams (SEALs).
- The U.S. Special Forces actually began as a psychological warfare operation, but switched to its current mission in the mid-1950s as American leaders realized that there was a major threat from communist guerrilla movements.
- The communists, especially the Chinese, invented what we now think of as guerrilla warfare. The United States invented, over several centuries of practice, the best methods for defeating guerrillas (but ignored that experience in Vietnam).
- The Vietnam War proved that commandos worked. Some 8 percent of the infantry in Vietnam were "Perfect Soldiers" (Special Forces,

LRRPs, or commandos), and they did a disproportionate amount of damage to the enemy.

- Today, the elite forces come in three flavors. First, there are the traditional commandos. The United States has Delta Force, Britain has the SAS, the Russians have their Spetsnaz, the Germans have KSK, and so on. Next come the large elite units. These used to be called "guards" units, because many of them were the elite units that guarded the king. The U.S. Marine Corps transformed itself into such an elite force as a way to avoid being disbanded. U.S. Army airborne divisions serve a similar function—as elite combat units— and were formed early in World War II after the successful use of German paratroopers was noted. The third category is a uniquely American one: the Special Forces. These fellows are a combination of commando and secret agent. First formed in the 1950s, they were meant to work with friendly (or potentially friendly) civilians in enemy territory.

- The Special Forces were first intended to operate in Eastern Europe, where the unpopularity of communist governments was expected to create people willing to fight as guerrillas, especially if the Soviet Union went to war with the North Atlantic Treaty Organization (NATO). This never happened, but there was Vietnam. South Vietnam was full of anticommunists, and the Special Forces did quite well among the tribal peoples of central Vietnam and, just to the west, in Laos. Beyond that, there weren't a lot of similar situations. But there were a lot of opportunities to provide military training in foreign countries, and it was found that the Special Forces were very good at this. It wasn't just that the Special Forces guys were knowledgeable soldiers and good instructors. Most important, the Special Forces were trained to relate to foreigners, and the foreign troops they trained really appreciated that. Still, the Special Forces are, first of all, elite infantry. When the war in Afghanistan broke out in 2001, the Special Forces were the first to go in, and they performed very well indeed.

- In Vietnam, Special Forces troops and regular infantry created numerous Long Range Reconnaissance Patrol (LRRP, pronounced *lurp*) units. The success of LRRPs in Vietnam led to the revival of the Rangers and the regular use of LRRP units. The Air Force also got into the game by upgrading and expanding units dedicated to rescuing downed pilots in enemy territory and parachuting into hot spots to provide target spotting for warplanes overhead.

- In response to increasing terrorist activity worldwide in the 1970s, the U.S. Army formed the 1st Special Forces Operational Detachment–Delta (SFOD-D) in 1977. Less well known is another unit formed about the same time, the Naval Special Warfare Development Group. SFOD-D came to be known as Delta Force and was basically an American version of the British SAS. The founder of Delta Force, Colonel Charles Beckwith, had served with the SAS (on an exchange program) in the early 1960s and long wanted to establish something similar in the United States.
- Unlike the SAS, which is constantly involved in operations that the British manage to keep secret (or at least out of the mass media), Delta has had opportunities to strut its stuff. Its first combat operation was in 1983 (Grenada), followed by Panama in 1989. Delta saw a lot of action during the Gulf War, and several Delta troopers were decorated for their work in Somalia in 1993. When the war in Afghanistan got under way, Delta Force was there.
- The United States has long maintained a huge force of elite infantry. Since the fall of the Soviet Union in 1991, the U.S. has the world's largest force of this type. This includes an airborne division, an airmobile division, and two divisions of Marines. Actually, American generals eventually discovered what the British have long known, that an all-volunteer force produces an overall level of excellence approaching that of the traditional elite units. This was seen during the 1991 Gulf War, in which all American ground units operated with a level of efficiency that startled even American brass. This despite the sometimes inept opposition by the Iraqi foe. Even the fairly good elite Iraqi units were quickly chopped up by American infantry and armor units. Military analysts in Moscow recognized what was going on in the Kuwaiti desert. Ever since the Soviet Union fell apart, Russian military reformers have been working to convince politicians that an all-volunteer force was the only way to go. Indeed, the trend is against conscription, with more and more nations dropping it and going for volunteer armed forces.
- The concept of volunteering for commando-type units is essential, for this type of service requires troops to train with an intensity that few people will tolerate. What made the noncommando units so

effective by the end of the twentieth century was the fact that so few people in the military were combat troops, so those who did seek out the kind of stimulation only combat operations provide gravitated to the elite units. There just aren't that many people in any society who have the physical, intellectual, and mental talents to be exceptional warriors. As the proportion of support troops began to outnumber the fighters in the course of the twentieth century, it became possible for the combat units to have a higher proportion of people who wanted to be there and were good at that sort of thing. Higher levels of health and education have also helped, for today's warriors have to handle a lot of technology, and they need robust health to endure the grueling, 24/7 pace of combat operations. While this selectivity has produced superior "regular" combat units, it has produced some spectacular commando outfits. And the reason for all this excellence is the same for both regular and elite units. It comes down to careful selection of the volunteers, years of constant and effective training, plus good leadership.

- Modern commando units are so effective because they have larger populations (of healthier people) to choose from and more efficient screening techniques to ensure that they get only the most capable people. Training methods are also much better. By historical standards, the current crop of commandos are the best to ever exist.
- Modern commandos are also allowed to select their own equipment. The quirky gadget master "Q" in the James Bond films is based on fact. During World War II, the first commandos began the tradition of getting the right tools for the job, especially if the armed forces didn't have what they needed. This tradition continues.
- Technology (computers, spy satellites, cell phones) has made it possible for commandos to more carefully plan their operations. This usually ensures that they can surprise their opponent, and surprise is always the most powerful weapon a military force can have.
- The United States has the largest force of commandos in the world. Some forty-six thousand troops are assigned to the American Special Operations Command (SOCOM). Only about a quarter of these men (they are largely men) are "operators"—troops that go out armed, into harm's way. The rest of the SOCOM personnel provide support. Most of this has to do with transportation and firepower support. There are also a lot of "Q" types supplying special equip-

ment, as well as communications geeks who ensure that the operators stay in touch wherever they are. The SOCOM also contains
Civil Affairs units (to deal with foreign civilians when the shooting
has stopped) and Psychological Warfare (propaganda and information war) units. The cutting edge of SOCOM is a Ranger regiment
(three battalions), seven Special Forces groups (twenty-one battalions) plus Delta Force (a small battalion), and nine SEAL teams
(equaling two small battalions). The Air Force provides a lot of specialized aircraft but also has a few hundred commando-grade troops
who can get on the ground and do really useful stuff.

- A major difference between today's commandos and those of the
  past is the much more intensive selection, training, and use of special technology. Even through World War II, most commandos were
  quickly selected (from volunteers), given some extra training (often
  only a few months), and sent off on special missions. Success was
  usually a matter of careful preparation for each mission and capable
  leaders. This led to many successes, some spectacular failures, and
  the feeling that "special operations forces" were something that
  would become a permanent part of most nations' armed forces.

- While commandos have become better trained, equipped, and more
  effective over the last half century, so have all the other combat
  troops. The trend has been to create all-volunteer armed forces full
  of Perfect Soldiers. It's expensive, but if you can afford it, it works.

AFGHANISTAN AND THE PERFECT SOLDIERS

Things always look easy when pros are doing them, whether this be
playing a piano, creating some really useful software, or pitching a no-
hitter. But it's not that easy at all. Becoming a competent professional
takes years of practice by people who have a talent worth improving
in the first place. The success of the Perfect Soldier in Afghanistan
was the result of new developments in many areas.

The revolution in air war control. AWACS aircraft (introduced in
the 1980s) made it possible for bombers to be over Afghanistan 24/7.
The AWACS concept has been in development for nearly sixty years.

Well-trained commandos. The Special Forces were on the ropes
after Vietnam because many senior generals did not like the idea of
commandos. But some did, and the idea caught on with many elected

leaders (presidents Kennedy and Reagan, for example). Special Forces survived attempts to eliminate them. SEAL forces were expanded, Delta Force was created, and eventually Special Operations Command and lots of specialized support from the Air Force came along. Without all that, there would not have been enough commandos to support the Special Forces, nor the specialized aircraft needed to move everyone around Afghanistan. It looked easy; it wasn't.

Experienced and battle-tested Special Forces troops. After Vietnam, the Special Forces had few supporters in the Army. Elsewhere, however, in the Department of Defense and other parts of the government (the Central Intelligence Agency and State Department in particular), there was support for the Special Forces. By the late 1970s, Special Forces strength had declined from a 1960s high of nine thousand down to two thousand. In the 1980s, the Special Forces were given more money and more than doubled in size. While only a few hundred Special Forces troops were needed to defeat the Taliban in two weeks, a far larger number were needed in order to have those with the specific language skills to work in Afghanistan.

Smarter bombs. Smart bombs were invented, and first used, during World War II. They were good enough back then to sink ships and knock down bridges, but not to provide the kind of close support provided to the Northern Alliance in Afghanistan. By 2001, smart bombs had become accurate and dependable enough to frighten even the battle-hardened religious fanatics fighting for the Taliban. It's the norm for a "revolutionary new weapon" to take half a century to become really effective.

More accurate reconnaissance. Drones (small, unpiloted aircraft that can circle for hours taking pictures) and JSTARS (larger aircraft with a radar that can pick up vehicles on the ground hundreds of miles away) made a murky situation a lot clearer. Both systems benefited from several decades of development and a lot of trial and error.

Satellite communications (SatCom). While recon satellites were not all they were cracked up to be, communications satellites were another matter. Recon satellites are in orbit and can take digital pictures of anyplace on earth as they pass overhead (several times a day). That info is not current enough to be really useful for the Special Forces. But the explosive increase in communications satellites—there are several hundred of them up there now—made possible all sorts of useful services. Satellite phones were essential for Special Forces and commandos. The Department of Defense "bought" (it was a complicated deal) the bankrupt Iridium satellite phone system in 2000, enabling it to provide lots of satellite phones and cheap rates (twenty-five cents a minute) to its troops. The Department of Defense was not able to get enough cheap satellite time to handle all the real-time video coming off the drones and spy satellites, but there was enough to get by. SatCom has been growing in importance since the 1970s. But in Afghanistan it was an essential component of the war-winning formula.

Agile diplomats and CIA agents. Like the Special Forces and commandos, the State Department and CIA like to work in the shadows. But both were essential players in the rapid victory over the Taliban. Afghanistan is landlocked and surrounded by nations that are, more often than not, hostile to the United States. This undoubtedly made many Taliban members think they were immune to any meaningful attack by America. But American diplomats promptly worked out deals to use airspace and bases in Pakistan and other nations to the north of Afghanistan. The CIA has been in the area all along, quietly developing contacts and sorting out who was who. This proved crucial when it came time to make deals with the Pushtun tribes in southern Afghanistan, and get most of them to rise up against the Taliban—or at least remain neutral.

Civil Affairs and Psyops (Psychological Warfare) units trained and ready to go. These two functions have long operated in the background, but the United States is one of the few nations to maintain a substantial number of units for this kind of work. This proved useful during the Gulf War, and crucial during the Afghanistan war.

The color purple. A major shortcoming of U.S. armed forces has long been rivalry among the services. But over the last twenty years, there has been a major effort to "think purple"—that is, to put aside rivalries and do what's best for the war effort. Combine the colors of each service's uniforms and you get a shade of purple. Like interservice cooperation, it ain't pretty, but it works. In Afghanistan, the Air Force shared its aerial tankers with the Navy and the Navy provided a carrier for Army Special Forces helicopters. The Army integrated Air Force controllers and Navy SEALs into the ground operations. Without all this cooperation, victory would not have been as swift, or decisive.

A HISTORY OF INNOVATION AND MILITARY EFFECTIVENESS

The development of the unique commando tactics seen in Afghanistan should not be surprising. Europe, and later the United States, has regularly introduced military innovations over the last seven hundred years. Other parts of the world have come up with innovations over the past few thousand years (China invented the crossbow, stirrups, and gunpowder), but once the Europeans got going at high speed four hundred years ago, the rest of the world gradually fell far behind in military capability. Often noted, but little discussed, this phenomenon has persisted to the present. This is why Western nations have most of the commandos and most of the useful commando gadgets.

It's not just a talent for war; the West has had an edge with innovation in many other areas as well—politics, engineering, entertainment, and religion. Until about four centuries ago, however, the West was as likely to borrow innovations from elsewhere as it was to come up with its own. But then things began to change with increasing rapidity. At first it was seemingly minor things. Germans reintroduced the cadenced step and invented the iron ramrod. Then bayonets and new forms of artillery were developed. More effective military organizations were implemented (first the brigade, then divisions and corps). The use of formal military staffs was developed, but constantly improved, like all previous inventions. By the nineteenth century, nearly all military innovations were coming from the West. During the 1930s, some non-Western innovations did occur. The Japanese developed the larger "long-lance" torpedo and better tactics to go with it. But the special torpedo tactics used in their Pearl Harbor attack were borrowed from a similar British attack on an Italian naval base a year earlier. The Japanese also showed how valuable hard, and well-thought-out, training could be. This was the main reason for their early victories in 1942. But it was Britain that developed the aircraft carrier, and an American who invented the modern submarine. Radar, nuclear weapons, military computers, communications satellites, guided missiles, and smart bombs and bombers were all Western inventions.

The concept of professional soldiers is ancient, but developing training and evaluation techniques to ensure that the professionals are effective is yet another Western innovation. Even the current tactics and techniques of loosely organized terrorist organizations were invented in Europe during the late nineteenth century.

Innovation is a weapon, and for thousands of years it has proved itself the most decisive weapon. Today's Islamic terrorism was derived from Soviet terrorist training manuals and European political philosophers. Most Western innovations are exported, and some come back to haunt us.

Western nations not only have an edge in developing new ideas first, but also have the money to recruit, train, maintain, and lavishly equip more commandos than anyone else. One innovation that is still in the works concerns new ways to use commandos. We'll all know what this means once it has played itself out. Meanwhile, we will see greater use of commandos and Perfect Soldiers by the nations that can afford it.

2 COMMANDOS THROUGH HISTORY

Commandos are an ancient military tool, but in the past they were selected quite differently than they are today. No matter. They were used much as they are today, for desperate situations requiring exceptional soldiers to deal with them.

FELLOWSHIPS AND ROYAL GUARDS

For thousands of years, successful military leaders ordered subordinates to "send me your best men" for particularly difficult tasks. Often, commanders already had several hundred of their best men employed as personal bodyguards. This was not being overprotective; until a couple of centuries ago, an army commander would often have to charge into a critical part of the battle himself or risk defeat. In this case, the quality of his personal bodyguard was a matter of life and death. Out of this practice came the establishment of "guards" units. The king (who was often the head of the army) paid careful attention to how his personal ("royal") guard was selected, equipped, and trained. These men protected the king in war and peace, so their loyalty, as well as their ability, was critical. This combination of qualities made the guardsmen natural candidates for special jobs, although some of these tasks might involve murder or kidnapping. But, come to think of it, some contemporary commandos have also been called on to do that sort of thing.

Some twenty-five hundred years ago we have the example of these royal guards in the Persian emperor's "Immortals" (so called because whenever a member of the ten-thousand-man unit died, a replacement was promptly provided). Another example was the several hundred horsemen who stayed close to the Persian empire's archenemy, Alexander the Great. These men—called, not unnaturally, the Companions—were hard fighters and selected for their ability to keep up with Alexander, who was often seen charging into the most critical (and usually most dangerous) part of a battle.

The Persian emperor's Immortals were not the kind of outfit from which you were likely to get commandos. There were thousands of them, selected for loyalty and reliability rather than their combat skills. Alexander, on the other hand, worried less about betrayal and more about competence. His Companion cavalrymen were often called on to perform special missions.

LEGENDS AND REALITY

While the names of fighters in the Immortals or the Companions have not been left to us, other early commandos have entered popular legend. The semifictional King Arthur's Knights of the Round Table, for example, were another form of royal guard. In this case, the knights were the king's closest companions, a group commonly called a fellowship. King Arthur wasn't real, but the way his key knights were used was. Today, when you see a celebrity's entourage or, in a more basic form, a gang, you're seeing the legacy of the medieval fellowship. The fellowship was an ancient custom whereby powerful warriors collected about themselves people they were comfortable with and when they could depend on. And in battle, or when there was danger of assassination or kidnapping, the guys in the fellowship were expected to protect their patron.

These fellowships, however, were more than bodyguards. They also undertook commando missions. Out of them came one of those standards of adventure fiction (and nonfiction): the quest. Some of the oldest literary works known to man describe these adventures, whether it be to find the Promised Land, the Holy Grail, a magical object, the monster Grendel, a secret of some kind, or the Golden Fleece. These quests are basically commando operations. What we now call a quest, or commando operation, goes back to the hunting party, or a group of explorers looking for better farmland or pastures. In any event, going on risky missions that often involved combat against heavy odds became something much admired. For thousands of years, these tales were passed down as oral tradition. Those that survived to get written down are now considered classics of literature and, in some cases, holy books.

One well-known example of a commando mission took place more than three thousand years ago, when a handful of Greeks hidden in a wooden horse were left outside the gates of Troy. The Trojans, believing that the Greek Army had given up its siege and was sailing away, thought the wooden horse was a way of acknowledging the Trojan victory. The Trojans hauled the horse into the city and held a great celebration. Then, while everyone was sleeping that off, the hidden Greek troops quickly killed the few Trojan guards, opened the city gates, and let the returned Greek Army in. This was a classic commando operation. Had any of the Greeks in the horse made a noise or moved around, their presence would have been given away and they would have been killed.

For thousands of years, the lure of the quest led a lot of enthusiastic men to their deaths. Most of these adventures ended in dismal failures, giving the vultures and jackals a free meal and accomplishing little else. You don't hear too much about this, except in some of the oral traditions describing how one band of adventurers wasted someone else's. Military recruiters have long used the appeal of "the adventure of a lifetime" to attract young men for war. And even though every village and neighborhood had its share of soldiers who had gone off and never came back, there were still some who thought they could beat the odds.

The reality of commando operations as finally codified in the twentieth century, however, was that you could only survive these high-risk operations if you were extremely selective about who joined the team, and equally diligent in your training and planning of operations. Until the twentieth century, this knowledge, while not unknown, proved highly perishable. At any given time in the past there was, somewhere, a sharp fellow who realized that if he chose the best men, trained them hard, and then carefully thought out what to do with them, he would succeed more often than not. But this brings up another aspect of commando operations: You really only get to fail once. Since commandos tend to go deep into enemy territory, or up against large odds, the price of failure is often death. So for centuries, people didn't think of commandos as a special type of military unit, but rather a bunch of heroes, blessed by the gods to be ever victorious. At least until they weren't. Even then, however, you got some great stories with which to entertain the kids.

PRIMARY GROUPS

Another characteristic of commandos is that they tend to operate in small groups, usually no more than a dozen men. Research into how soldiers fought during World War II reveals that the key to combat success was the "primary group" comprised of from half a dozen to a dozen troops. The more skillful, coordinated, and loyal to each other they were, the more effective their primary group was. Commandos learned to enhance the effect of the primary group as much as possible, making sure that all members of each squad knew and trusted each other's abilities. Many commando operations depend on only one, or a few, of these squad-sized groups.

Making a dozen men into a successful primary group depends on establishing trust among them. Everyone talks about "teamwork" and its positive effects, but putting together a good team, as any sports fan knows, isn't easy. Moreover, combat teams have a hard time training for what they will actually do when they go into harm's way. In the past, successful commandos tended to be people who spent a lot of time hunting, or had plenty of combat experience. Today, that experience is replicated by well-thought-out exercises that accomplish the same thing. But until the twentieth century, few military commanders realized that this was an alternative to hiring small groups of warlike hunters to perform dangerous missions.

Even though ancient armies soon found that large masses of archers, spearmen, and cavalry were superior to small hunting bands, these larger groups still drew their strength from the smaller groups of men that made up the larger groups. Even the Romans, who fought in large (but highly disciplined) groups, divided their five-thousand-man legions into eight-man squads. The squad members knew each other well and took care of one other in and out of combat.

Although the infantry squad is thought of as a twentieth-century invention, it actually goes way back. Of course there was the hunting party, which had to be small lest a larger crowd scare all the game away. During the thousand-year period when knights ruled the battlefield in Europe, the basic unit was the "banner," consisting of the knight (whose banner displayed the knight's coat of arms), a squire or two (a less well-equipped knight in training), one or more armed commoners ("men at arms") to help keep the knight alive in combat, plus some servants who would only join the fight if there was a siege. All members of the banner looked out for each other; they were selected for compatibility and the ability to work together. Like any other squad, they lived or died according to how well they performed as a group.

What makes a good squad into commandos is the ability to travel undetected, and this brings us back to the origins of commandos as hunters.

HUNTERS AND COMMANDOS

That these small groups are so important in warfare should come as no surprise. A primary group is basically a hunting party. While mankind grew and created advanced cultures based on success at agriculture, man was always a hunter. Okay, before agriculture was invented, most humans got along as "hunter-gatherers"—most of the food came from the gathering of edibles out in the bush. There are still a few hunter-gatherer cultures left that can be studied, and some anthropologists were surprised when they discovered that hunting brought in the minority share of calories. Not that hunting is just a sport for these cultures. Without the game trapped or killed, food supplies would be smaller, and the youngest and oldest members of the tribe might starve. Moreover, hunting is almost always a male thing, and there is a competitive aspect to it. The best hunters attract the best-looking women and eat better (they get the choice bits from what they kill). The women stay at home, gathering the bulk of the family's calories and inventing agriculture.

Apparently the women don't mind the men going off to hunt. It keeps them out of their hair and brings in something edible, and different, from time to time. But these bush skills also provide a means to detect and deal with predators (lions, large bears, and hostile tribes) that hunt humans. Primitive tribes are sophisticated enough to make war on each other, and from the very beginning, hunting was practice for war. Hunting skills are what commandos need to survive in enemy territory. A good hunter can track prey over all sorts of ground and not be detected while doing it. The first wars were feuds between different groups of hunters. The men stalked each other, and the less skilled got killed (and sometimes eaten).

While ancient warfare got away from the tactics used by the hunting party, this was not always the case. The most successful army in all history was that of the Mongols. In less than two centuries, the Mongol forces conquered everything from Eastern Europe to China, northern Russia to Thailand. Mongol combat methods were adapted from techniques used in hunting.

Hunting was a serious business to the Mongols. Strict discipline was taken for granted, and the leader of the hunt could enforce obedience with harsh punishments. This was carried over to Mongol warfare. The Mongols institutionalized this traditional discipline throughout their entire army, adapting it to local customs as needed. The Mongols were able to use their hunting techniques in their warfare because they generally operated on the vast plains of Eurasia. Their armies approached and defeated enemy forces the same way a hunting party would go after a small herd of deer. The Mongol armies moved quickly, while using deception and tight coordination to surround, confuse, and eventually destroy their opponents.

Guerrilla warfare also goes back to the hunting party for its tactics and methods, as do commandos. But in getting from there (ancient hunting parties) to here (twenty-first-century combat), a lot of commando outfits throughout the history of warfare have developed techniques that are still useful today. For example, basic bushcraft skills such as tracking, camouflage, and the ability to strike fast are still taught to commando recruits. Animals that have a lot of predators either become hard to catch or become extinct, as do successful guerrillas. Commandos, at least the successful ones, keep this in mind as they hone their skills.

THE HEROES OF LEGEND WERE REAL

The original commandos were expert and effective hunting parties who also engaged in the occasional raid on their human neighbors.

Some of the spectacular exploits of these groups still get passed down orally in those few hunting cultures that continue to exist. These stories all contain the same elements: exceptional hunting skills by all members of the party, excellent leadership by the guy in charge of the group, and much derring-do and risk taking. These people still exist. They are the "tribal warriors" who show up so frequently in both history books and the daily news.

This is the sort of warfare practiced in Afghanistan to this day. In the 1980s, the Russians had a hard time dealing with the Afghan habit of going into battle as a "hunting party." The Russians were trained to deal with an enemy that was controlled by one commander and used a supply system. Afghan hunting parties had neither. Each small group of Afghans was on its own and scrounged its own supplies. The Russians responded with their own hunting parties (using Spetsnaz commandos) to counter the Afghans. Eventually, however, the Russians got tired of fighting the Afghans and left the country. A similar situation occurred in Somalia in the 1990s. The better-equipped peacekeepers eventually left, even though they could have easily killed off all the Somali "hunting parties" they encountered.

American history is full of hunting parties that were successful in war. The American Revolution (1770s), the Civil War (1860s), and the Indian wars (1860–1900) all saw success going to small groups of fighters. During the Revolution, guerrilla groups in New York, New Jersey, and the southern states all drove the British nuts. In the South (the Carolinas and Georgia), the rebellious guerrillas eventually beat the British regular troops. The British had noted, before the Revolution, that many Americans were enthusiastic hunters and spent much of their time in the wilderness. The British also noted how the Americans had used their hunting skills to their advantage in combat during the earlier wars with the French and Indians. Most British officers thought this American skill would not amount to much in a "real war." In practice, however, American hunters controlled the roads between British-occupied towns and cities, making it difficult to feed troops and keep them supplied. The situation was so acute that the British had to bring much of the food for their troops from England. Trying to get food from the farmland surrounding New York City meant facing constant ambush and harassment from American raiding parties.

Americans in the eighteenth century were not tribal warriors, but there was still the threat of hostile Indians operating outside the few big cities (Boston, New York, Philadelphia). As a result, there was an active militia, especially outside the cities. The abundance of game made hunting a popular pastime and an economical way to supplement the diet. Thus Americans were unique in that they had access to the most modern weapons of the day (muskets and cannon) and regular practice at operating (hunting) in wilderness areas. The militia's training—and there wasn't a lot of it—was devoted to fighting formal battles (lining up and shooting at massed enemy infantry), but most militiamen also knew how to move stealthily through forests, or anywhere else, and get a shot off at a target, be it a white-tailed deer, an Indian, or a British soldier.

TRIBAL COMMANDOS

Tribal warriors have a lot of skills that commandos can use, and often some tribesmen are trained to be commandos. About 10 percent of the eighteenth-century American Rangers, for example, were Indians recruited for that duty. On their own, however, tribal fighters are a mixed bag. The best of them, especially a crew of very good tribal warriors, can make life difficult if you're fighting them. Even the most inept of tribal warriors know a lot about tracking people through the bush, staying hidden, and surviving in what looks like a wilderness. Tribal hunters are exceptionally good at ambushing more civilized warriors and avoiding superior firepower and helicopters. Fortunately, tribal forces do not take advantage of their most skilled members. Tribal military forces are very informal affairs.

The biggest problem tribal warriors have is that they rarely operate with large groups of fighters. Their most successful "units" are hunting parties. Coordination or cooperation among hunting parties is not much practiced or used. Tribal warriors are, by definition, undisciplined and individualistic. Think of tribal warriors as a sports league, where each team (crew of a dozen or so warriors) is out to score more points against the enemy than the other tribal crews. War for most tribal groups is considered a form of recreation, and an opportunity to build a reputation and become more attractive to women. Tribesmen are often insulted when soldiers from industrialized countries come by and make war as if it were a business, not a competitive sport.

Still, among some tribes there developed the idea of an elite crew. In ancient America, and through the end of the Indian wars a century ago, some tribes had elite hunting parties. Warriors competed to demonstrate their prowess so that they would be selected to join the elite group. These highly skilled groups would often undertake commando-type operations, such as stealthy raids to steal an enemy tribe's horses. This tradition is found in most tribal cultures. But the tribes rarely developed military leaders who thought to use their elite groups for militarily useful operations.

SEND ME YOUR BEST MEN FOR A SPECIAL MISSION

Armies developed when mankind shifted to agriculture and building cities some six to eight thousand years ago, and along with them came more interest in strategy and tactics. This led to interest in using brains instead of brawn to win battles. Several thousand years ago, military writers began to note that a battle won without fighting was a lot cheaper and less risky. While many of the great generals simply used various deceptions and fancy maneuvers to defeat their enemies, there were times when a little muscle, applied in the right place, was needed to gain a victory. This called for what we now refer to as commando operations. But the idea of special commando units, constantly pulling off special operations, didn't appear until the twentieth century. Thus for thousands of years, the general wishing to pull off commando operations would ask his subordinates to "send me your best men."

In this way, impromptu commando operations were organized. Missions often involved scouting deep into enemy territory, or special assaults on fortresses (seizing a gate via deception, coming in via the water supply, and so on). Attacks on walled cities or castles were often successful only because of some commando-type operations. Getting over the walls successfully usually involved having a small group of men who were particularly agile and good fighters. Movable towers and other machines were often used in a successful siege, but it all came down to getting those first few men over the wall, making it possible for more attacking troops to follow. Not every army besieging a fortress was able to put together a commando team for this work. As a result, those who made the attempt were often called the "Forlorn Hope." Translation: "You poor devils are probably going to die trying."

A more survivable form of pre-twentieth-century commando work was riding out to find the enemy before he found you—in other words, scouting. For good reason, many light cavalry units were regarded with the same awe now accorded commandos. The light cavalry, used mainly for this scouting, tended to attract the kind of quick-thinking and tough individuals who succeed in modern commando units. Americans early on (during the colonial period) learned the value of hiring Indians to help with the scouting. This had the benefit of allowing the non-Indian members of a unit to learn better scouting techniques. This approach was carried over to foreign wars Americans were involved in. The most successful American commando operations during the Vietnam War were long-range Studies and Observation Group (SOG) patrols in which the majority of the troops were local tribal volunteers.

Spying, assassinations, and kidnappings of key enemy personnel have also been typical "commando" operations for thousands of years. All of these are still typical tasks for elite forces. In the past, the people to whom these crucial jobs were given were those who had proven themselves. Often, they were mercenaries who followed the money and went to great lengths to maintain anonymity. This has always been a tricky business—you often want these jobs done without any chance of being tagged as the mastermind. Since this was all a shady business to begin with, not much has survived in the written records about who did what and how they prepared for it. But there were obviously some capable commando-type people available throughout history, for the results of their work (spectacular espionage, assassinations, or kidnappings) were recorded.

ARMIES OF COMMANDOS

The lack of separate commando units was often due to monetary, political, and cultural restraints. Maintaining commando units was expensive, and until the last few centuries these armies were usually touch and go in terms of financing. It wasn't until the Industrial Revolution of the nineteenth century that nations had enough money to maintain large armed forces on a regular basis. Commando-class troops are even more expensive to create and keep on the payroll. You really don't need them much unless there's a war going on. But there are other reasons as well. Commandos were (and still are) capable of removing a king from power. In the past, there weren't a lot of police and secret police organizations to detect and prevent such operations. So it didn't benefit a king to have an elite military organization sitting around, getting bored, and perhaps developing ideas about staging a coup. Kings and emperors had enough trouble making sure their royal bodyguards stayed loyal. Another problem was that, in wartime, when the word went out to "send me your best men," many of them were the sons of nobles or commanders of military units who didn't want to spend any more time than necessary in a temporary, and quite dangerous, organization.

Another form of ancient commando organization we are seeing reappear today is entire armies comprised of elite troops. It was organizations like this that enabled kingdoms and empires to survive for centuries. Without an elite military force, empires could still survive with a large number of lesser-quality troops, and most ancient empires did just this. But an elite group of troops tended to be easier to control. As long as you made sure the elite troops were paid, you didn't have to worry about what the people thought. With a mass army, however, a period of unpopularity among the population could be fatal for the emperor. The earliest of these "armies of commandos" were the "heavy horse." We think of these as medieval knights, but such forces appeared more than a thousand years before Europeans came up with the idea.

The major problem with raising an army of knights was money. Horses are expensive to maintain, and the soldier riding the horse had to devote most of his time to learning how to fight on horseback, and then maintaining those skills. Under the feudalism system of the Middle Ages, a king gave each knight enough land and farmers to support the knight and his family. This system developed before there were knights, simply as a way to control a large area and be able to get troops when needed. Warriors were given control over a village in return for always being ready to go to war for their overlord (king, prince, whatever). But eventually, exceptionally effective mounted warriors came along. The first of these evolved in modern-day Iran some twenty-five hundred years ago. Although lacking stirrups (a special saddle was used to keep the knight on the horse when fighting), these men had armor and used a lance, sword, and, most important, bow. We know these warriors as the Parthians (an Iranian tribe). By the time the Romans ran into them twenty-two hundred years ago, they had also developed plate armor (which wasn't seen in Western Europe until the fourteenth century). These well-armed mounted warriors were known in the East as cataphracts, and eventually the Romans adopted this type of soldiering, as well as feudal distribution of land to pay for it. Actually, only the eastern portion of the Roman army raised cataphract units. The western portion of the Roman empire fell apart in the fifth century. The eastern, or Byzantine, portion of the Roman empire lasted until the 1400s primarily because it had one of the more efficient fighting forces.

The mainstay of the Byzantine army was that Middle Eastern version of the medieval knight, the cataphract. The Byzantine cataphract had stirrups and plate armor, and was equipped with a very powerful bow, a lance, a heavy sword, a shield (with three heavy and fairly deadly darts behind it), and sometimes even an ax. These men could fight mounted or dismounted. They could also use a bow either way. All this made for a pretty deadly combination and probably the most effective of the medieval warriors. But because of the expense, the Byzantines could never maintain enough of them. This reminds us that commandos can help win a war, but they can't fight it all by themselves.

Armored horsemen weren't the only type of elite, and expensive, army. Some twenty-four hundred years ago, Philip of Macedon managed to unite Greece, at spearpoint, by finding a way to pay for an army of well-trained and -equipped infantry. Philip did this by seizing some lucrative gold mines and using his army to run a large-scale extortion racket in Greece. Philip's son, the conqueror Alexander the Great, found that he couldn't afford to meet the army payroll; that was one of the reasons he went off and invaded the (much wealthier) Persian Empire. A century later, the Romans figured out a better way to pay for a professional army: taxes, plus a share of the loot from defeated opponents. Eventually the Romans ran out of money, however, and lost their elite army. Fighters gathered together quickly in an emergency were not able to keep the empire going, at least the western part of it.

Never lose sight of the fact that exceptionally good soldiers are professionals, and professionals have to be paid. Otherwise they go off and serve someone else.

WHEN BEING THE BEST ISN'T GOOD ENOUGH

For about a thousand years, highly trained and very expensive knights were the foundation of military power in Europe. But this demonstrated another limitation of commandos. If everyone has an elite fighting force, no one (except the side with larger numbers, or much better leadership) has an advantage. There were three striking examples of how this worked during the past.

The Mongols arrived in Eastern Europe in the thirteenth century. A huge army of knights from Hungary and Poland was assembled to stop them. Nevertheless, the Mongols won. They actually would have kept moving west had it not been for political problems back home that caused them to withdraw. How did the Mongols beat the knights of Eastern Europe? They had better organization and leadership, and they used mounted archers (which the Europeans had never adopted). The Mongols also had heavy cavalry—perhaps not as good, man for man, as the European knights, but good enough when part of a better army. The problem with European knights was that, unless led by a very good leader, they didn't operate in a very disciplined fashion. It was like herding cats. Knights worked on their own, while the Mongols operated like a disciplined army.

Unfortunately, European knights learned nothing from their unpleasant encounter with the Mongols, and they attributed it to God's will that the heathens departed and never returned. It took another, this time homegrown, lesson for Europeans to learn the practicality of the Mongols' war methods. During the Hundred Years' War (1337–1453), England almost conquered France. At the time, France had a population three times that of England. How did English troops manage to rampage around France for more than a century? By having a larger pool of higher-quality troops. England also had a lock on longbowmen (yeomen), who made excellent infantrymen and light cavalrymen as well. Thus the English had mobility and quality advantages. The English also had an edge in leadership and tactics, all the result of their own recent history.

For more than two centuries before the Hundred Years' War, the English had been engaged in constant warfare in Wales, Scotland, and Ireland. As a result, they had developed a professional military force using part-time soldiers. Unlike the rest of Europe, where the nobility attempted to monopolize military service, the English had a large number of well-off farmers who were willing to train on their own and serve as longbowmen and light infantry. This training was organized, and the longbowmen were gathered into units of a hundred archers. The system took most of the thirteenth century to evolve. England had very few knights (less than a thousand), but lots of trained commoners who would serve the king for pay and the prospect of pillage. The English troops were disciplined and trained well to do their jobs—a sharp contrast to the unruly mobs of feudal warriors commonly found on the Continent. The English also had superior leadership. Many of the English military commanders were excellent. Edward III and his son Edward the Black Prince, for example, were among the most capable of the medieval generals.

France, on the other hand, had to contend with poor generalship. The French looked down on armed commoners, but this was not the case with the English nobles, who often entered service as commoners and worked their way up. Late in the Hundred Years' War the French did develop some good generals, and the English ran out of exceptional commanders. The French also fortified most of central France (at horrendous expense), making it more difficult for the English to live off the land and provide enough pillage to attract large numbers of those still-superior English men-at-arms and yeomen. The French thus wore the English down—sort of like Napoleon or the Germans going into Russia, only in slow motion.

Before the English lost the war, however, they demonstrated how some kinds of elite troops can defeat other types of elite troops by being smarter and more practical. European knights, having long forgotten the Mongols by the fourteenth century, had enjoyed centuries as a preeminent military power (aside from a larger army of knights). When this new English Army came along, the results were, well, shocking. For one thing, the English Army was composed mostly of well-organized and disciplined archers. The English appointed "officers" (in the modern sense of the term), and the French marveled at how the English soldiers obeyed their officers. The odd behavior of the English, however, didn't end there. The English rarely fought mounted; they used their horses mainly for transportation. France was a larger country with far more knights than the English, and the French were sure this gave them an insurmountable advantage. But the English used a technique typical of all successful commandos: They didn't fight the way the enemy expected them to. Moreover, the English took advantage of what the French knights thought was their own biggest asset: the massed charge of thousands of knights. The English archers would form a line, pound pointed stakes into the ground in front of them, and then let loose with thousands of arrows. These English archers didn't fire straight at the French, but up, at an angle, so the plunging arrows hit more of the French horses. The French quickly learned that you could not launch a cavalry charge against this. No problem, thought the French, we'll come at them on foot. But that was slower, giving the archers more time to work the French knights over with their arrows. Then the French discovered that the English archers were also good infantry, and had worked out excellent tactics for going after heavily armored knights on foot. The preferred weapon of the archers was what we would today call a kind of sledgehammer. Applying one to the side of a French knight's helmet would knock the poor fellow unconscious, or at least make him incapable of doing much for a few minutes. Another archer would then go in with a sharp knife and slide it between one of the gaps in the armor. Why didn't the knights gang up and rush the archers? Because they were dead tired after trudging several hundred yards, often in summer heat, while being shot at with armor-piercing arrows.

We don't often think of these medieval "yeoman archers" as commandos, but in many cases that's what they were. By law, English farmers holding a certain amount of land were required to regularly undergo military training (mainly archery). When the king needed troops for operations in France, he would hire the best of these part-time warriors. The pay was good; also, the yeomen knew they were among professionals and that the prospects of getting rich from loot and ransomed French knights were excellent.

What ultimately destroyed the concept of knights was not the bow. There were never enough yeomen archers to seriously threaten all the knights in Europe. What did kill feudalism was a weapon that had gone out of favor more than a thousand years earlier. This was the pike, and it was first used in the thirteenth century by Swiss farmers and herdsmen who were tired of being oppressed by German knights. The pike is a long spear—up to eighteen feet long. You would have men holding these pikes in multiple ranks (a dozen or more) in such a way that the front rank had a wall of spearheads in front of it. Simple, yet effective—but it requires great discipline and practice to pull off. The Swiss practiced moving around quickly in these formations, so mounted knights couldn't hit them in the flank. Since the pikemen weren't wearing much armor, they could take off running in these formations and go crashing into enemy infantry (or horsemen) with devastating effect. From the fourteenth century until guns and cannon became common in the seventeenth century, the Swiss pikemen de-feated knights wherever they encountered them. For several centuries, the Swiss served as well-paid mercenaries for whoever could afford them (including the pope). They had imitators in Germany, but the Swiss were always the best, a truly elite force. Not commandos, how-ever. In fact, commandos saw little action for several centuries as ar-mies of men with firearms, fighting set-piece battles (lining up opposite each other and going at it), dominated warfare. That other common form of combat during this period, the siege (of fortresses or walled cities), was also dominated by gunpowder (cannon) rather than the occasional commando operation to seize a fortress. For example, it was such a thirteenth-century raid that brought the current rulers of Monaco (the Grimaldis) possession of that principality in the south of France—they snuck into the castle at Monaco disguised as monks and took over. But by the time gunpowder and muskets began to dominate warfare in the 1500s, fortresses were better built to defy commandos.

THE GRENADIERS

The desire to gather "your best men" in elite units did not entirely disappear when gunpowder came into wide use four centuries ago. It brought not just guns and cannon, but also the first hand grenades. These were crude devices—just a container (often metal) filled with gunpowder with a burning fuse to detonate it. You had to be careful when throwing it, because if too much fuse was left when it landed among the enemy, it could be thrown back. But if the fuse was too short when you threw it, it could explode while still in the air and injure the thrower. Grenades were commonly used during a siege, which now meant digging trenches and moving your own cannon close enough to the fortress walls to get a good shot at them without being destroyed by the cannon inside the fortress. These operations often involved counterattacks by infantry from within the fortress, and this was where the grenades came in as troops fought from trench to trench. Grenades were also used when troops were fighting within a town or city. Recognizing a need for specially trained troops to handle the grenades, not to mention the more difficult trench and house-to-house fighting, it became common to place the best men in each battalion (three to four hundred men) into one or two companies of "grenadiers." Initially, these "best men" comprised about 10 percent of each infantry battalion. But after a few generations, generals were forming entire battalions of grenadiers. These men were, in most cases, not only skilled at using grenades, but also more accurate with their muskets and often taller and more muscular than the average soldier. Once you had battalions of grenadiers, their commando functions pretty much ceased, although the grenadier battalions were often used for difficult situations during a battle.

COMMANDOS ON HORSEBACK

While there was less work for commandos when the newfangled gunpowder ruled the battlefield, there was still a need for fast-thinking, fast-moving troops. These were largely on horseback and were used to scout ahead of the army. Scouting has always been a commando function, and the best scouts during this period could be considered highly skilled and resourceful fighters who deserved the name. Still, the light cavalry used for scouting was a mixed bag. If a commander paid attention to whom was recruited for scouting, he would end up with a pretty elite force. Then, as now, however, a general had a lot of things to worry about, and the horsemen used for scouting were often just the ones who could not afford to equip themselves with the breast-plates, more extensive training, and larger horses of the heavy cavalry (all very useful during battles). It was noticed that men from certain areas made better light cavalry. Hungarians, whose origins as Central

Asian nomads survived in their devotion to horsemanship, became known as good scouts. The Hungarian scouts were called Hussars, and they maintained their ancient customs of riding fast and avoiding fighting anyone they couldn't easily beat. Eventually, just the concept of Hussars remained, with units of non-Hungarians being formed. When real Hussars were not available, there were similar hard-riding groups (especially Croats, Pandours, and Serezhans from the Balkans) available. But the Hussars were, for many centuries, the most professional and reliable light horsemen available. They served as scouts and, occasionally, as commandos.

The Hungarian experience was not unique. The Russians also had their Cossacks—horsemen from the Eurasian plains who were Russian, part Russian, or non-Russian, and who relied on the same tactics as the Hussars. Not all Cossacks were elite, but all of them could be depended on to range far and wide, and plunder whenever they had the opportunity. Some groups of Cossacks, under good leaders, were very useful for daring raids or scouting missions.

The need for a good leader to turn a bunch of hard-riding warriors into commandos has been a common situation for centuries. During the American Indian wars of the nineteenth century, the danger posed by a group of mounted warriors was largely dependent on their leader. A good one could make the band a lethal (to any civilians they encountered) nuisance and a very difficult group to round up. In the Indian wars, the American Army eventually resorted to recruiting expert Indian scouts to lead cavalry units going after the commando-quality warrior leaders. Sometimes bribes would work. That's another ancient technique used by, and against, commandos. But often you had to chase down exceptional Indian leaders like Geronimo.

MAMELUKES AND JANISSARIES

There was another way to create an elite military force, but cultural restrictions prevented Europeans from training slaves to be supersoldiers. Muslims had no such problems with this. In the thirteenth century, Egyptian leaders, needing more reliable soldiers, imported Turkish and European slaves and trained them long, hard, and continually as soldiers. This was nothing new. Nor was the fact that by the end of the thirteenth century the slave soldiers took over Egypt themselves, and continued to import and train slaves as soldiers. These superbly trained troops, known as Mamelukes, were formidable. They defeated European crusaders and the Mongols. In the sixteenth century, they were defeated by the Turkish Empire.

The Turks had noticed how the Mamelukes operated and in the fourteenth century formed a similar body of soldiers, the Janissaries. The Turks used Christian children taken from the territories they ruled in the Balkans. The Turks imposed more discipline on their Janissaries, and didn't allow them to marry. Since the Janissaries were trained from childhood (and converted to Islam), they tended to be a lot more loyal than the Mamelukes. The great wealth of the Turkish Empire allowed the sultan to maintain the Janissaries as a standing army. By the sixteenth century, there were twenty thousand of these soldiers. Those who survived their service were retired to administrative jobs in the imperial government. While some Janissaries had children out of wedlock while in service, these were not legally recognized. Unlike the Mamelukes, then, there never developed a Janissary class—at least not at first. The children of Janissaries knew who Daddy was and became a political force. Unfortunately, they were a conservative force and did much to block needed reforms in the Turkish Empire. The Janissaries increasingly got involved in the civil strife that often accompanied the death of the Sultan. The Janissaries themselves—there were more than 135,000 in uniform by the early nineteenth century—also backed whichever son of the sultan seemed most likely to look after them. By this time, most of them were no longer Christians taken at a young age and converted to Islam. Instead, Muslims were allowed to bribe their way in. Discipline had declined. By 1826, the sultan declared war on the Janissaries and destroyed the organization (and many of its members). It was a nice idea while it lasted. For several centuries, however, the Janissaries were the most formidable troops in Europe and the Middle East. An army of commandos, as it were.

THE LESSONS OF THE PAST

No matter how good your special troops are, their effectiveness depends on how they are led and used. The Janissaries were very well trained and disciplined, but they were rarely used for commando operations and normally just thrown into battle. This was not stupid; the

Turks organized the Janissaries so that the government would have a loyal and effective standing army. That these superb troops could also undertake commando operations (as they sometimes did) was not a major consideration.

There were a few commando organizations before the twentieth century. Most were rather temporary—a group of capable men always available to do some nasty bit of business for the king or emperor. But in the eleventh century, in what is now Iran, there developed a very capable commando organization. Actually, it was more of a politically motivated "Murder, Inc.," but that diminishes their skill and effectiveness. Hasan, the founder, was the son of a noble family. He had a grudge against the powers-that-be and a genius for organization and persuasion. Using religion, sex, and drugs (a formidable combination), capable young men were persuaded to become assassins. These killers, however, unlike your average medieval hit man, were not bothered about getting killed in the act. And this made the *ashishin* (from "users of hashish") not just killers, but highly effective terrorists. However, willingness to get yourself killed while doing a job was not enough. Hasan developed an organization that was able to get the hit man to the right place (where the victim was) at the right time (when the victim was vulnerable). Each killing was a classic commando operation using a team of skilled operatives to get the hit man into position to do the job. The sect maintained a number of mountain fortresses and, over the two centuries it existed, came to control considerable territory in Iran and Syria. Terror was its main weapon, for its hit men were known to be virtually unstoppable. Finally, in the thirteenth century, Mongol and Arab armies went after the "assassins," destroying their castles and killing their leaders. The sect continued as a religious organization but gave up the use of murder and terror. Some 150,000 sect members still live in the Middle East, where the methods of the medieval suicide terrorists continue to be practiced by other groups.

Hasan's organization was unique because it was one of the few such operations to develop before the twentieth century. Entering the twenty-first century, we have dozens of special commando organizations all over the planet, and most of them can carry off an assassination if need be. Hasan would appreciate that what he created has not completely disappeared.

WILDERNESS WISDOM

During the late 1750s, American Indian fighter Robert Rogers formed what we would today call a commando unit of several hundred troops. This was during the French and Indian War, which France lost. That outcome was in no small part due to the activities of Major Rogers and his Rangers. Robert Rogers had a keen understanding of how to operate and fight in the wilderness.

Today, the three hundred or so Rangers (organized into "companies" of thirty men each) would be considered commandos. The British recognized the value of the Rangers. The term *Rangers* comes from the American term for long-range scouts, *ranging men.* Operating deep in a wilderness inhabited by hostile Indians was considered quite an accomplishment, and it was. Rogers not only fought Indians but he was also able to negotiate with them. After the French and Indian War ended in 1760, Rogers went on to work out peace deals among tribes, and between Indians and colonials.

Rogers was one of many officers who served in North America and realized that they had experienced a different way to fight. During the eighteenth century, military thinkers were developing what they thought were the ultimate in logical and devastating combat tactics. The fighting in North America showed that these splendid new ideas might work well against other Europeans, or civilized (but less well organized for war) peoples in India and China. But out in the wilderness, the Indians knew a few tricks as well. What Rogers did was combine the warrior techniques of the Indian tribes with the discipline and technology of European armies. In other words, Rogers invented modern commandos.

When the American Revolution broke out, Rogers offered his services to the rebels but was turned down. The rebels were suspicious of Rogers because he had worked with the colonial government for so long. Rogers then went and offered his services to the Crown, and the Rangers fought for the British throughout the Revolution. Despite that detail, the Rangers were revived as an American army unit during World War II; the 75th Ranger Regiment continues in service today. While the World War II Rangers were commandos, the current rangers are more accurately described as elite assault infantry. Today's Rangers operate in larger numbers, although in a pinch they can carry out classic commando operations.

MAJOR ROBERT ROGERS'S RULES FOR HIS RANGERS

The rules Robert Rogers established for his Rangers are remarkably relevant even today. Well, you could say the same thing for just about any successful combat unit from the last few thousand years. To demonstrate this, below are Major Robert Rogers's Rules for his Rangers (in his own words, as published in the 1760s), along with commentary to connect these rules, laid down 250 years ago, with notes on their application to twenty-first-century military practice.

Rogers's original rules are in italics.

1. *All Rangers are to be subject to the rules and articles of war; to appear at roll-call every evening, on their own parade, equipped, each with a firelock, sixty rounds of powder and ball, and a hatchet, at which time an officer from each company is to inspect the same, to see they are in order, so as to be ready on any emergency to march at a minute's warning; and before they are dismissed, the necessary guards are to be draughted and scouts for the next day appointed.*

Discipline and readiness are stressed here. Modern commandos have an attitude of "check, and check again." You don't just trust your fellow commandos to be ready, you constantly check each other. It worked then, and it works now.

2. *Whenever you are ordered out to the enemies' forts or frontiers for discoveries, if your number be small, march in a single file, keeping at such distance from each other as to prevent one shot from killing two men, sending one man, or more, forward, and the like on each side, at the distance of twenty yards from the main body, if the ground you march over will admit of it, to give the signal to the officer of the approach of an enemy, and of their number &c.*

The spacing rules are a result of the widespread use of firearms in the eighteenth century. Before that, being bunched up was not that critical. Even with a powerful bow, you weren't going to get two men with one arrow. Rogers also revealed his awareness of posting someone on the flanks to avoid ambushes, and the use of a point man for the same reason. While such procedures were not unique to Rogers, he made his men aware that they must operate this way all the time. This gave the Rangers an edge that was often the difference between victory and defeat.

3. *If you march over marshes or soft ground, change your position, and march abreast of each other to prevent the enemy from tracking you (as they would do if you marched in a single file) till you get over such ground, and then resume your former order and march till it is quite dark before you encamp, which do, if possible, on a piece of ground which that may afford your sentries the advantage of seeing or hearing the enemy some considerable distance, keeping one half of your whole party awake alternately through the night.*

These rules were followed with great success by Special Forces long-range patrols deep in communist territory during the Vietnam War. It's another reason why, once in combat, the young troops learn to listen to older soldiers or, in this case, someone who has read a two-century-old list of battlefield guidance.

4. *Some time before you come to the place you would reconnoiter, make a stand, and send one or two men in whom you can confide, to look out the best ground for making your observations.*

Rogers is pointing out that, even if your patrol consists of only a dozen men, it's safer to send only one or two ahead to find a safe place from which to observe an enemy position (or enemy-controlled town or village). Rogers's attention to security will be found again and again throughout his rules.

5. *If you have the good fortune to take any prisoners, keep them separate, till they are examined, and in your return take a different route from that in which you went out, that you may the better discover any party in your rear, and have an opportunity, if their strength be superior to yours, to alter your course, or disperse, as circumstances may require.*

Rogers points out two important practices here. The first has to do with not letting prisoners be together so they may agree on what lies to tell to deceive their captors. Criminal investigators have known this one for thousands of years. The second item again addresses security. When deep in enemy territory, you cannot afford to be predictable. Never use the same route twice. The enemy often has trackers, and a route you have passed over twice makes it that much easier for the tracker to pick up the signs (bent grass and branches, displaced pebbles, and footprints).

6. *If you march in a large body of three or four hundred, with a design to attack the enemy, divide your party into three columns, each* *headed by a proper officer, and let those columns march in single files, the columns to the right and left keeping at twenty yards distance or more from that of the center, if the ground will admit, and let proper guards be kept in the front and rear, and suitable flanking parties at a due distance as before directed, with orders to halt on all eminences, to take a view of the surrounding ground, to prevent your being ambuscaded, and to notify the approach or retreat of the enemy, that proper dispositions may be made for attacking, defending, &c. And if the enemy approach in your front on level ground, form a front of your three columns or main body with the advanced guard, keeping out your flanking parties, as if you were marching under the command of trusty officers, to prevent the enemy from pressing hard on either of your wings, or surrounding you, which is the usual method of the savages, if their number will admit of it, and be careful likewise to support and strengthen your rear-guard.*

This advice is somewhat dated. Back then, muskets weren't very accurate, and effective firepower came from groups of men firing at once (a shotgun effect). Note that all of the Rangers were also equipped with tomahawks for hand-to-hand combat. But Rogers's attention to security can be seen in how he directs a group of attacking troops to approach the enemy while avoiding the possibility of ambush.

7. *If you are obliged to receive the enemy's fire, fall, or squat down, till it is over; then rise and discharge at them. If their main body is equal to yours, extend yourselves occasionally; but if superior, be careful to support and strengthen your flanking parties, to make them equal to theirs, that if possible you may repulse them to their main body, in which case push upon them with the greatest resolution with equal force in each flank and in the center, observing to keep at a due distance from each other, and advance from tree to tree, with one half of the party before the other ten or twelve yards. If the enemy push upon you, let your front fire and fall down, and then let your rear advance thro' them and do the like, by which time those who before were in front will be ready to discharge again, and repeat the same alternatively, as occasion shall require; by this means you will keep up such a constant fire, that the enemy will not be able easily to break your order, or gain your ground.*

Here Rogers is taking advantage of the way the weapons of the day operated. You could see a group of enemy troops preparing to fire at you; they had to go through a loading routine that took twenty to thirty seconds, and then their leader would give the order to aim their muskets and fire all at once. Rogers knew that this gave his men time to hit the ground and avoid getting hit. This advice is still useful if you know how the enemy operates. An example of this was seen in the movie *Saving Private Ryan*. When paratroopers attacked the German radar station, the captain pointed out that the German machine gun (an MG-42, a design later adopted by the American and post–World War II German armies) would overheat after a while, and its barrel would have to be changed. This gave the American troops enough time to rush the German position. When all the shooting was over in that scene, you could still see the steam coming off the overheated German machine-gun barrel. More important, the two-hundred-year-old tactic still worked. The other lesson Rogers imparts is one that was not widely accepted until World War I: fire and maneuver. That is, while one part of a unit (usually a squad of six to twelve men) advances, the other covers them by firing at the enemy, or simply standing ready to shoot at any enemy troops who show up. The American Army later refined (a bit) and renamed this tactic "bounding overwatch." Rogers would still have recognized it.

8. *If you oblige the enemy to retreat, be careful, in your pursuit of them to keep out your flanking parties, and prevent them from gaining eminences, or rising grounds, in which case they would perhaps be able to rally and repulse you in their turn.*

Here Rogers recognizes that his opponent is often going to be as clever as the Rangers. Pursuing a retreating enemy can be dangerous if the enemy troops are a disciplined force. Such troops, like the Rangers, can ambush the advancing troops, and sometimes turn a defeat into a victory.

9. *If you are obliged to retreat, let the front of your whole party fire and fall back, till the rear hath done the same, making for the best ground you can; by this means you will oblige the enemy to pursue you, if they do it at all, in the face of a constant fire.*

Rogers recognizes that, even in defeat, there is opportunity for the better-trained and -disciplined soldiers. Less well-prepared troops make what is called a "headlong retreat"—everyone runs as fast as they can to get away from the victorious enemy. But not the Rangers.

Here Rogers advises using "fire and maneuver" even in retreat, knowing that most enemy troops will rush out into the open if they think they have you on the run. This will give your troops better opportunities to even up the odds. The tactic also makes the advancing enemy cautious, allowing you a better chance of getting away to fight another day. These tactics only work with well-trained, -disciplined, and -led troops.

10. *If the enemy is so superior that you are in danger of being surrounded by them, let the whole body disperse, and every one take a different road to the place of rendezvous appointed for that evening, which must every morning be altered and fixed for the evening ensuing, in order to bring the whole party, or as many of them as possible, together, after any separation that may happen in the day; but if you should happen to be actually surrounded, form yourselves into a square, or if in the woods, a circle is best, and, if possible, make a stand till the darkness of the night favors your escape.*

This is a standard tactic for commandos, who usually operate in situations where they can find themselves vastly outnumbered. Operating at night or in a forest, you always have the option of scattering. Some of you will get away, and the enemy will spend a lot of time trying to catch you. The key is having troops who have been trained to move without being detected and are capable of finding their way across unfamiliar ground. Most of Rogers's Rangers grew up in a wilderness area and picked up these skills as they grew up. Today, providing commandos with equal skills takes several additional years of training and constant practice.

11. *If your rear is attacked, the main body and flankers must face about to the right or left, as occasion shall require, and form themselves to oppose the enemy, as before directed; and the same method must be observed, if attacked in either of your flanks, by which means you will always make a rear of one of your flank-guards.*

Rogers realized that he was not the only stealthy fighting force in the forest and that no matter how good the Rangers were, the other guy could always get lucky. So he trained his Rangers to be aware that they might have to quickly reposition their forces if the enemy catches them as they are moving through the wilderness. The above rule not only warned his men of a possible worst-case situation but also served as a description for training exercises. Rogers didn't just recruit men who already had wilderness skills, but also trained them for situations they were unlikely to face just growing up out in the bush.

12. *If you determine to rally after a retreat, in order to make a fresh stand against the enemy, by all means endeavor to do it on the most rising ground you come at, which will give you greatly the advantage in point of situation, and enable you to repulse superior numbers.*

This is a reminder to observe one of the oldest rules of warfare: "Seize the high ground." By doing so, you can better see what the enemy is up to, and, if you're attacked, the enemy must move uphill to get at you.

13. *In general, when pushed upon by the enemy, reserve your fire till they approach very near, which will then put them into the greatest surprise and consternation, and give you an opportunity of rushing upon them with your hatchets and cutlasses to the better advantage.*

This particular advice is not for the faint of heart, but it is decidedly practical. The eighteenth-century musket was about as accurate as a modern pistol. If you wanted every shot to count, you had to open fire when the target was less than thirty feet away. Doing this required discipline and confidence that your fellow Rangers would also be as accurate at shooting as yourself. Firing at close range ensured not only that most of your musketballs found a target but also that the enemy was shocked and disorganized long enough to let you at him with your tomahawks or short swords (cutlasses). Such a strategy also meant that the enemy would not have a chance to fire back at you. Accurate and lethal use of your weapons, along with surprise, makes a lethal combination in combat.

14. *When you encamp at night, fix your sentries in such a manner as not to be relieved from the main body till morning, profound secrecy and silence being often of the last importance in these cases. Each sentry therefore should consist of six men, two of whom must be constantly alert, and when relieved by their fellows, it should be done without noise; and in case those on duty see or hear any thing, which alarms them, they are not to speak, but one of them is silently to retreat, that proper dispositions may be made; and all occasional sentries should be fixed in like manner.*

Here Rogers pays attention to an important detail that is often missed on the battlefield. It's not enough to have sentries posted at night; they must also carefully conceal themselves so that they spot an approaching enemy before the sentries themselves are spotted. The old movie cliché of sneaking up and killing a sentry only works for those sentries dumb enough to let themselves be seen. Ranger sentries are hidden and motionless while an approaching enemy is moving around in the dark. Guess who will find who first?

15. *At the first dawn of day, awake your whole detachment; that being the time when the savages choose to fall upon their enemies, you should by all means be in readiness to receive them.*

You can still tell if combat troops are above average by noting whether they customarily "stand to"—have every man awake and armed just before dawn—when out in the field. Rogers understood this and made it part of his regulations.

16. *If the enemy should be discovered by your detachments in the morning, and their numbers are superior to yours, and a victory doubtful, you should not attack them till the evening, as then they will not know your numbers, and if you are repulsed, your retreat will be favored by the darkness of the night.*

Rogers's regulations were nothing if not common sense. Here he points out that if you're attacking a larger force, it's better to do so at night. The Rangers are better able to operate at night (something that's still true). Rogers points out not only that chances of defeating the larger force are better at night, but also that if the attack doesn't work out, the Rangers are better able to get away.

17. *Before you leave your encampment, send out small parties to scout round it, to see if there be any appearance or track of an enemy that might have been near you during the night.*

This advice is still valid today, and one of the reasons why American combat troops are trying to get handheld drone recon aircraft widely distributed to combat units. The idea of sending scouts out before the rest of the unit hits the road makes even more sense now. Peacekeeping missions, or wars like those taking place in Afghanistan, feature small units of bad guys skulking around where you don't expect them—unless you send out scouts or, better yet, a small drone aircraft to work with scouts on the ground. Rogers would have loved those small drone aircraft.

18. *When you stop for refreshment, chose some spring or rivulet if you can, and dispose your party so as not to be surprised, posting* *proper guards and sentries at a due distance, and let a small party waylay the path came in, lest the enemy should be pursuing.*

Another bit of advice on the need to always post guards to avoid being surprised. Rogers correctly observed that you only had to screw up in this department once and you were toast.

19. *If, in your return, you have to cross rivers, avoid the usual fords as much as possible, lest the enemy should have discovered, and be there expecting you.*

Another bit of advice that boils down to "Don't do the expected."

20. *If you have to pass by lakes, keep at some distance from the edge of the water, lest, in case of an ambuscade or an attack from the enemy, when in that situation, your retreat should be cut off.*

This is another angle on Rogers advice to "always have an escape route handy."

21. *If the enemy pursue your rear, take a circle till you come to your own tracks, and there form an ambush to receive them, and give them the first fire.*

Not only is this an ancient trick, but some large, nasty animals (like the African Cape buffalo) are known to use it to lethal effect against human hunters as well.

22. *When you return from a scout, and come near our forts, avoid the usual roads, and avenues thereto, lest the enemy should have headed you, and lay in ambush to receive you, when almost exhausted with fatigues.*

This trick was rediscovered during the Vietnam War, and would be something to watch out for in any anti-guerrilla war.

23. *When you pursue any party that has been near our forts or encampments, follow not directly in their tracks, lest they should be discovered by their rear-guards, who, at such a time, would be most alert; but endeavor, by a different route, to head and meet them in some narrow pass, or lay in ambush to receive them when and where they least expect it.*

Another admonition not to underestimate the enemy, especially one who is also out sneaking about in the bush.

24. *If you are to embark in canoes, bateaus (flat bottom boats), or otherwise, by water, chose the evening for the time of your embarka-tion, as you will then have the whole night before you, to pass undis-*

covered by any parties of the enemy, on hills, or other places, which command a prospect of the lake or river you are upon.

Rogers again recognizes the importance of moving by night, when you are least likely to be spotted, and thus still able to sneak up on the enemy. Surprise, as Rogers notes, is very important. Surprise allows a smaller force to attack and win.

25. *In paddling or rowing, give orders that the boat or canoe next the stern most, wait for her, and the third for the second, and the fourth for the third, and so on, to prevent separation, and that you may be ready to assist each other on any emergency.*

In eighteenth-century North America, the quickest way to travel was by water (via a river or lake). Rogers' advice here is maintain your discipline even when on the water.

26. *Appoint one man in each boat to look out for fires, on the adjacent shores, from the number and size of which you may form some judgment of the number that kindled them, and whether you are able to attack them or not.*

On the water, there's no need for a point man and flankers, but you do need to watch out for the enemy. As you move over water at night, the foe is likely to be camped somewhere, meaning there will be one or more campfires. But you won't be sure of seeing those fires unless you make sure someone is looking.

27. *If you find the enemy encamped near the banks of a river or lake, which you imagine they will attempt to cross for their security upon being attacked, leave a detachment of your party on the opposite shore to receive them, while, with the remainder, you surprise them, having them between you and the lake or river.*

In the eighteenth-century wilderness, the major obstacles—if you didn't have a boat handy—was water. Any military operations had to deal with this. In this case, Rogers points out how to deal with an enemy force that might flee by water when you attack.

28. *If you cannot satisfy yourself as to the enemy's number and strength, from their fires, &c. conceal your boats at some distance, and ascertain their number by a reconnoitering party, when they embark, or march, in the morning, marking the course they steer, &c. when you may pursue, ambush, and attack them, or let them pass, as prudence shall direct you. In general, however, that you may not be discovered by the enemy upon the lakes and rivers at a great distance,* *it is safest to lay by, with your boats and party concealed all day, without noise or show; and to pursue your intended route by night; and whether you go by land or water, give out parole and counter-signs, in order to know one another in the dark, and likewise appoint a station for every man to repair to, in case of any accident that may separate you.*

Rogers's last regulation is telling, as he emphasizes again the need for secrecy and gaining surprise. Throughout history, the easiest way to win a battle has been to surprise the enemy. You may not always win, but you will be less likely to lose.

FIGHTING TOWARD THE FUTURE

Commandos before the twentieth century were rare, because the kinds of missions twentieth-century commandos carry out rarely existed back then. Moreover, the tools that make modern commandos possible—aircraft, fast ships, automatic weapons, and explosives—are also twentieth-century developments. But going into the nineteenth century, some of the technology began to appear, and commando-type operations naturally increased as well.

One aspect of commandos that is often overlooked is that they are largely a Western development. Actually, the modern concept of professional soldiers developed some five hundred years ago in Europe. Thereafter, Europeans (and Americans) took it for granted that this was what soldiers were. When these well-equipped, well-trained, and well-led troops consistently stomped all over soldiers elsewhere on the planet, Europeans tended to assume that they were simply culturally superior to the "lesser breeds." The real reason was more pragmatic. The Western world had institutionalized effective military forces. Europeans and Americans just assumed that this was the way you raised an army, and to do it any other way was simply a waste of time. But nearly everyone else in the world still accepted slapdash, "just make it look good" armies that were cut to pieces by the more professional European troops. This was not a problem until the Europeans showed up. Before that, the lackadaisical local troops would flail away at one another until one side gave up.

But once the Europeans arrived, warfare became a much more serious business. The Europeans had rules and regulations. Not only were their troops well equipped, but the soldiers were expected to take good care of their weapons and equipment. And then there was the training. It seemed the crazy Europeans were always marching around or firing their guns at targets. This last habit seemed particularly wasteful. Why fire expensive ammunition at pieces of wood with circles (bull's-eyes) drawn on them? Ammunition was expensive; why not save it to fire it at enemies? And what kind of officers didn't steal some of the ammunition to sell on the black market? The locals were even more surprised to find that the officers didn't steal part of the soldiers' pay. And when these crazy Europeans fought battles, the officers got in front, waving their swords, urging their troops on, and often getting killed in the process. All of this was incomprehensible in most parts of the world, where warfare was practiced as a rather more casual affair.

This collision of casual, and ancient, attitudes with the no-nonsense new European style took place mainly in the eighteenth and nineteenth centuries. The speed with which European soldiers conquered the Native American empires in the sixteenth century was one of the first examples of what professional soldiers could do. It was during the sixteenth century that most of the concepts found in a modern army—organization, officer ranks, training—were developed and became a permanent part of European culture.

Out of this tradition of professional military organization, training, and leadership arose the concept of taking these practices to the extreme to create commando units.

3 OUT OF AFRICA AND INTO THE TRENCHES

The word *commando* is a Dutch term meaning "a command," usually referring to a small military unit. The term came into use during the nineteenth century as the Boers (Dutch settlers in South Africa) organized self-defense forces against the native population and then the British during the Boer War at the end of that century. The commandos were organized as fast-moving mounted riflemen and the British copied the concept, developing the idea right up into World War I. During the late nineteenth century, the Boer War between the British and the Dutch settlers changed the British Army in a profound way. At first the British had only contempt for the Boers, who were basically part-time soldiers. But there's nothing more instructive than defeat. The British changed their tactics and their multicolored uniforms (adopting khaki-colored clothing to avoid being seen by Boer sharpshooters), as well as developing a taste for the fast-moving and hard-hitting commando-type operations the Boers favored.

The modern concept of commandos took a lot more than just the name from the Boers.

The Boers were Dutch settlers who arrived in South Africa in 1652. They found a dry, temperate climate and not much of a local population. The native Khoisan tribes were hunter-gatherers who had been in the area for thousands of years. Bantu peoples from the north had been slowly moving in for several centuries. The Bantus didn't like the cooler climate of South Africa, and found that they had to develop new farming methods to survive. As a result, most of the Bantus in South Africa were herders, tending large numbers of cattle. The Boers (the

Dutch word for "farmer") were better armed and organized than the Bantus or Khoisan, and when the culture clashes led to warfare, the native Africans lost.

The Boers enslaved some of the locals, which was part of the culture clash, but the population was so sparse that most slaves were imported from Indonesia, India, and Madagascar. For the Boers, life was good. Their superior farming technology and political organization made them relatively rich, and the local tribes were not encouraged to modernize. The Khoisan and Bantus learned to keep their distance from the Boers. Any raids on Boer farms led to savage retaliation by gun-toting Boers on horseback. Able to raise hundreds of armed men on short notice, the Boers were the kind of force the tribesmen, armed with spears and shields, could not match.

This was a pattern that was quite common during this period. The Europeans, with their superior weapons and organization, were showing up all over the planet, and the locals were getting the worst of it. The Europeans began to believe that they were successful because there was something that just naturally made Europeans superior. This was just a comfortable (for the Europeans) myth. In actuality, the Europeans had developed a technology-based culture that broke with tradition and encouraged change. One of these changes was the commando tactics the Boers developed and the British (and other European nations) adopted. Most of the other ancient cultures on the planet still showed enormous respect for traditions, even if many of them were counterproductive. Despite seeing that the Boers lived longer by using better sanitation and farming methods, the local tribes still clung to their traditional (and less healthy) customs. Even when some native Africans did adopt European technology, they did so in the face of disapproval from their family and tribe. When tribespeople, ultimately, did begin using guns, they never went the extra step, as the Boers did, to practice until they became accurate shots. Nor did the tribes adopt the Boer custom of putting experienced riflemen on horseback and carrying out well-planned operations. The Boers had it made, until other Europeans showed up.

In 1795, the British moved into South Africa and took over, just like that. The British had the world's most powerful Navy, and their soldiers were a match for the Boers. At first, the Boers just put up with British rule. It didn't really change their situation all that much, and it didn't seem worth the effort to fight the British. Then the British outlawed slavery in 1808. That hurt the Boers, and encouraged the Xhosa Bantu tribes to engage in a little payback by encouraging their warriors to raid Boer farms. The British government did little to help protect the Boers and would not allow them to carry out their usual reprisal raids. So the Boers, in 1834, just up and moved away from the British (whose control was largely confined to the coastal areas).

The Great Trek had one major obstacle, however: the new Zulu kingdom. At about the same time that the British were colonizing South Africa, Shaka, king of the Zulus, was establishing a radically new military culture to the north. Shaka was what you call an original thinker. Starting with one small band of Bantu, he developed a highly disciplined military and social system. He began conquering nearby tribes and literally founded a nation—modern-day Zululand in South Africa. Shaka died in 1828, but his new empire, and military system, lived on.

As good as the Zulu military machine was, however, it met defeat against the emigrating Boers at the Battle of Blood River in 1838. Thereafter, the two groups tended to leave each other alone. But the British were still determined to control the Boers, so they came north and took control of the new Boer republic in 1843. In response, the Boers moved on and established two new republics by 1852. The British left the Boers alone until 1877, then tried to seize control of the independent-minded states once more. The Boers fought back, and the British gave up in 1881. But gold, diamonds, economic development, and British nationalism were making the United Kingdom increasingly irritated about the continued existence of these two republics. In 1899, war broke out again. The British, forgetting past experience with the Boers, thought it would be over quickly.

While ignorance may be comforting, when the shooting starts, it becomes very embarrassing. What hurt the British the most was not the hard-riding Boer commando tactics but recent improvements in the rifle. In the twenty years before 1900, the infantry rifle underwent enormous changes and emerged a weapon so superior that it is still used to this day, virtually unchanged. There were three major changes that brought this about. First, engineers and rifle designers, especially Peter Paul Mauser, developed very easy-to-use and reliable mechanisms for loading bullets into the rifle from a magazine (holding five to ten rounds). Second, chemists developed a "smokeless gunpowder" (which was not a powder, but it was smokeless). Not only did these new propellants keep the battlefield free of smoke, but the guns themselves were also kept cleaner, which allowed bullets to move along at higher speeds and longer ranges. Third, advances in metalworking enabled more precise parts to be made for faster and cheaper assembly. Soldiers could now fire faster (up to twenty shots a minute), farther (a thousand yards or more), more accurately (no smoke), and with more lethality (faster bullets do more damage).

The Boers, whom the Germans saw as heroes for standing up to the British, had been equipped with the marvelously deadly new Mauser rifle. This weapon changed warfare in many ways. It greatly strengthened the defense. The Mauser rifle, for example, could regularly pick off enemy soldiers several hundred yards away. A group of Boer riflemen firing together could "cover" an area more than a thousand yards wide. The smokeless powder made it difficult to see where the Boers were. Many British troops were still using black (very smoky) powder. The British also tended to attack by just lining up, fixing bayonets on the ends of their rifles, and marching toward the Boers. This had worked for the last century against tribal foes on several continents. The British, however, forgot that the Boers operated like Europeans. Several battles, and hundreds of British soldiers, were lost before the British reconsidered their strategic options.

The Mauser rifles also made sniping more common. Sniping in the past was dangerous, because black powder exposed the sniper's location after the first shot. The modern rifle changed everything. More accurate, with a longer range and smokeless powder, it allowed a single sniper to keep dozens, or even hundreds, of enemy troops pinned down. The Boers were always good shots, and as snipers with Mausers they were very lethal.

With their superior scouting and tracking skills, a few Boers on horseback were now capable of doing great damage to British troops. Worse, the Germans had also sent the Boers modern light artillery and high-tech (for the time) explosive shells. In the first few months of the war, the Boers were better armed than the British.

Unfortunately for the Boers, who expected to grab territory and then call for a peace conference, the British were not good losers. Over the next three years, the British poured half a million troops into the struggle. With the British Navy making resupply from Germany difficult (whatever the Boers received had to be smuggled in overland from Germany's African colonies), the Boers were eventually reduced to using guerrilla tactics.

It looked as though the commandos might still win the war, even though they lost several major battles (which killed twenty-two thousand British and four thousand Boer troops). Nevertheless, the Boer riflemen were able to obtain food from local farms and disrupt the railroads the British depended on for supplies. They also did well in fighting small units of enemy troops. But the British demonstrated they could be ruthless and imaginative as well. They went around to the Boer farms and moved the people found there (mostly women, children, and older men) into concentration camps. Some 150,000 Boer civilians were rounded up, of whom 27,000 died from disease and privation. The British rounded up a smaller number of blacks who were on friendly terms with the Boers (some ten thousand blacks joined the Boer armed forces), and fourteen thousand of these people died in the camps. To protect the railroads, some eight thousand blockhouses were built and manned. The men assigned to this duty were more effective than the British cavalry, which vainly scoured the countryside looking for the Boer commandos. In the end, the commandos lost.

The British learned much from their two wars with the Boers. The commando tactics were particularly attractive to them, because their empire still had vast areas that needed pacification from time to time. The Boers' clever use of new weapons also taught the British not to ignore, or underestimate, new technology. This attitude came in handy in 1914, when World War I began.

The two Boer wars also changed the way the British dressed for war. No more fancy uniforms, just plain old khaki. Actually, khaki first became popular in northwest India, where the British Indian Army was constantly fighting the Pushtun tribes. *Khaki* means "dust" in Hindi. Initially, the rest of the British Army resisted leaving their colorful uniforms behind when they went off to fight. The Boers changed everyone's mind, and not just because they shot at officers first. Another Boer innovation was placing white rocks, marking the distance from their trenches (the better to adjust their aim), in front of them. Thus British troops in South Africa adopted the saying, "When the shooting starts, avoid officers and white rocks."

The British learned how to handle commandos and guerrillas, which they continued to do with success several times in the next century. The most important lesson was that it was critical to cut off the guerrillas from their sources of supply and support. While the concentration camp worked in South Africa, that was only because there was a relatively small number of Boer farms. In Malaya after World War II, the British cut off supply in more numerous villages by installing trustworthy and competent police to protect villagers from the guerrillas and win their trust. The British also learned that to run the guerrillas down, you had to fight like guerrillas. British mounted units never matched the skills of the Boer commandos, but they came close enough to get the job done. Most important, the British learned that regular troops alone cannot defeat a guerrilla army. This is a hard lesson for generals to accept, but no one has ever found a way to refute this particular bit of wisdom.

STOSSTRUPPEN AND SPECIAL UNITS

World War I saw the first wide-scale use of commandos and the creation of many basic commando techniques still in use. A lot of these developments had nothing to do with the war. In the first decades of the twentieth century, for example, the concepts of industrial engineering, quality control, and methodical training programs (for all sorts of job, military and civilian) flourished and were eagerly accepted new developments. It was also a time of rapid-fire invention. The automobile was rapidly evolving, as was the airplane and industrial chemistry. There was an attitude that anything was possible. Then World War I broke out in 1914, and Europeans were confronted with a seemingly intractable stalemate. Trenches and troops stretched from neutral Switzerland to the sea, and neither side seemed able to figure out how to move forward.

While it appeared to be a hopeless stalemate, much brainpower and imagination were being applied to a solution. Poison gas, aerial reconnaissance and bombing, tanks, massed artillery fire, elaborate attack plans, and clever fortifications were all seemingly useless. Then the infantrymen themselves came up with a solution that did work. As the old saying goes, "It's the workman, not his tools, that makes the difference." The result was new infantry tactics that cracked the stalemate wide open.

The Germans are generally credited with inventing infiltration tactics—sneaking past enemy strongpoints—and using them to nearly win the war in 1918. But it's a myth. In fact, German military men to this day are generally unfamiliar with the term *infiltration tactics*. What German soldiers have recognized, instead, throughout the last century is steady progress in just improving their infantry tactics. It was startled British reporters who coined the term *infiltration tactics* when they interviewed shocked British soldiers in 1918 and heard tales of Germans "coming out of nowhere." The Germans had indeed developed tactics that used a lot of deception and moved around enemy positions whenever possible. Even the Germans admitted that these new tactics were not new, but had been in development by all armies since 1915. Moreover, many of the ideas for these tactics came from techniques developed piecemeal by French and German troops. The difference here was that, while many of the troops in the trenches were constantly working out new ways to fight and survive, only the German leadership recognized these innovations and implemented them on a large scale.

In the first three years of the war, tactics had fallen into a wearily repetitious pattern. Masses of troops moved forward to be mown down by machine guns and artillery. The defenders had an enormous advantage, because their positions were well-built trenches, plus even deeper bunkers in which to survive the attackers' extensive artillery bombardment (often lasting days, and sometimes even weeks, thereby totally losing the element of surprise). The attackers knew, however, that when they finally came out of the trenches, there were always some defenders left shooting at them with machine guns. Since the defenders were often in cleverly concealed positions, the attacker was constantly deceived as to where all this lethal firepower was actually coming from.

Within a year of the war's beginning in 1914, German, French, and British troops had developed a better tactics. For example, Andre Laffargue, a French infantry captain, developed effective small-unit assault tactics in 1915 and wrote up his techniques in a pamphlet that was distributed throughout the French Army. These techniques were only intended to deal with the local business of combat patrols and raids, but contained all the basic ideas that later came to be known as infiltration tactics. The Germans captured one of these pamphlets in 1916 and distributed it throughout their Army. Meanwhile, the Germans assigned infantry captain Willy Rohr to develop new unit organization and tactics for *Sturmabteilung* (assault detachments). While somewhat similar to Laffargue's work, the Germans were thinking of larger-scale operations.

All these efforts dispensed with the traditional idea of masses of troops marching across no-man's-land. Instead, small groups of troops were trained to operate like a patrol. Effective patrolling techniques had developed during the war, if only because the generals didn't bother themselves with minor details and thus left the troops to use their judgment. A major attack was hard to miss, and was often announced by several days of artillery fire. But a patrol could slip out into no-man's-land at night, enter the enemy positions, grab a prisoner or two, and scurry back to friendly lines without suffering any casualties. Patrols depended on deception, sneaking around at night when they could not be seen, and generally staying out of sight as much as possible. Actually, snatching a prisoner was often the culmination of a series of patrols. Night after night the patrols would go farther into no-man's-land to map the area and determine the easiest route into the enemy positions. The final assault would be well rehearsed, and a complete surprise.

These are classic commando tactics, and the small groups of soldiers who were best at this were every bit as competent and skilled as today's commandos. These developments were not given the attention they deserved, however, by the generals commanding British and French armies.

By 1917, the Allies had worked out new tactics to reduce their casualties—though not to break through the trench lines. For that, they were betting on the mass use of tanks (which didn't work). But as the Germans demonstrated in 1918, it was men, more than machines, that provided the solutions.

The Germans adopted patrol tactics on a large scale for their *Stosstruppen* ("storm" or "assault troops"). Then the Germans went a lot farther. They revolutionized the way infantrymen were organized, equipped, and led. The basis of infantry organization now became the squad, which was equipped with at least one machine gun. The soldiers were trained to rely more on hand grenades than firearms when it came to fighting in trenches. Most important, the role of the sergeants who normally were in charge of squads (which had long been administrative organizations within infantry units) was changed. In the past, sergeants had generally been behind the troops, making sure there were no stragglers. The new German doctrine called for the squad being trained so that the sergeant would lead from in front. Moreover, several of the more promising soldiers in the squad were trained so that they could take over if their sergeant was killed. This required a lot more training, and the troops had to be specially selected for initiative, enthusiasm, and physical fitness. This was very much like the approach taken during World War II when commando units were formed.

But the Germans were looking beyond better tactics for the troops stuck in the trenches. For one thing, they'd learned a lot from the Boer War. Many German volunteers served during the 1899–1902 Boer War, and when these men got back to Germany, the Army wanted to know more about the innovative new tactics the Boers had used to defeat the highly respected British. The Boers demonstrated the need for initiative and the unforeseen uses of new weaponry. The Germans also paid close attention to the battles of the Russo-Japanese War of 1905. Here portable mortars and flamethrowers were used for the first time, especially in the trench warfare that characterized several battles in that war. The Germans were thinking beyond improved patrol tactics and assault detachments. They wanted to create an army that would be transformed by the use of storm troopers, and by 1918 they did just that.

Captain Laffargue's methods spread through the French and British Armies, making patrols, raids, and small-scale attacks more often successful. Captain Rohr's work was also widely adopted in the German Army. By 1916, most German divisions had formed their own assault battalions, or at least assault companies, and these were used successfully in the 1916 Battle of Verdun. Then the following year, on the Russian front, German general von Hutier was the first to use storm trooper units on a large scale. In September 1917, von Hutier used multiple assault battalions to infiltrate past Russian strongpoints, causing nine thousand Russian troops to panic and surrender. The battle was won with minimal casualties to both sides. The French and British blamed the defeat on poor Russian morale, and Russia did collapse later in the year. Two months later, the same tactics (now called "von Hutier tactics" by the Allied press) were used against the Italians during the Battle of Caporetto. This resulted in a major defeat for the Italians. The Allied generals in France, however, blamed the catastrophe on the ineptness of the Italians.

The German 1918 offensive, which put an entire British Army out of action and advanced an unprecedented twenty-five miles within a week, nearly won the war for Germany. There was no magic involved. The heretofore impregnable trench lines were penetrated by some twenty thousand commandos. These *Stosstruppen* were assigned in numbers from a company or two (one to two hundred men) to a battalion's worth (five hundred men) to each of the thirty-two infantry divisions making the attack on March 21, 1918. More *Stosstruppen* were in reserve so that the offensive could be kept going when the first wave of storm troopers were worn out from fatigue and casualties. Thus each division attacking the British trenches was led by hundreds of storm troopers, who took the British by surprise and cleared the way for the regular German infantry that followed.

The *Stosstruppen* force had been created over the past three years, as division commanders told their subordinates to "send me your best men" and used these troops to create companies and battalions. But in 1917, the Army high command realized it had a superweapon in the *Stosstruppen,* and trained more of them. The 1918 spring offensive was the largest use of "special operations troops" ever undertaken.

That was not all there was to it. Like their enemies, the Germans also developed radical new artillery techniques to support the storm troopers. Unlike past attacks in which the artillery would pound enemy positions for days before an attack, the Germans kept the bombardment short and used novel new methods. The most prominent of these new techniques was the "hurricane" barrage. This was a fifteen- to three-hundred-minute shelling of key enemy positions. The objective was to fire quickly and put as many shells on the enemy position in as short a time as possible. Experience had shown that most of the damage to the target was done in the first hour or so of shelling. After that, enemy troops were either underground in their bunkers or dead where they were caught in the open. The hurricane barrage actually consisted of several different patterns of shelling on different kinds of targets. One especially useful artillery technique was a rolling barrage, in which the artillery fired a line of shells in front of the advancing *Stosstruppen,* and then moved the line of exploding shells one to two hundred yards closer to the enemy every four minutes. This hid the advance of the *Stosstruppen* groups of ten to twenty men, who were ready to leap into the enemy positions shortly after the German barrage lifted.

The new artillery tactics were actually the first demonstration of the World War II *blitzkrieg* (lightning war). The initial minutes of the hurricane barrage sought to go after enemy headquarters and communications (radio sets, and areas where telephone lines were). The next target was to destroy and interrupt enemy artillery. After reaching the defenders' artillery (which was usually a couple of miles behind the trench lines), the artillery hit roads, or open areas, over which enemy reinforcements could approach. While all of these artillery techniques had been used before during World War I, the Germans spent more time on air reconnaissance and ground patrols to pin down the exact locations of targets. They were destroyed or damaged in less time with fewer shells. This is similar to the revolution in bombing that has occurred over the last two decades as more accurate bombs have been developed.

Trained to move fast, the *Stosstruppen* were equipped with a lot more firepower than other World War I troops. The light machine gun was in wide use by 1918; the standard machine gun weighed fifty to sixty pounds and was difficult to move forward, or in any direction. The new versions weighed from eighteen to thirty pounds, and the *Stosstruppen* had lots of them. The Germans also took the lead in developing submachine guns like the MP-18, a weapon that would eventually evolve into the modern assault rifle. By the end of World War I, about thirty thousand MP-18s were in use. Had there been ten or twenty times as many MP-18s available a year earlier, they actually might have changed the outcome of the war. As it was, the MP-18 demonstrated the devastating effect of automatic weapons in the hands of infantry. It fired the standard 9mm pistol round, used a thirty-two-round drum magazine, and fired six to seven bullets a second. The Germans kept developing this type of weapon; by World War II they had the MP-38 and MP-40. The short range (fifty to one hundred yards) of the 9mm pistol round prevented the Germans from attempting to rearm all their infantry with this weapon; infantry often had to hits targets farther away. Additionally, there was a shortage of production facilities to build that many MP-18s.

But for the tactics the *Stosstruppen* used—sneaking up close before attacking—it was ideal. Several members of a *Stosstruppen* squad would have MP-18s. It wasn't until they saw the Russians using similar weapons on a mass scale during World War II that the Germans realized the short range of the 9mm pistol round was not as great a shortcoming as they'd thought.

The experience with 9mm submachine guns in World Wars I and II led the Germans to develop the StG-44 in 1943, which used a more powerful bullet. This weapon looks a lot like the Russian AK-47, and in fact heavily influenced that gun's design.

The key element of *Stosstruppen* tactics was that the troops did whatever they could to keep advancing. Once they broke through enemy lines, the *Stosstruppen* kept going. Bypassed enemy troops were left for the second or third wave of Germans. In the months before the 1918 offensive, the Germans had given troops in all their fifty-six first-line divisions special training on how to exploit the advances made by the *Stosstruppen,* such as clearing out enemy trenches with grenades and encouraging the now surrounded troops to surrender. This included practice on how to manhandle the heavier weapons (light artillery pieces) and ammunition over the pockmarked and generally torn-up battlefield terrain.

The first groups of *Stosstruppen* only attacked enemy fortifications if they could not be bypassed. If the *Stosstruppen* could go around the enemy, they did so. Unlike the traditional World War I offensive, the *Stosstruppen* attacks did not put a lot of troops in the initial assault. The defenders knew something was up when they saw a rolling barrage coming at them, but when the shelling stopped, the *Stosstruppen* were usually into the defenders' trenches with grenades and submachine guns before the defenders could climb out. These attacks were more like trench raids. The *Stosstruppen* kept going until they got a few miles behind the enemy trenches. That was where the enemy supply units and artillery were. Once these were captured or destroyed, there was no food, ammunition, or artillery support for the defending troops in the trenches. After they were into the enemy rear area, the

Stosstruppen would indicate (usually by a flare signal) that they were through. That group would then be reinforced immediately by the regular troops (who also took care of any bypassed troops). Because the ground had not been torn up by days of shelling, the *Stosstruppen* were able to move quickly, dragging in small carts containing ammunition and heavy weapons (flamethrowers and mortars). A *Stosstruppen* attack quickly broke through the lines of enemy troops who did not know what they were up against. Unlike the World War II *blitzkrieg*—which used tanks to make and exploit the breakthrough, and trucks to keep it going—once the *Stosstruppen* were past the enemy front lines, they usually caused a panic among the enemy, with many of the frightened troops fleeing.

The Allies had generally ignored the 1917 *Stosstruppen* operations in Russia and Italy and were generally unprepared for these attacks on the Western Front in early 1918. The allies had their own assault companies, but never thought to use them as boldly as the Germans did. The large-scale German use of commandos was a success, and the offensive almost succeeded. The only problem was the enemy's ability to quickly reinforce the area where the Germans were breaking through.

By March 24, 1918, three days into the battle, the *Stosstruppen* had broken through thirty-seven miles of British trenches, often putting German troops up to twelve miles into the British-held rear area. But by the first week of April, the Germans had penetrated twenty-five miles into enemy territory. At this point, the Allies stopped the German offensive. It wasn't just the desperate Allied defense, but also the Germans' own lack of mobility. Once the Germans had gone six to nine miles past the enemy trenches, they were out of range of their own artillery. The several hundred yards of bombed-out terrain between the German and British trenches ("no-man's-land") was difficult for wheeled vehicles (artillery and supplies) to get across. In addition, the Germans had to build roads across their own and the British front-line trenches. This took time, and the Allies used that time to rush in reinforcements via their own rear-area road network railroads. It was this difference in mobility that stopped the German advance. Several of the new divisions sent to stop the Germans were American, because the United States had entered the war in 1917. By this time in the war, in early 1918, the Americans were just beginning to arrive in large numbers, and they were fresh and eager. Looking back, if the Germans had had cross-country trucks (something developed after World War I), they would have won. That would have been the first modern *blitzkrieg*. As it was, more than four hundred thousand troops from both sides were killed, wounded, or captured in this German "Victory Offensive."

The lessons of the German *Stosstruppen* tactics were generally lost on the Allies after World War I, yet these new tactics revolutionized infantry warfare. Twenty-two years later the Germans used the same (well, slightly improved) tactics, but with tanks and trucks, to successfully conquer France in six weeks.

After World War II, the German *Stosstruppen* tactics did finally sink in, although it took until the 1980s before it became generally known, by non-Germans, that *infiltration tactics* was a misleading term. By the 1970s, American military professionals began to realize that it was the German infantry, not the German tanks, that accounted for most of the German Army's success during World War II. What the Germans did between World War I and World War II was change their infantry organization and training to maximize the number of commando-grade troops in units. The Germans were very involved in training for their NCOs and officers. Many American infantry officers were shocked (but not surprised) when they discovered that new German sergeants received more training than new officers in the American Army. By the 1970s, these policies were being adopted by the U.S. Army, and the result was the Hundred Hour War against Iraq in 1991.

While most people recognize commandos as exceptionally well-trained and capable troops, it is generally ignored that it is also possible to train large numbers of troops to a high standard. In other words, an army of Perfect Soldiers. This will be ignored no longer, for it is the trend of the future.

UNDEFEATED IN AFRICA

World War I, for all its stalemated trench warfare and reputation for stodgy thinking, was actually a hotbed of new ideas. By the time the war ended, mechanized warfare had been invented, infantry tactics were revolutionized, and paratroopers were not just an idea, but in training. Lost in all this is the creation of the first modern commando units. Still, it wasn't just the *Stosstruppen* battalions, but also an army of German and African troops who were outnumbered but never defeated during four years of fighting in Africa.

How did the Germans end up with commando-quality troops in Africa in 1914? It was mainly a fortuitous combination of talents. On the German side, there was the efficient and honest attitude toward civil administration that Germans had developed over the centuries. The same attitude was also applied to military training, which was strict and effective. On the African side, there was a warrior culture and training in fieldcraft (how to survive in the bush) that most African men received from childhood. In 1914, the Germans had several colonies in Africa, the largest being German East Africa (occupying the area of modern-day Tanzania, Rwanda, and Burundi). The area had a population of 7.7 million, of whom only 5,400 were European (and 4,100 of those were German). The Germans had actually only been in East Africa for thirty years, but they had already introduced mandatory elementary school for boys and eliminated several diseases through vaccination. While Germans held most of the senior positions in the civil administration, more Africans were being trained. The colonial police, or *Schutztruppe* (security troops), numbered four thousand—a few hundred German officers and NCOs, with the rest of the troops and some of the NCOs being African. They maintained law and order in an area the size of modern-day Nigeria (about four hundred thousand square miles). The commander of the *Schutztruppe* was German army lieutenant colonel Paul von Lettow-Vorbeck. The African troops were called Askaris, and it was considered a choice occupation. Not only were Askaris the law, but they got to dress like Europeans and use European weapons (although these were older models; the Askaris had black-powder, 11mm rifles). The Askari recruits received the same tough training German recruits received back in Germany. The discipline was actually the hardest thing for the Askaris to accept, because they were from a warrior culture that did not favor this kind of rigidity. But those who wanted to become Askaris made the effort.

In 1914, as in the Boer War, the British, who were the major colonial power in Africa (along with Belgium, France, and Portugal), gathered a force of eight thousand Indian troops and sent them off to take control of German East Africa. Von Lettow-Vorbeck met the invading British force with some twelve hundred men and won a lopsided victory, killing, wounding, or capturing half the invading force. The captured British weapons enabled von Lettow-Vorbeck to recruit more Askaris. He would need them, because the British spent the next eighteen months raising a larger army of forty-five thousand troops to invade German East Africa overland from the south. To oppose them, von Lettow-Vorbeck never had more than fourteen thousand troops (80 percent Askaris), and with this army he defeated the 1916 invasion.

The British were not amused. Von Lettow-Vorbeck was a hero back in Germany, and he was quickly promoted to the rank of major general. So the British attacked again. In 1917, they came at German East Africa from every direction, with the Belgians and Portuguese joining in. This massive effort to catch von Lettow-Vorbeck failed, and at great cost. By the end of World War I, it had actually cost the British more than three hundred thousand military casualties and some fifteen billion (in 2002 dollars) chasing after the Germans. Von Lettow-Vorbeck did lose sixty thousand men, mostly from disease, but the British were never able to defeat him. Still, the British pressure did drive von Lettow-Vorbeck and his Askaris into the bush, where by 1918 they began waging guerrilla war against the British. Finally, several days after World War I ended in Europe, von Lettow-Vorbeck found out about it and offered to cease operations—but not surrender. He was allowed to return to Europe with his German officers and NCOs. His Askaris were interned for a while and then released. In the 1920s, the German government paid the Askaris their back wages; their pensions were paid in the 1960s. As for von Lettow-Vorbeck, he was the only German general to get a victory parade after World War I.

What saved von Lettow-Vorbeck time and again was the high skill levels and resourcefulness of his troops. Since von Lettow-Vorbeck was cut off from Germany, he had to get new weapons and ammunition from his enemies. He did this with regular raids on enemy camps and forts. Many of these attacks went off without any German casualties. The troops were well trained and led, and the operations carefully planned. They were classic commando operations.

WHY EVERY NATION DOESN'T HAVE COMMANDOS

Von Lettow-Vorbeck's success in training rural tribesmen to the highest standards of military effectiveness should give pause to Western nations that think they have a monopoly on commandos. While Western attitudes toward discipline, training, and technology do not spread quickly to many parts of the world, the people there, with the right motivation, can overcome their cultural traditions and became as effective as Western troops. This has typically happened when Western supervisors (officers, and sometimes NCOs) were provided. If the Westerners stayed around long enough, however, the locals eventually picked up enough knowledge and cultural attitudes to train their own efficient officers and NCOs without outside help.

But unless the society the officers come from is keen on efficiency and discipline, the officers won't maintain the necessary standards. This happened in many African countries after the colonial powers left in the 1960s. Even India, with two centuries of exposure to British administrators and officers, lost some of its military edge in the decades after the British left in 1947. India is a large collection of cultures with three times the population of Europe. Some parts of India provide world-class military officers, but many others do not. Moreover, India developed a stifling bureaucracy similar to the one it had before the British showed up, and this discouraged the strict discipline and high degree of organization needed for exceptionally good military units. Stories of corruption and laxity in the military are common features in the Indian media. But a nation like India has the human resources to develop world-class military units. All nations have the potential. As the old military saying goes, "There are no bad troops, only bad officers." If a nation gets some hotshots into the officer corps, exceptionally capable units can follow.

4 RAIDERS, GUERRILLAS, AND PEACEMAKERS

The experience of World War I, especially trench raids, specialized assault units, and storm troopers, got soldiers to thinking about new infantry tactics for future warfare. One military organization in particular, the U.S. Marine Corps, not only gave the issue a lot of thought but also started to try out new ideas. The Marines wrote about what they did, how they did it, and what it all meant for the future and, unsurprisingly, they became an early proponent of commando operations.

MARINES AS PEACEKEEPERS

Even before World War I, the Marines were being used quite a lot as peacekeepers—troops sent into a hot spot to keep quiet things down without a lot of fighting. So much so that the Marines were often referred to as "State Department Troops." The Marines saw service in China and five Latin American countries between 1901 and 1934. While they saw about a year of heavy combat in World War I, the many more years of peacemaking missions had a greater impact on how their tactics and leadership developed.

Below are countries the Marines served in before World War II, and where they learned that well-planned and rapidly executed commando missions were all the combat needed, if that, to keep the peace. The rest of the time, the Marines concentrated on getting to know the locals and helping to improve their lives.

Panama (1901–1914). After the United States backed the Panamanian rebellion against Colombia that set the country up as an independent nation, civil unrest persisted while the various factions maneuvered for power. The Marines were sent in to keep the peace, which they did without having to fight anyone. Early on, the Marines realized that a show of force (just being there with guns and an attitude) and a lot of talking with the locals was more effective than coming in with guns blazing.

Cuba (1906–1909). Same situation as Panama, although in this case U.S. troops had liberated Cuba from Spanish rule in 1898. The Marines again kept the peace without having to fight anyone.

Nicaragua (1912). Brief intervention to restore order.

China (1912–1941). Battling warlords made China unsafe through the 1920s. Then a civil war erupted between the republican government and the communists. The Marines were there to protect Americans (mainly merchants and missionaries) and keep the major rivers and coastal areas safe for shipping. Most of the action was "show of force" and negotiation. The 4th Marine Regiment arrived in 1927 and stayed until November 1941.

Haiti (1915–1934). After Haiti sank into anarchy (a fairly normal event there), the Marines were sent in. Because local politicians could not put together a national government, the Marines were assigned to protect American administrators who helped run the country until 1934. When the Marines left, Haiti limped along under one dictator or another until, well, until the present. The Marines learned a lot about how to deal with chaotic situations while in Haiti.

Dominican Republic (1916–1924). Sharing the same island as well as political problems as Haiti, the Marines again intervened until a national government could be established in the Dominican Republic. In this case, however, the Marines were allowed to depart earlier.

Nicaragua (1926–1933). This was a civil war. Like so many others in Latin America, it was among a handful of clans that owned most of the country. The Marines, however, never were able to run down one of the rebel leaders (a former army general named Sandino). Nevertheless they restored peace and supervised elections. After they left, the sniping among the ruling families continued (and continues to this day).

The Marine Corps wasn't very large during the 1920s and 1930s, never more than twenty thousand men. After World War I, a growing interest in marine aviation fueled growth in this branch of the service. One thing noted was that the techniques the Marines used certainly kept their casualties down during this period. The 1912 Nicaragua operation incurred only twenty-one Marine casualties. The 1926–1933 Nicaragua occupation saw only 113 Marines killed or wounded. The twenty-year operation in Haiti caused only thirty-six Marine combat casualties, and the Dominican Republic operation only sixty-seven. The losses to those who opposed the Marines with force were higher; in fact, the Marines lost more men dead and injured to disease than to combat.

Why? The Marines had quickly learned that words were more effective than bullets. Public works, efficient government, and maintaining order became as much a part of the Marine playbook as aggressive patrolling and maintaining a tough demeanor.

The many Marines who participated in these peacekeeping operations (which usually consisted at least a few thousand troops) discussed their experiences among themselves during the late 1930s. Even though another world war was looming and attention was turning to amphibious warfare, the Marines prepared and published the *Small Wars Manual* in 1940. This was a remarkable document, especially since it showed a noteworthy degree of insight on how to conduct peacekeeping operations. For example, the manual noted that:

The goal is to obtain decisive results with the least application of force and the consequent minimum loss of life.

Tolerance, sympathy, and kindness should be the keynote of our relationship with the mass of the population.

A force Commander who gains his objective in a small war without firing a shot has attained far greater success than the one who resorted to the use of arms.

Although the Marine interventions were later used by local politicians to demonize the "imperialistic" United States, when the Marines were there the people had better government than when the Marines were absent. Which is why the local politicians like to denounce

American intervention, not why there was intervention (corrupt politicians) in the first place. One lesson of the *Small Wars Manual,* however, is that the intervening force is only a temporary fix. All the nations the Marines operated in still have the same problems they suffered from more than sixty years ago.

What the Marines did demonstrate, however, was that tactics later adopted by the Army Special Forces were valid. Indeed, the *Small Wars Manual* was avidly studied by the early Army Special Forces troops for useful information. The manual contained much practical information based on actual experience.

World War II and the Cold War diverted the Marines from their peacekeeping missions. As soon as the Cold War ended, however, the Marines went back to "special operations" (the fancy term for commando operations) and trained units so that Marines could fight, perform peacekeeping missions, or undertake many different commando-type operations.

MARINES AS RAIDERS

The U.S. Marine Corps realized, since its establishment in 1775, that a part of its mission was going ashore for short periods to accomplish various operations in support of the Navy. This is something Marines in all nations have always done. Because of this, until World War I, the Marines rarely operated in more than battalion strength (five hundred men). When the Marines went ashore, there were often much larger enemy infantry units in the vicinity. To survive, they had to hit hard and hit fast and then get out. This is what raiding is all about. This mentality carried over to all Marine operations on land. During peacekeeping operations before World War II, this attitude made it difficult for local opposition to thwart the Marines. With the exception of the Nicaraguan guerrilla leader Sandino, the Marines managed to counter all the irregular forces they encountered.

During the last hundred years, most navies used their Marines as onboard police, gun crews, and, occasionally, landing parties.

Marines were originally organized, back in the days of sailing ships, as onboard close-combat specialists, at a time when ship crews still boarded each other's ships to decide naval battles. When landing parties of infantry were infrequently needed, they were largely sailors led by Marines. The twentieth century, and especially World War II, brought forth the capability to quickly move hundreds of thousands of heavily armed troops long distances by sea and to land them on an enemy shore. This is what most people still think of when you mention the U.S. Marine Corps. But all of this was only invented during the 1930s, when modern amphibious warfare techniques were developed. The first Marine division was not organized until 1942. By the end of World War II, there were six American Marine divisions. Since then, the Marine Corps has maintained three divisions, plus a large aviation force. Although all the ships and aircraft, as well as the Marine Corps itself, are nominally under U.S. Navy control, the USMC manages to maintain an individual identity.

The U.S. Marine Corps always attracted innovative and determined officers. In fact, it was these leaders who created the "can-do" spirit and dedication to professionalism that allowed the U.S. Navy's marines to turn into one of the largest commando-class fighting forces in the world. Even when the Marines were a six-division force during World War II, they still had a raider spirit. Indeed, the raiding battalions raised early in the war were eventually disbanded because, as many Marine generals eventually concluded, "All Marines are raiders."

The Marines concentrated on being very good at some key tasks that called for commando-type operations. These included:

- **Raiding.** These are classic commando-type operations. The British Royal Marines also excel at this, because all Marine forces are highly trained and somewhat elite. Raiding especially requires troops with above-average combat skills gained through long and tough training.
- **Spearheading amphibious operations for Army troops.** Something like a raid, except you don't always have to fight your way out. If the job is done right, the non-Marine troops coming ashore behind you will bail you out. Marines are often called upon to make the initial beachhead on an enemy-held shore. Functioning like assault troops, they use a variety of special skills and equipment so that the Army troops can get ashore later with a minimum of trouble. At that point, the Marines can be withdrawn. Often they have to stick around, though, to become part of the infantry (they're very capa-

ble) battle. While the Marines still practice attacking a defended beach, they prefer the pre–World War II method of landing where there is no opposition. Today, they do this by going in via helicopter. The head-on amphibious assault techniques the Marines pioneered in the 1930s were developed because armies had gotten so big (or because some Pacific islands were so small) that all landing areas were covered. There was no choice but to assault the heavily defended beaches. Once the Marines got their helicopters, they had a lot more landing options.

- **Getting there first with the most.** Often military action is needed and regular ground forces either are not available or cannot get there fast enough. The Marines are trained, equipped, and often used as a rapid intervention force. They are basically light infantry, trained to move quickly on foot over any kind of terrain. Until paratroopers became practical during World War II, the fastest way to get troops to any part of the world was by ship. The U.S. Navy has had ships in every part of the world for the last century, and this has included Marines being brought along for any work that needs to be done ashore. Despite the availability of paratroopers and long-range transports to carry them to any part of the world, the battalion of Marines that accompanies most U.S. carrier task forces still tends to be the troops closest to an emerging hot spot on the other side of the planet.

REELING IN THE RAIDERS

One ancient, and much-feared, tradition that largely disappeared in the twentieth century was that of raiding. For thousands of years, people like the Vikings, Magyars, Comanches, and others considered it their right to periodically raid their neighbors for money, food, women, and whatever could be stolen. Colonialism, police states, radios, and aircraft all worked against raiding in the twentieth century. But it's not completely gone. Somalis, Afghans, and pirates in Southeast Asia and areas embroiled in civil wars or revolutions still see a lot of raiding. The soldiers who dealt with these raiders, particularly after World War I, began to view the issue in a different light, and developed new ways to cope with these troublesome raiders.

After World War I, Britain and France inherited colonies and former fragments of the defunct Ottoman Empire. Afghanistan was still a problem, but Somalia and Iraq were now major headaches. So the British tried something different: some of the proven warplanes left over from World War I, piloted by experienced aviators. This was a new technique for dealing with tribal raiders. And it worked. As one British officer put it, the Royal Air Force (RAF) took twenty-one days to solve a problem that had eluded the Army for twenty-one years. The problem in question was Somali rebel leader Sayyid Muhammad Ibn Abdulla Hassan, referred to by the British press as the "Mad Mullah."

Sayyid Muhammad was a popular religious teacher and adherent of the militant and ascetic Salihipa sect of Islam. The Mad Mullah's followers were similarly inspired and, since they were all Somali tribesmen, raised to use guns and horses to get what they wanted; the British had a tough time suppressing the group's raids on local people who were under British protection. Once the British mounted troops got close to the Mullah's boys, the Somalis would disappear into the desert. In 1919, the RAF changed that, quickly finding and machine-gunning the Mullah's raiders. The Somali horsemen could neither outrun nor hide from the RAF aircraft. The Mullah's force dispersed, and Sayyid Muhammad fled to exile in Ethiopia (where he would have to behave); he died the next year.

The success of the RAF in Somalia led to a similar campaign in Iraq two years later. The RAF leaders were not just looking for something to do now that "The Great War" (as World War I was known until World War II came along) was over. The RAF was also fighting the Army's attempt to absorb it, and the British Air Force had to prove that it deserved to exist as a separate service. It was 1921, and the RAF had just been put in charge of Mesopotamia (now Iraq) and Jordan. Since the Turks, who had ruled the area for centuries, departed in 1918, the local tribes were fighting among themselves to establish a new pecking order. Now the British were trying to install a member of the Hashemite clan (the same family that still rules Jordan) as king of the newly established nation of Iraq. The tribes were not happy with this. The British had 135,000 troops in the country, trying to deal with 130,000 tribal raiders. The British were losing.

Then along came the RAF, which for the first time in history was being placed in charge of defending a (soon-to-be-former) colony. The techniques used were a variation, but an important variation, on the ancient techniques ground troops had used. In the past, when a tribe became troublesome, raiding trade routes and attacking civilians, troops marched into the tribe's territory and let it be known that if the tribe did not behave, its villages and crops would be burned. While this often worked, it was very expensive. You needed a large enough ground force to appear invincible to the tribe in question. And in most places where this was going on, you lost a lot of your own troops to disease. Iraq was an even worse situation because many of the rebellious tribes were nomads, so there were often no villages or crops to threaten, just fast-moving horses and herds.

The RAF had a solution for all that. Instead of sending a few thousand infantry to deal with a rebellious tribe, an aircraft would drop leaflets warning the villagers that, until their elders agreed to make the tribe behave, RAF warplanes would bomb or machine-gun anyone found in the tribe's villages, fields, or herds. After one air raid, the tribesmen would try to flee. After a few weeks out in the wilderness, cursing the daily reconnaissance flights by the RAF, the tribes would agree to behave. For the nomadic tribes, the RAF warplanes scoured the desert and hills until they found their camps. Leaflets were dropped. A few air raids usually followed until the tribesmen realized they could not hide from the RAF. Submission soon followed, and the raiding ceased. Thus with a fraction of the manpower, and at much less risk to British servicemen, the tribes of Iraq were pacified.

The RAF proceeded to use its new tactics in such places as Iran, Yemen, the Sudan, India's northwest frontier, Palestine, and Jordan. Suddenly, tribes found that raiding was no longer as easy as it used to be. The RAF experience did contain a catch: You had to be sure whom you were attacking from the air. You couldn't just fly out and shoot up targets you suspected were hostile. If you hit the wrong people, you turned a friendly tribe into a hostile one. The British were very keen on this point, largely because the British colonial officials had always emphasized trying to settle disputes by negotiation. Part of this was just cultural custom, but part was because most British colonial operations were initially organized as commercial endeavors. Thus everyone kept in mind that fighting was expensive and bad for business. That said, the RAF got its chance to use airpower against troublemakers because of the potential cost savings. As other proponents of airpower discovered, however, you can cause more problems than you solve if you are indiscriminate when applying death from above.

Many soldiers saw other opportunities in the air. Military thinkers in the industrialized nations saw new opportunities for raiding by using aircraft, lighter-weight radios, and the raiding experience of World War I. All of this was coming full circle, for it was the peacetime soldiers operating in colonial situations who had learned the benefits of raiding and how a well-executed raid could be more effective, and a lot cheaper, than sending out a larger force.

RAIDERS FROM ABOVE

Aircraft, in particular, caught everyone's imagination after World War I. And along with this came imaginative ways to use aircraft. For example, the modern parachute was perfected during World War I, and plans were made to use paratroopers against the Germans if the war extended into 1919. After World War I, the first nation to actually do anything with the concept was the Soviet Union. The Soviets made the first military drop in 1927, but it was a clumsy operation because it took too long to get the primitive parachutes off. This problem was solved when the quick-release harness was developed in Britain in 1929.

The Soviet Union formed the first parachute units in the early 1930s. At this point, the newly created Soviet Union was open to all manner of technological innovations, particularly military ones. The Soviets took the lead, and the rest of the world followed. By 1932, after several years of planning, the Soviets had a thousand paratroopers and were enthusiastically working out the technical details of airborne operations. During the 1930s, the Soviets sent their new paratroopers on demonstration tours throughout Europe to show off their new combat capability.

British officers were impressed and tried to start their own parachute infantry (or "airborne") force. But the Great Depression, was on and the British government did not see the need to pay what it would cost to imitate the Russians. Germany was different, because the Nazis had just taken over. The Germans began organizing a parachute regiment, which went on to some spectacular success in the first two years of World War II.

The Soviets, meanwhile, decided that it wasn't enough to have the first paratrooper force; they wanted the largest. So they kept training more and more paratroopers.

YEAR	NUMBER OF RUSSIAN PARATROOPERS
1932	1,000
1933	8,000
1934	10,000
1935	10,000
1936	10,000
1937	12,000
1938	18,000
1939	30,000
1940	50,000
1941	55,000

By 1934, the Soviets come up with a paratrooper organization they would retain for more than ten years. The basic unit was a brigade that contained 3,000 to 3,500 men (four 450- to 550-man infantry battalions, a recon company, an artillery battalion, and support units). The Soviets pioneered the use of gliders, and the airborne brigades had combinations of parachute and glider battalions (usually two of each). Gliders allowed the landing of light tanks and artillery. These "two and two" brigades each had eleven light tanks and seventeen pieces of artillery (four 75mm guns, with the rest combinations of mortars, anti-aircraft, and anti-tank guns). The brigade also had sixty to seventy trucks, which usually weren't brought in by air.

While Russian paratroopers had trained hard and performed well in maneuvers, they had yet to fight. In 1939, one brigade fought as infantry against the Japanese in Mongolia. They did well as infantry but were not able to use their parachutes. The problem, which would persist into World War II, was a lack of sufficient air transports.

In 1940, two brigades fought (again, as ground troops) against the Finns. Although the Russians had plenty of warplanes and transports for this war, the Finnish Air Force fighters had demonstrated an uncanny habit of showing up at the wrong time (for the Soviets). So rather than risk an embarrassing air attack on Russian transports full of paratroopers, the paratroopers were sent in on the ground. The Russian paratroopers were, as always, brave and determined. But the dictator of the Soviet Union, Joseph Stalin, had killed off most of the competent senior Army officers during purges in the late 1930s. Lacking commanders who were smart enough to use them, the paratroopers were used ineptly in the war against the Finns.

The closest the paratroopers came to an airborne combat operation was in 1940, when three brigades were dropped ahead of ground troops during the Russian reoccupation of the Romanian province of Bessarabia. There was no opposition during this operation, so it was basically another training exercise.

In late 1940, airborne divisions (called "corps") were formed in Russia, each with three brigades (three thousand men each) plus support units (light tank battalion, artillery battalion, and anti-tank battalion). A full-strength airborne corps had 10,500 men. While these Russian units were the first paratrooper divisions to be formed, and the most numerous, they would go on to have a very mixed record during World War II. The Russian paratroopers could have been Perfect Soldiers, but poor leadership prevented this from happening.

The big mistake the Russians made was not developing their paratroopers as a raiding force. Stalin's killing off many of the officers who had organized and led the airborne units didn't help, because these men would have been capable of planning and carrying out raiding-type operations. The Russians also had a tendency to think big, even when more modest-sized forces were more appropriate. The Germans demonstrated this in 1939 and 1940, when small numbers of paratroopers carried out classic, and very successful, commando operations.

The Russian experience with paratroopers was one of those rare cases in which being "first with the most" was not the best solution. The major lesson from all this is that it's not enough to have well-trained commandos; you also need combat leaders who know what to do with them.

AIRBORNE QUALIFIED

Those nations that did develop airborne forces realized that most people (men and women) in good physical condition could be quickly trained to safely make parachute jumps. This turned out to be a crucial factor in World War II espionage operations. Agents could be dropped into enemy territory rather than risking the landing of an aircraft to let them off. Even commando operations benefited from this new capability: Dropping them deep into enemy territory was now possible. While it became common for all commandos to be airborne qualified (trained to use a parachute), there were times when commandos had to go in with some civilian technical expert in tow. Because airborne schools could train just about anyone to jump, the commandos could go anywhere and take their noncommando specialists with them.

Intelligence agencies didn't have much need for airborne-qualified agents in peacetime. It was easier, and safer, to travel by ship and train. Moreover, parachutes were a new technology, and it was feared that most landings would result in some kind of injury. So the intelligence people had to learn about parachutes in a hurry once World War II broke out.

Meanwhile, the military was thinking about airborne raids from the beginning. In the early 1930s, a common script for Russian paratrooper demonstrations was a "vertical attack on an enemy headquarters." However, the Russians really preferred large-scale operations and soon moved away from such paltry missions to airborne attacks featuring thousands of paratroopers landing at once. This turned out to be, if not a mistake, not the best way to use airborne forces. The raid, using a hundred or so paratroopers, was the most effective way to go. The Germans saw this immediately in the 1930s when they began to build their airborne force. But even the Germans, as well as the other nations that raised large airborne forces (the United States and Britain), soon turned to large airborne forces. The mass drops had a Golden Age during World War II, but were quietly shelved after the war. What has survived since the 1930s is the use of airborne raids. Although parachutes were eventually replaced (in most cases) by helicopters, the concept of the "vertical raid" remains a frequently used tactic by commando organizations.

Parachute training, however, remains. Even though most people who undergo it rarely get to use their skills in action, the training itself has proven a useful way to prepare troops for the rigors and uncertainty of combat. You might say it has been concluded soldiers that who will jump out of an airplane will be capable of doing just about anything.

THE GUERRILLA REVOLUTION

It wasn't just the professional soldiers who were rethinking raiding and commando operations during the 1930s; many armed political organizations also came up with new ideas. The twentieth century was a period of many revolutions, and this meant a lot of guerrilla wars. The term *guerrilla* only appeared in the early nineteenth century, but this form of warfare goes back at least as far as written records of warfare.

The most successful guerrillas were always the ones who could stay out of the way of better-armed and more numerous soldiers while continuing to stir up trouble among the population. This gave guerrillas on horseback a big edge. But whether mounted or on foot, guerrillas have long been confronted with a very effective countermeasure: group punishment. If guerrillas were identified with a specific tribe, or even suspected of coming from a certain group, the powers-that-be (usually a king or some feudal aristocrat) would inflict punishment on the entire tribe or community. This approach has gone out of fashion—but not disappeared—over the last century. As a result, guerrilla warfare has become more common, and soldiers usually find themselves unable to cope.

Military professionals have tended to ignore guerrilla warfare. After all, guerrillas are not professional soldiers, and will not come right out and fight. Soldiers tend to consider guerrillas bandits and criminals, which is why captured guerrillas are often not accorded any prisoner-of-war status. But history has shown time and again that guerrillas are often formidable adversaries. Unsuccessful guerrillas are frequently just bandits with some kind of political agenda. The successful guerrillas, however, usually have many accomplished commandos in their ranks. Such a force can be deadly for a regular army, even with nations that have long experience being, and fighting, guerrillas.

A good example of how this amnesia works can be seen in the history of guerrilla warfare in the American Revolution. Actually, little has been written about this compared to the larger number of books on George Washington and his Continental Army. But the American guerrillas (both rebels and loyalists) did most of the fighting during the war. The guerrilla operations in the South (from southern Virginia to Florida) do get some coverage because those rebels, fighting against loyalist American troops and guerrillas, won the war down there. Up north, however, it was rebel guerrillas operating in New Jersey and the areas north of New York City who tied down thousands of British troops throughout the war. All the cities occupied by the British were quickly surrounded by American guerrillas who made life dangerous for any of the king's troops who ventured into the countryside. The British adapted by staying in the cities and using their command of the sea for transportation, sending mail and moving supplies. This made the war in America a lot more expensive—an expense that proved a major incentive for the British to finally give up trying to suppress the rebellion.

Interestingly, even the guerrillas looked down on being guerrillas. Any degree of success tended to encourage them to organize themselves into regular military units—and usually get smashed by the professional soldiers in a stand-up battle. But ignoring the history of guerrilla warfare won't make it go away. No, such ignorance just makes it more costly the next time you encounter guerrillas and have to relearn (at great cost) how to deal with them.

Again, American history provides the example of the Civil War, in which guerrilla operations provided significant military advantage to whoever was using them. In this case, the most effective guerrillas were actually soldiers operating as guerrillas. The Confederates, for example, controlled the Shenandoah Valley in Virginia through most of the war with hard-riding groups of Confederate cavalrymen operating as guerrilla raiders. These men were supplied by the local (pro-Confederate) civilians. The Union generals were never able to deal with the problem until General Sheridan burned the valley down in 1864.

The major lessons for fighting a guerrilla war are to avoid the political problems that get them started and, failing that, to realize that you have to fight fire with fire. If not the kind of fire General Sheridan applied to the Shenandoah, than the heavy use of commandos to meet the guerrillas in their own element. It's easier to deal with the political angles, as the Marines point out in their *Small Wars Manual*. The American Special Forces of today were set up to deal with the local political situation and, failing that, to go commando and outguerrilla the guerrillas. In Vietnam, the Special Forces were very successful with this approach, as were the Marines. But the senior American military commanders kept trying to fight the war as if guerrillas didn't really exist. That didn't work.

Guerrilla operations, like any other form of warfare, changed over the centuries. The twentieth century saw a lot of progress in the development of new political and military tools for guerrillas. In the past, effective guerrilla movements arose when a lot of people in one area suddenly felt angry about something. It might be a new tax, a new (and unpopular) ruler, an invasion by particularly nasty foreigners, or unhappiness with a corrupt government. Africa and South America are still full of guerrilla wars because of this.

Historically, once the cause was gone, the guerrillas disappeared. Sometimes the ruler or invader literally killed all the unruly people, or drove them off to somewhere else. What was new in the twentieth century for guerrillas was a higher degree of political organization, the use of formal training and indoctrination, plus the development of professional guerrillas. We can thank the communists for most of this. In the past, ethnicity (or "race") and religion were the two major driving forces behind guerrilla movements. The communists made revolution and guerrilla operations a way of life; a career choice, so to speak. The professionalization of guerrillas made them a lot more effective. It allowed more effective operations against governments that, in the past, would have been able to suppress the uprising. But a major reason for these new, more powerful, guerrillas was the attention paid to logistics.

When the communists could establish training and supply bases across the border from a country under attack by their guerrillas, they would usually win. This, of course, is an ancient tactic. Many times in the past, one nation would annoy, or weaken, an unfriendly neighbor by providing protection for rebels fighting against the rulers of their neighbor. This would often lead to a war. The new wrinkle the communists added was great attention to public relations and running a media campaign that denied—often successfully—that logistical and other support was being obtained from a neighboring nation. While the "Who? Us?" angle has been used in the past, the communists took it to new heights of effectiveness. All of this was employed during the Vietnam War.

By employing professional (trained and supervised) guerrillas, the communist forces were even more effective in combat. Moreover, soldiers, and governments, who paid attention to the history of guerrilla warfare found that the usual methods for suppressing the unrest did not work as well, if at all, against communist guerrillas. The communists made fewer mistakes that local soldiers could take advantage of and sent out better-trained and -equipped guerrilla commandos to hit government targets. Most of these new techniques were developed between World War I and World War II, although most people didn't become aware of this new age in guerrilla warfare until after World War II.

It wasn't just the communists who made professionals of guerrillas, the United States and Britain, too, would learn much about this during World War II, where the American OSS and British SOE supplied weapons and advisers to guerrillas opposing the Germans and Japanese. After World War II, the United States used this experience to develop a new type of military unit, the Special Forces, whose main job was to create more effective guerrillas and defeat hostile ones.

5 THE GOLDEN AGE: COMMANDOS

While the 1930s saw much thinking and speculating about commando operations, a lot of strange ideas put forth on the subject were quickly sorted out when World War II came along and clarified everything. World War II turned out to be a Golden Age for commandos, as well as an opportunity to develop most of the concepts for creating and using them that are employed to this day.

BRITISH STORM TROOPERS

When World War II broke out in late 1939, the idea of forming commando units was widespread in most nations' armed forces. But the senior commanders felt that these units were largely a waste of resources and discouraged the formation of specialized units.

In true commando style, these units did get formed through the initiative and efforts of a few enterprising individuals. Winston Churchill, the energetic prime minister of Britain during World War II, got wind of a proposal by artillery lieutenant colonel Dudley Clarke for the establishment of raiding troops. Clarke had made his proposal on June 4th, 1940; Churchill found out about it two weeks later and promptly wrote a note to the general commanding troops in Great Britain:

What are the ideas of C.-in-C., H. F., about Storm Troops? We have always set our faces against this idea, but the Germans certainly gained in the last war by adopting it, and this time it has been a leading cause of their victory. There ought to be at least twenty thousand Storm Troops or "Leopards" drawn from existing units, ready to spring at the throat of any small landing or descents.

These officers and men should be armed with the latest equipment, tommy guns, grenades, etc., and should be given great facilities in motor cycles and armoured cars.

British generals already had learned, the hard way, that when Churchill made a suggestion, you had better act on it. By the end of June, the first twelve commandos (as the commando units were called) were not only formed but sent off on missions as well. The British Army had just been thrown out of France by the victorious German Army, so there were plenty of British soldiers eager to volunteer for a unit that was going to fight back right away. The major problem was the resistance of commanders reluctant to see their best troops volunteer for these new units. This was partly solved by forming two of the units from independent companies raised earlier in the year from reservists. These "independent companies" were sort of commandos, but mainly they were to be used when a small unit of infantry (an infantry company has about 150 men) was needed to land in a coastal area and destroy something an approaching enemy might want (port or communications facilities, airfields and the like). These independent companies were formed using men who had been discharged from the Army over the past few years after seven-year enlistments and were now in the reserves. These men were thus experienced, a little older (and wiser), and not already part of a unit that didn't want to lose them.

The eleven independent companies were used for raids from the sea against German facilities, or small garrisons, in Norway. Four of these companies had already been used in May 1940 as part of the British operations around Narvik, Norway. So there were already many officers in the Army who were open to the idea of commandos. But the independent companies were just volunteer infantrymen who were willing to undertake very risky raiding operations.

The British had a tradition of raiding-type operations, especially over the last two centuries. This sort of thing was not seen as totally alien. Officers who served in Britain's numerous colonies had developed and used raiding-type operations to deal with bandits or guerrillas. British historians had made much of the experience with "Rangers" in North America (both before and during the American Revolution) and light infantry units during Napoleon's campaigns in Spain in the early nineteenth century. More recent experiences against

Boers at the turn of the century, with von Lettow-Vorbeck's Askaris in Africa during World War I, and among the German storm troopers at the end of World War I had made a strong impression on the current generation of British generals. While some commanders muttered about commandos being "private armies," there was enough enthusiasm for the project to see that it got going with a minimum of interference.

Initially, each "commando" was a battalion-sized unit of some six hundred men, with the fighting elements being ten fifty-man troops (a British term for platoons). In early 1941 this was changed to six troops of sixty-five men each. This was dictated by the capacity of the newly developed amphibious landing craft the troops used on many of their raids. An assault landing craft (LCA) could hold thirty-five troops (or eight hundred pounds of equipment), so each commando needed two LCAs.

The timing for the formation of the commandos was excellent. Britain was on the defensive, expecting a German invasion within the year, and under attack by the German Air Force (the Battle of Britain, which began in July and was not decided until October 1940). About all British ground forces could do was get ready to repel German invaders or volunteer to raid the Germans. Since the German Army controlled the coastline from the Spanish border with France to the northern tip of Norway (and many islands along the way), there were plenty of targets. The Royal Navy was strong enough to operate in the waters off German-controlled coasts, so this provided raiding opportunities.

Britain had always maintained a high level of training for its troops and a tradition of thorough preparation and innovation in military matters. So the commando concept was in the hands of the right people. Officers selected their men and looked for soldiers who were in good physical shape, well trained as infantrymen, and able to carefully prepare for operations and then carry them out aggressively. Training was intense, and everyone knew that the job was to be raiding, striking into the edges of occupied Europe.

COMMANDO TRAINING

While most volunteers for commando duty were already trained soldiers, often with several years of service, and combat experience as well, a training program was set up for them in early 1942. The purpose of the thirteen-week course (later shortened to five weeks) was to make sure everyone used the same techniques the same way. This reduced the possibility of fatal misunderstandings in combat. There was also an additional two-week course for officers and NCOs being trained as instructors.

The training concentrated on the special aspects of commando operations that would less likely be encountered in regular combat units. These items included instruction in use of explosives. Commandos were often called on to destroy structures such as bridges, enemy equipment, or buildings with explosives. In the Army, these tasks were usually left to engineers.

Much attention was paid to close combat, both unarmed and with a variety of weapons. The unarmed combat training drew from a large reperatory of brawling techniques. Actually, many of the techniques came from combat veterans who had developed—or discovered while in a tight spot—some new hand-to-hand combat trick they wanted to pass on. Normally, these techniques would spread slowly from soldier to soldier, but by collecting these tricks of the trade and showing them to all new candidates, knowledge spreads faster.

Because commandos made most of their raids from the sea, there was also amphibious training. Since these landings were often under fire, there was a lot of live-fire training, as well as instruction on how to find and destroy mines. There were obstacle courses as well as practice with scaling ladders and using small boats.

There was also training in small-unit tactics, exposure to special food (concentrated food bars), and instruction in how to prepare food in the field. Night operations, battle drills, and ambushes were practiced. They also developed some tactics that only worked with particularly dedicated and well-trained troops, and these were the ones taught at the commando school. The battle drills were in things a small group of troops might do on command (deploying for attack or defense, or getting out of a tight situation), or automatically (reacting if ambushed). Camouflage and field fortifications were covered, as well how to set up roadblocks and other obstacles. Techniques of street fighting were taught (except for the recruits headed for Burma, who were given more training on navigation and maps).

Field training covered such typical commando skills as stalking (quietly sneaking up on enemy troops). Trainees were also shown how to kill a man quietly, with either a knife or a garrote (strangling with a wire). Map reading and mapmaking (how to sketch a map that another soldier would understand) were covered.

Attention was also paid to leadership techniques. Commando units had a much higher proportion of men who were, or could easily be, combat leaders. So it was emphasized that any man could, and should, take over in a tight situation.

The training was intense, with periods of several days in which no one got any sleep. The instructors were looking for men who couldn't take it, and these were RTU'd (Returned to Unit—sent back to the unit they were in before they volunteered). This was not an option in the Royal Marine commandos (at least in most cases), as all Royal Marines were volunteers and the Marines already screened their volunteers (and rejected some of them).

The training program evolved during the war and became the basis for most commando training since. The attrition rate during wartime was low, mainly because most of the candidates had combat experience. But there *was* a war going on, and that motivated everyone. In peacetime, the lack of combat experience quickly became a major problem, and led to the current training and selection programs that flunk out up to 90 percent of candidates. This is another example of how important actual combat experience is.

COMMANDOS IN ACTION

Winston Churchill's suggestion that these new troops be called "Storm Troopers" or "Leopards" was shelved. Initially, the units were called Special Service battalions. In 1941, these units were renamed Commandos (a name that was applied to them unofficially early on). There was also a desire to prevent confusion with the notorious German Nazi Schutz Staffel (SS) battalions, which specialized in war crimes.

The Commandos, as trained and organized, were elite infantry. They were to be used for raids from the sea. Until 1944, this is mostly what they did. But casualties were often high, as senior commanders could not help sending in the Commandos to salvage desperate situations. They were usually able to put things right, but often at great cost to themselves. The problem was that it's hard to find enough raiding work for the four-hundred-man Commandos, and leaving that many well-trained troops sitting around waiting for work is extremely tempting for commanders.

Most generals in the period had been trained to keep a reserve of combat units for emergencies. Historically, the reserve was often made up of the best units in an army. This custom arose from long experience. Having your best troops as your reserve made it more likely that they could handle any emergency (such as enemy troops breaking through your front line, or showing up unexpectedly on your flank). Putting the best units into the reserve was also something of a reward. If the battle could be won with the regular troops, the elite units avoided getting banged around in yet another battle, and that was great for their morale. The Commando units were definitely elite troops, and when there weren't raiding duties for them, the local senior commander tended to use them as his reserve.

But in many cases, there were raiding jobs for the Commandos. Between 1941 and 1943, they staged raids, usually successful, along the French and Norwegian coasts. Moreover, the 10th Commando was staffed with non-British troops—French, Norwegian, Belgian, and even some anti-Nazi Germans. These were used to good effect, particularly for raids in Norway. These raids scared the Germans so much that they kept increasing the garrison in Norway until they had three hundred thousand troops up there. They could have gotten away with a third of that, but the raids made them think otherwise.

The Commandos were basically what Americans would think of as Marines, and the U.S. Marine Corps disbanded its commando ("Raider") battalions before the war ended when it decided that "all Marines are raiders." The British Royal Marines did have battalion-sized units in wartime, but did not go on to form amphibious divisions like the U.S. Marines did. The Royal Marines did realize, as did the U.S. Marines, that they were trained to a high standard and could easily operate as commandos. So the Royal Marine battalions were converted (mainly renamed and reorganized) and expanded to create, between 1942 and 1944, nine Royal Marine Commandos (numbered 40 to 48). Other Royal Marines continued to serve, as they had for centuries, as detachments on ships and to provide security for Navy land bases.

In 1941, a brigade of three Commandos was sent to North Africa. Known as Layforce (after its commander, Colonel Laycock), it got caught up in the desperate (and unsuccessful) battle to defend the island of Crete from invading German paratroopers. By the end of 1942, all the Commando units in North Africa were disbanded. But in late 1943, two Army and two Royal Marine Commandos were sent to Italy to form the 2nd Commando Brigade, which spent the rest of the war fighting in Italy, the Adriatic Sea islands, and the Balkans. These troops thus engaged in both amphibious raids and the classic World War I storm trooper operations against the formidable German fortification in the mountains of Italy.

The 3rd Commando Brigade (with two Army and two Royal Marine Commandos) was formed in late 1943 and shipped off to India, where they fought to defend India from the Japanese and liberate Burma.

For the D-Day invasion, five army and three Royal Marine Commandos were formed into the 1st and 4th Commando Brigades. Both brigades were part of the D-Day invasion force, and undertook several additional amphibious and river crossing assaults for the rest of the war.

In 1946, all the Army and most of the Royal Marine Commandos were disbanded. The Marines continued their commando tradition until the present, but the Army didn't get back into the commando business until 1952, when the SAS (Special Air Service) was revived.

COMMANDOS UNDERWATER

Commandos are specialists, and sometimes even specialists need specialists. The 30th Commando was formed in the summer of 1941 and included divers and intelligence specialists. These men were also trained Commandos, because their job was to be the first into enemy headquarters (after the enemy had been killed or chased away). This sometimes meant that fighting would still be going on, and enemy attempts to burn important documents were incomplete. Thus the commando nature of such operations: to snatch valuable documents before the retreating enemy could destroy them. The divers were to go into sunken enemy ships looking for useful intelligence material.

The unit operated in Italy and Sicily in 1942 and 1943. But in early

1944, the 30th Commando was taken over by the Royal Navy and renamed the 30th Assault Unit. During the D-Day invasion, the 30th Assault Unit was often the first one into smoldering enemy bases, looking for valuable documents, and often finding them. The Army formed a similar unit called T Force, which sometimes was in competition with the 30th Assault Unit to be first into enemy headquarters. Both units were kept busy during 1944 and 1945 as Allied armies moved across France and into Germany. In late 1944, the 30th Assault Unit was again renamed as the 30th Advance Unit, but was disbanded at the end of 1945.

BATTLES IN THE SURF ZONE

Many new forms of warfare in World War II were the result of new technology that was not designed for military use. One example of this was the development of scuba (self-contained underwater breathing apparatus) gear in the decades before World War II. Actually, the first true scuba equipment was developed in 1876, but it took a while before the equipment became reliable and rugged enough for military use. What was also needed was the rubber mask with the glass lens, along with the rubber flippers, and these were not developed until the 1930s. Interestingly, scuba gear was not finally perfected until 1943, when French Navy officer Jacques-Yves Cousteau developed the automatic regulator so that the diver no longer had to manually adjust the airflow. Cousteau gear is what is used to this day.

France was where most of the scuba developments occurred during the 1930s, and not surprisingly Italy (where scuba diving was also popular) took the lead in the military use of scuba gear. The Italian Navy formed a skilled and daring collection of military divers. These men carried off several raids on British Mediterranean bases during World War II. The Italian divers approached the British bases at night via small submarines or boats, than swam in to place explosives on the hulls of enemy merchant vessels or warships. These explosives had timers on them, so they would not go off until the ships were at sea, thus leaving the British in doubt about just how the ships were destroyed. The Italians also pioneered the development of torpedolike devices that the divers could ride, like a horse, for longer distances while carrying larger amounts of explosives.

Out of all this came the current U.S. Navy SEALs. These first appeared during World War II as Navy Combat Demolition Units (NCDUs). In 1943, volunteers from a Naval Construction Battalions (SeaBees) were selected and trained as the first NCDU. This came about because the Navy found that the new amphibious warfare ships, which ran right up on the beach, were vulnerable to steel pillars driven into the sand so that they were just below the surface at high tide (when the amphibious ships would be used, so that they hit the sand at the shallowest angle). Underwater Demolition Teams (UDTs), as the NCDUs were soon renamed, went in and used explosives to destroy these obstacles before the amphibious ships came in. UDTs were also used to go ashore to scout the beaches for other defenses (especially minefields, which were not visible from the air). Another essential scouting chore was taking a sample of the sand, because sand from different beaches has different carrying capacities. If the sand is too soft, you have to lay down some metal mats before trucks can drive across it.

As stealthy as the scout UDTs were, the enemy often figured out they had been there (and sometimes caught them in the act). So the Navy also used UDTs as a deception. These "beach jumpers" were sent to reconnoiter beaches that were not going to be invaded in order to confuse the enemy. This worked quite well.

Even before World War II was over, many UDTs were pointing out that they could do a lot more damage to the enemy because of the stealthy way they operated. Divers were trained to destroy (with explosives) any target that was near a coastline. During the Korean War (1950–1953), UDTs went after bridges and tunnels that near the coast. In the 1960s, elite UDTs were selected and trained as SEALs, and in 1983, the remaining UDTs were converted to SEALs.

The World War II experience also saw the development of special light boats and "underwater motorcycles" (descendants of the transport torpedoes) and even submarines specially equipped to transport and deploy SEALs. This unique form of warfare, "from the sea," was unexpected before World War II, but an established tool by the end of the war.

LONG RANGE DESERT GROUP

World War II reminded the generals that a few well-trained and resolute men could be extremely useful undertaking long-range patrols. This was first demonstrated in the North African desert and led to the current concept of Long Range Reconnaissance Patrols (LRRPs).

Some of the officers serving with the British Army in North Africa during World War II had lived in the area before the war. These men had come to know their way around the Sahara Desert, the largest desert in the world. But the desert is a severe and unforgiving place. As such, it has always appealed to those with the adventurous spirit. Even before World War II broke out, some British officers stationed in Egypt suggested establishing long-range desert patrols, using trucks instead of camels. For thousands of years, tribesmen had wandered the desert on camels, becoming the first long-range desert reconnaissance units. But using trucks allowed the unit to move faster, carry more equipment, and cover more ground in a shorter time. To do this you had to know how to navigate using the sun and the stars. You also needed extensive knowledge of the many kinds of ground you would encounter. Some you could cross, and some you couldn't. You had to know how to conserve water and how to deal with the various tribesmen you might run across. Like the tribesmen, you had to be able to read tracks, to determine who was coming from and going to where.

Once World War II began, the foremost "desert officer," Major Ralph Bagnold, was allowed to form what was first known as the Long Range Patrol Unit. These men went out on their first patrol in September 1940, about the same time that Italy decided to invade British-controlled Egypt. The patrols not only sneaked through "impassable" desert terrain but also staged attacks on undefended rear-area installations. These attacks cost the enemy valuable equipment and supplies as well as causing much nervousness and caution among troops who thought they were far from the front-line combat.

The LRDG (as it eventually came to be known) was never a large organization, rarely having more than three to four hundred men. Each patrol had twenty to thirty men and five or six trucks (or jeeps). Eventually, the LRDG formed its own Air Force by purchasing two civilian biplanes for flying important items (radio parts, captured documents, medicine) between their base and patrols out in the desert.

The LRDG demonstrated that the development of aircraft did not replace long-range ground reconnaissance. Even with sharp eyes and good cameras, recon aircraft would miss things. Moreover, aircraft could not sit around for days watching a road, and were pretty useless at night or in bad weather. The LRDG patrols could do all the things aircraft could not, and more. One of the more common LRDG missions was road watch. Two men, often without weapons (which would not do them much good if spotted by a larger enemy force), would sit by a road for twenty-four hours, taking notes of whatever passed. Once relieved, they would scurry back to their hidden camp and radio what they'd seen back to headquarters. At this point, the patrol would move on, for the Germans were good at radio direction finding (RDF, using two or more listening stations to pinpoint where a transmission was coming from). Often, the LRDG patrols would move by night, and hide by day, to avoid air patrols. But most of the LRDG time was spent deep in the desert. The average patrol lasted two weeks and covered some twelve hundred miles. Patrols did get attacked from time to time, and in one epic case, nine survivors of an air attack walked 186 miles back to base.

The LRDG were not considered commandos, but rather superb scouts. However, the patrols did carry explosives and lots of weapons (including 20mm or 37mm anti-aircraft guns), and would always put up a stiff fight if cornered. While all patrols were out looking for information, they would destroy any lightly guarded enemy camps or supply dumps they came across. Some of the first Special Air Service missions were carried out by riding into the enemy rear area with an LRDG patrol and then hooking up with the patrol later to make an escape. It was usually the LRDG that showed the SAS team the best way to reach an enemy airfield or camp. The LRDG maps of previously uncharted desert wastes allowed British units to outflank German units who thought the desert to the south was impassable. It was, unless an LRDG patrol had found the one track a combat unit could move along.

After the North African campaign ended in 1943, the LRDG moved on to scouting in the Aegean and Italy. Not having a desert didn't slow them down much. A good scout will always find a way.

What the LRDG accomplished during World War II was not forgotten. The U.S. Army set up long-range patrols into North Vietnam–

controlled territory during the Vietnam War. The Army Special Forces carried out a lot of those and are still trained and ready to go the long route into the enemy rear area for information or a fight.

POPSKI'S PRIVATE ARMY

In any war, extraordinary individuals will, by force of personality, create and lead exotic commando-type units. One of the most exotic was officially known (at various times) as the 1st Long Range Demolition Squadron and the 1st Special Demolition Squadron. But it was more commonly known as Popski's Private Army (PPA). Formed in North Africa at the outbreak of the war by a forty-three-year-old British officer, Vladimir Peniakoff ("Popski"), it specialized in going out into the desert and raiding distant enemy bases. Peniakoff was a Belgian (with a Russian father) who studied at Cambridge and served in the French Army during World War I. After that war, he went to Egypt and became a sugar manufacturer. While living in Egypt, Popski spent a lot of time traveling in the desert. Like T. E. Lawrence before World War I, he was much taken by desert life and became quite an expert in navigating the wastes. As World War II approached, he joined the British colonial forces in Egypt as an officer. Initially he served in the Libyan Arab Force, which mostly performed internal security duties as the British advanced into Libya.

Popski soon tired of this dull routine work and joined the Long Range Desert Group. The LRDG specialized in hitting Axis air bases well behind the front, and actually destroyed more enemy aircraft than did any Allied fighter squadron in the campaign. Popski, however, found this too tame, for the "long" in LRDG was not long enough. So he recruited his own specialized raiding group of about 120 men. The 1st Long Range Demolition Squadron made really deep penetration raids behind Axis lines, often striking hundreds of miles into the enemy's rear. Popski and his daredevils fought throughout the North African campaign and in Italy, making thousands of rear-area Italian and Germans troops decidedly uncomfortable.

Eventually, Popski was given his own unit. It was officially called Popski's Private Army and was recognized as the smallest independent unit (twenty-nine men at the time) in the British Army during World War II. Never let it be said that the British don't have a sense of humor.

But Popski got this kind of treatment mainly because he consistently produced results. He thrived in the British armed forces because the British have always recognized, and appreciated, "eccentrics." For this reason, the British were the first to field new weapons (like tanks and aircraft carriers) and let capable, if a bit odd, commanders do their thing unhindered. This is a long tradition. In the eighteenth and nineteenth centuries, the British were the first to use rifles, rangers (in North America), and artillery rockets.

Popski, and his bosses, also recognized that there was a certain kind of warrior who actually enjoyed war. The prospect of getting killed or maimed was secondary to accomplishing impossible feats and having an exciting time of it. Popski's Private Army actually had an unofficial recruiting slogan that reflected this: "Join Popski's Private Army and Enjoy the War." Popski knew what kind of men he was looking for, and he got them.

After the North African war ended in early 1943, Popski's Private Army moved to Italy, where they rampaged through the German rear area for the rest of the war. Popski wrote of his exploits after the war, but his private army was disbanded when peace came. Popski's spirit and capabilities live on in the SAS, which was revived in 1952.

There were several dozen small commando outfits like Popski's Private Army, none as small or as outrageously successful. World War II was notable for the adventurous attitudes of the senior commanders. There was a need for commandos in this war, and whenever the need arose, a strong leader, and equally adept followers, seemed to appear to do what had to be done.

SPECIAL AIR SERVICE DURING WORLD WAR II

The SAS are the current elite commandos of the British armed forces. The SAS developed from the Commandos during World War II, and were so successful that they provided the model for British postwar commandos. SAS differed from the original World War II Commandos in three respects:

- They operated in smaller units, usually a five-man team.
- They were trained to use parachutes (to land in enemy territory) and infiltration techniques (so they could sneak past enemy units to do

their work in the enemy rear area). In general, SAS troopers had more skills and were better trained than Commandos.

- Candidates for the SAS had to be more qualified than your average Commando.

The SAS began when a member of the 8th Commando, Lieutenant David Stirling, while in North Africa (after his unit had gotten banged around in the Crete battle), came up with the idea of using small units of Commandos to parachute deep into enemy territory and stealthily attack airfields and destroy enemy aircraft on the ground. The proposal was made in July 1941, and approved. To deceive the Germans, the new unit was called L Detachment, Special Air Services Brigade.

The parachute angle did not prove practical in North Africa, especially after a disastrous jump by five SAS teams in November 1941. So the SAS rode into the desert in armed jeeps and trucks, often with the Long Range Desert Patrol. This worked much better. In one week during December 1941, SAS teams destroyed sixty-one German aircraft and thirty vehicles. An even more spectacular raid was made in January 1942, when SAS hit a German fuel depot near the coast, destroying seventy-two thousand gallons of fuel, several docks, and warehouses holding thousands of tons of German supplies. Perhaps most important, eighteen large fuel transport trucks were destroyed as well, seriously limiting the ability of the Germans to keep their tanks and trucks moving in an offensive they had just launched.

By the summer of 1942, the handful of SAS troopers had destroyed more than two hundred German aircraft on the ground, more than the Royal Air Force had managed to destroy in the air. By the end of the North African campaign a year later, the SAS had destroyed over four hundred German aircraft. The Germans were very upset with this sort of thing, and had to divert thousands of troops to increase the security around their airfields. Sometimes this stopped the SAS raiders, but often it didn't. The SAS also attacked German targets on the island of Crete, in addition to raids all over North Africa.

In March 1943, SAS strength stood at 580 men, and all were members of the 1st SAS Regiment. At that point, some reorganization took place. This was caused largely by the capture of SAS founder David Stirling and several other key officers. The French SAS troops, and some non-French men, went off to form the 2nd SAS Regiment for the expected invasion of France in 1944. Another group formed the Special Raiding Squadron (SRS), which went off to fight in Sicily with 287 men. Unfortunately, they got into commando-type fighting, not SAS-style operations, and took sixty-eight casualties in their first action. The SRS went back to Britain in December and reconstituted themselves as the 1st SAS. Back in England, the need for expert commandos, and reputation of the SAS, was such that after the 2nd SAS was formed the French formed the 3rd and 4th SAS and the Belgians the 5th SAS. All this activity was to support the invasion of France.

The remainder of the March 1943 SAS went on to form the Special Boat Squadron (SBS). This is an SAS outfit that specializes in raids from the sea, using small teams—something like the modern-day U.S. Navy SEALs. The SBS still exists.

THE ORIGINS OF THE U.S. SPECIAL FORCES

At this point, it became apparent that SAS members were turning into something other than commandos. In fact, the highly skilled and talented SAS men were seen as capable of helping the espionage agencies that were working with the French resistance. As part of the preparations for the D-Day invasion, British (Special Operations Executive, or SOE) and American (Office of Strategic Services, or OSS) were landing (by boat and aircraft) hundreds of agents in France (and other occupied countries) to assist the guerrilla organizations that had developed to fight the Germans. Most of these guerrillas were poorly armed, trained, and led. In France, twenty-five three-man Jedburgh teams were parachuted in to work with the guerrilla organizations. These teams concentrated on establishing regular radio contact between the guerrillas and SOE and OSS headquarters in Britain, making it easer to get the guerrillas weapons, equipment, and instructions for their part in supporting the D-Day invasion. The modern-day equivalent of the Jedburgh teams are the CIA and U.S. Army Special Forces teams sent to Afghanistan in late 2001. The OSS also had seven thirty-four man Operational Groups (OGs) that were sent in after the invasion to work with the guerrillas. The OGs were doing pretty much what the U.S. Army Special Forces do today: training the locals and fighting as needed.

While SOE and OSS had nearly three hundred people behind

enemy lines during the 1944 battle for France, the SAS had more than twice as many. Often, the SAS went in with the SOE or OSS teams, and regularly worked with these teams. While the SAS men were also there to work with the local guerrillas, they also did a lot of fighting. SAS troops had lots of training and experience in sabotage, and a major job for the guerrillas was destroying railroad equipment, bridges, and communications (telephone wires, radar stations). Naturally, the SAS and the guerrillas tried to avoid battles with the more numerous and better-armed Germans. But a smaller number of Germans— say, couriers driving along a road on a motorcycle, or a small convoy of German trucks—was considered a good target for an ambush. As throughout the war, however, the main SAS mission was reconnaissance and sabotage.

In 1945, the SAS was disbanded, only to be re-formed in 1952 to deal with communist guerrillas in Malaya (then a British colony). From that point on, it was realized that an organization like the SAS was useful in peacetime, and it has been in operation ever since. Americans who served in the OSS and saw the SAS in action came out of World War II with their own ideas on how to use this new form of warfare. And out of that came the current U.S. Army Special Forces.

THE ORIGINS OF THE GREEN BERET

For the first year of the British Commandos' existence, there was no common headdress for the troops. In the British Army, each regiment has its own headdress that's worn when not in the field. Each regiment tries to be distinctive, using a wide variety of head covering (caps, berets, tam-o-shanters, and so on). Since the men were all volunteers from other infantry units and the Commandos were still thought of, by some, as a temporary wartime assignment, every Commando unit featured a wide array of different headgear when back at its base. This did not please the sergeant majors—the senior NCOs in charge of seeing that the unit ran smoothly. So in the summer of 1942, Commando officers sought to come up with a common headdress for all commandos. Actually, the 1st and 9th Commandos had already standardized on the tam-o'-shanter. But this was seen as something that identified the wearer as Scots, and that would not do for the English,

Irish, and Welsh Commandos. Then it was noted that the tank and parachute troops—two other rather recent British military organizations—had adopted the beret. The tank troops, who first saw action in 1915, adopted the black beret before World War I ended. The parachute troops, who were being formed about the same time as the Commandos, had adopted the red beret. Since those two colors were already taken, everyone seemed to agree that a green beret would be just right. This quick consensus came from the history of the British Army, where light infantry and colonial ranger units all used a lot of green in their uniforms, since these troops were trained to sneak around the woods and surprise, or avoid, the enemy. In 1953, as the U.S. Army Special Forces were being formed, some of the first members were veterans of the OSS and had seen the SAS and British Commandos in action. These men got green berets and began wearing them as unofficial headgear. It wasn't until the end of the 1950s that the Army finally allowed the Special Forces to wear the green beret as part of their uniform.

U.S. ARMY RANGERS

Ranger battalions were the U.S. Army's version of the British Commando units, created in light of the British success. Unfortunately, the Americans lost sight of the key elements in the British concept of commando operations. The Americans allowed the Ranger units to turn into units that were neither commandos, nor regular infantry. The British concept was of very well-trained infantrymen who were basically amphibious raiders. The Commandos went ashore in small groups, hit an enemy installation, and then departed as they had arrived, by sea. Perhaps the Army was too afraid of being identified with the U.S. Marine Corps, which had formed its own Raider battalions but still considered every Marine a "raider."

In 1942, America decided to form its own commandos and called them Rangers. The name was taken from the eighteenth-century American unit Rogers's Rangers—also one of the inspirations of the British Commandos. That summer, a group of American volunteers (forty-five men and six officers) went off to train with the British Commandos. These troops formed the training cadre for the 1st Ranger Battalion, which was ready for action by the end of 1942.

The Rangers also adopted the British form of organization, which was shaped by the amphibious landing craft the Commandos used on their raids. Since an assault landing craft could hold thirty-five troops (or eight hundred pounds of equipment), the Commando (and Ranger) platoon contained thirty-two men. Two platoons made up a company (which had a headquarters of four men), and six companies made up the battalion. The battalion headquarters and support troops came to 108 men, giving a total strength of 27 officers and 489 men. With this form of organization, the Commandos (or Rangers) could be sent ashore in twelve to fifteen LCAs. It was in terms of equipment that the Rangers began to differ from the Commandos.

American Rangers performed successfully during the U.S. 1943 invasion of North Africa. The first battle was against French and Italian troops, and the Americans did well. The Rangers stormed ashore in their first action against the French and later carried off a spirited series of attacks, interspersed by long hikes over mountain trails, at night, to successfully attack surprised Italian units.

During the summer of 1942, as America and Canada prepared to attack the Japanese bases in the Aleutian Islands off Alaska, the 1st Special Service Force was formed from American and Canadian volunteers. The Japanese evacuated their Aleutian bases before they could be attacked, so this brigade-sized force ended up fighting in Italy and was disbanded in late 1944. The unit was considered a Ranger-quality force, but was mainly used for conventional infantry fighting.

In late December 1942, the 29th Provisional Ranger Battalion was formed in Britain from eighteen members of the 1st Ranger Battalion and volunteers from the 1st Infantry Division. In April and May 1943, the 2nd and 4th Ranger Battalions were formed in the United States. About the same time, the 3rd Ranger Battalion was formed in North Africa. In September 1943, the 5th Ranger Battalion was formed in the United States. In the Pacific, the 6th Ranger Battalion was formed in August 1944 from an artillery battalion. This process was difficult, because most artillerymen are not eager to join the infantry, much less an elite and hard-fighting outfit like the Rangers. Some of the artillerymen didn't work out, and more infantry volunteers had to be obtained to get the unit ready for action.

The 29th Ranger Battalion worked with British Commandos on several operations, but the unit was disbanded in October 1943. The

1st, 3rd, and 4th Battalions were collectively known as "Darby's Rangers" (after the founder of the 1st Rangers) through 1943, when they operated together in Italy. The 1st and 3rd Rangers took part in the Sicily invasion during the summer of 1943. There they used daring assaults to tear up enemy units and keep their casualties down. All three battalions of Darby's Rangers landed south of Naples in the fall of 1943 for the invasion of Italy. This involved a lot of hard infantry fighting, and in forty-five days of combat, the three Ranger battalions suffered 40 percent casualties.

Pulled out of the fighting for rebuilding, Darby's Rangers were then sent in to lead the amphibious invasion of Anzio (south of Rome). Two British Commandos went in as well, and these five battalions of elite troops made the landing, against opposition, a success. But a week later, the three Ranger battalions tried a risky infiltration of German positions at night and were caught in a desperate infantry battle. Two battalions lost 60 percent of their men (dead and wounded), and all but eighteen of the remainder were captured. The 4th Rangers took 40 percent casualties, but the survivors avoided capture. However, after the Anzio campaign ended in June, the 4th Rangers were disbanded, as were the 3rd Rangers (after the January 31st disaster). Survivors of the 1st Rangers were disbanded as well.

The 2nd and 5th Ranger Battalions were already in Britain; both took part in the D-Day invasion and subsequent fighting across France and into Germany. Both battalions were disbanded in June 1945.

In all these campaigns, there was an increasing tendency to use the Rangers as very competent infantry (which they were). But this caused heavy casualties that could not be replaced by men of the same caliber. The quality of the Ranger units declined throughout 1943.

Senior commanders did not grasp the essence of commando operations: Get them in against a target regular infantry can't handle, and then get them out again. Like many of their British counterparts, American commanders tended to use Rangers as elite infantry. This was what Rangers were, but this was not the way they were designed to be used. They were raiders, and that's what they had to be trained, equipped, and used as.

The British equipped the Commandos with light machine guns, submachine guns, and (in the battalion headquarters) light mortars and other heavy weapons as needed. British practice was to take only what was needed on a mission. Usually, the Commandos used only small arms and machine guns. The British realized that these troops were raiders who were not being sent to duke it out in a sustained infantry fight. American commanders missed this point and loaded up the Rangers with heavier weapons. Instead of twenty-pound automatic rifles (BARs), the rangers got forty-five-pound machine guns (M1919A4s). Instead of 60mm mortars, the Rangers had to lug around 81mm mortars. The Rangers added bazookas, even though they kept the obsolete British anti-tank rifles. The Commandos remained lean and mean; the Rangers continued to pile on the stuff to be carried. The Rangers also became less mean, because there were too many of them and too many casualties that could not be replaced with qualified troops.

"Too heavy to move and too light to fight" is how many put it at the time. But the Rangers, and the senior commanders who used them, learned from the Anzio disaster. The remaining three Ranger battalions fought on throughout the war. The Rangers continued to be used as infantry, but not as often and not in situations where their lighter armament would prove troublesome. Rangers continued to train for, and occasionally pull off, commando-type operations. Ironically, members of the sixth Rangers, who were recruited and trained in haste, had some of the most spectacular successes. They were nearly always used as raiders. In January 1945, 121 men of the 6th Rangers, working with 240 Filipino guerrillas, rescued 513 American prisoners held since the Japanese captured the Philippines in 1942. Some two thousand Japanese troops were guarding the prison camp, but the Rangers got in, grabbed the prisoners, and got out while suffering only twenty-six dead. It was an impressive operation that any commando would have been proud of. The 6th Rangers were disbanded in Japan at the end of 1945.

Some have blamed many of the Rangers' problems on their first commander, Lieutenant Colonel William Darby (he was promoted from captain in two weeks after being given the job in 1942). An artilleryman, Darby was held responsible for loading up the Rangers with a lot of heavy weapons that slowed them down. But it wasn't just Darby. The Army didn't grasp the fact that commandos were specialists, to be held in reserve most of the time until they were needed to pull off some desperate mission. The Rangers provided excellent infantry and fought well throughout the war (or until battalions were practically wiped out and disbanded). The only things lost were opportunities, opportunities for Rangers to do what Rangers do best.

Perhaps the most lasting, and valuable, lesson to come out of the World War II Ranger experience is that well-trained and well-led infantry can be very effective. But such men are not bulletproof, and heavy casualties can be expected. Many U.S. infantrymen remembered the Rangers, and starting during the Korean War, small, informal and unofficial units of Rangers were formed to do what Rangers do: scout and raid. Eventually, three Ranger battalions were created in the 1970s.

U.S. MARINE COMMANDOS

The U.S. Marines, a rough bunch to begin with, noted the success of the British Commandos and, like the U.S. Army, decided to form their own commando units. The Marines were also impressed by the German use of paratroopers, and decided to create some "paramarines" as well.

It's good to remember that, while World War II began in September 1939, the United States did not get into the war until December 1941. Thus for more than two years, U.S. military men were watching with intense interest (and taking notes about) the startling new military developments. The Marines decided in 1940 that they needed some airborne troops, and in August 1941 the 1st and 2nd Marine Parachute Battalions were formed. The 3rd Battalion was formed in 1942, and the 4th in early 1943. By early 1943, the 1st Marine Parachute Regiment was seeing heavy combat in the Southwest Pacific. But by then the brass noted that, while the Marine paratroopers were excellent fighters, they had yet to come across an opportunity to use their parachutes. And it did not look like there would be many such opportunities. So in late 1943, the regiment was shipped back to California and disbanded. The paramarines were used to create the 5th Marine Division. The 4th Battalion never left California, and was also used to help build the 5th Division. The USMC continued to train individual Marines for parachute duty, sending them to the Army Airborne School for that. But once helicopters became practical for sea duty in the 1950s, the Marines saw that this was the better way to move troops into combat.

The Marine generals also noted the success of the British Commandos and decided that this was just the sort of thing Marines could handle. The idea was further encouraged by Marine lieutenant colonel Evans Carlson, who had served as U.S. military observer with Chinese communist forces in 1937 and 1938. The Chinese had developed some excellent commando tactics, and Carlson was taken by their motto, "Gung Ho" ("work together" in Chinese). Carlson also knew President Roosevelt, having been in charge of a security detachment guarding the president during a visit to Warm Springs, Georgia. He and the president continued to correspond. By 1941, selected Marines began training to be Raiders. The training was based on what the British Commandos went through. Eventually, some 5,000 Marines would receive Raider training. Four Raider battalions were formed: the 1st and 2nd Raiders in February 1942, the 3rd Raiders in September 1942, and the 4th Raiders in October 1942. The 1st and 2nd Raider Battalions were in combat by August, with the 1st Raiders as part of the force that attacked Guadalcanal and 221 men of the 2nd Raiders taking part in a raid on Makin Island. These two battalions continued to fight in the Solomon Islands until they were disbanded in 1943. The 2nd Raiders was commanded by Lieutenant Colonel Carlson. The 3rd and 4th Raiders also went to the Solomons, where they fought until disbanded in late 1943. While the Raiders fought well, there weren't many specific commando missions in the Pacific. The Marines began a series of amphibious assaults on heavily defended Japanese islands in late 1943 (Tarawa was the first). It was obvious during the training of Marines for this first assault that some commando techniques were required, but commandos themselves would not have been of much additional use. So it was decided to use the Raider battalions to form a Marine regiment for a new division. By early 1944, the Marine Raider battalions were no more. As far as many Marines were concerned, "All Marines are commandos."

THE MAKIN MISTAKE

While the U.S. capture of Guadalcanal on August 7, 1942, was the first American offensive operation of the Pacific war, it tends to overshadow a spectacular raid by American troops ten days later. On August 17, 221 U.S. Marine Raiders landed on the Japanese-held island of Makin. The Marines were landed from two submarines. Within hours, they had destroyed a newly built seaplane base (for reconnaissance of the surrounding waters). The ninety-man Japanese garrison of the small island was wiped out. The Marines lost thirty dead and fourteen wounded. But the Japanese had gotten off a radio message before they were killed, and the Marines made haste to leave before Japanese reinforcements could arrive from nearby islands. The raid was mainly for propaganda purposes, although it did serve some military function by destroying the seaplane base. The Japanese occupied a lot of small Pacific islands only so they could build an airfield or seaplane base. With these, they could easily keep an eye on large areas of the vast Pacific. In this case, the Japanese were able to quickly replace what was destroyed on Makin.

Unfortunately, the raid backfired badly on the Marines. It made the Japanese aware of how vulnerable their many small island garrisons were. As a result, the Japanese decided to install larger garrisons on many of these islands and set the troops to work building extensive fortifications. When the Marines began invading these islands in late 1943, they encountered far heavier fortifications than might have been there if Makin had not been invaded. Of course, once the heavily fortified island of Tarawa was taken by the Marines in November 1943, the Japanese began to rethink their defensive tactics. This led to the bloody fighting on Iwo Jima, Saipan, and Okinawa, where the Japanese left the beaches undefended and instead placed their troops inside bunkers inland, away from the naval guns that had been so devastating at Tarawa. If Makin had not occurred and a less well-fortified Tarawa was more easily overrun by the Marines, the Japanese probably would have tried beach defenses at least one more time before eventually withdrawing their troops into the interior of islands they were defending.

This was always the downside of raids, which often exploited some mistake the enemy made in deploying his forces. The enemy, if he has any brains at all, changes his tactics to make that particular raiding tactic useless. Which is why raiders have to be smart, so they can always be one step ahead of their opponents and able to find one new enemy vulnerability after another.

There was another American raid in 1942 that had a better long-term outcome. The Doolittle raid (April 18, 1942, when sixteen B-25 bombers flew from a carrier to bomb Japan) caused the Japanese to keep hundreds of combat aircraft on the home islands to prevent another attack. The United States had no intention of repeating the Doolittle raid, but the Japanese could take no chances. It was very embarrassing for the government to have American bombers over Tokyo at the same time Japanese forces were so successful elsewhere. Those aircraft that were kept in Japan provided less opposition for American forces closing in from the east and the south.

Even the Makin raid had a similar impact. While the Marines had a harder time taking the heavily fortified Tarawa, the Japanese put thousands of additional troops on Pacific islands that America did not invade. The American strategy was to take only those islands needed for air bases. The other Japanese islands were bombed to destroy any aircraft they had on them and sink any ships in the area. The islands were then blockaded by warships and aircraft and left to wait for the end of the war, when the garrisons surrendered.

But the lesson should never be forgotten: Raids will always have consequences, often unintended consequences.

SNEAKING IN BY AIR

Two bits of technology made the vast number of special operations during World War II possible. First, there were relatively lightweight, cheap, and reliable radios. Being able to keep in touch with agents deep in enemy territory eliminated a problem that had long made it difficult to keep a lot of spies, commandos, and partisans going. But equally important was the availability of air transport. Agents and supplies could be brought in at night and parachuted to their operating areas. Long-range bombers were used for much of the parachute work. B-17s and Halifax bombers could carry several tons of matériel and many personnel nearly anywhere in Europe. In addition, it was also possible to fly in, land deep inside enemy territory, pick up people and matériel, and fly out. But flying in and out was a tricky business in this period just before the introduction of the helicopter. Only aircraft that could land on unprepared fields (clover turned out to be the best vegetation to land on), and take off from them as well, were capable of this. Flying in was particularly dicey in Europe, because the Germans had troops everywhere and soon figured out which open fields were suitable for impromptu landings. Because of the range of the aircraft capable of making these landings, most took place in France.

As the war went on and Allied ground forces advanced closer to Germany, landings could be made in more distant German-occupied territory. The favorite aircraft for these missions was the British Westland Lysander. This was a large (three-ton, fifty-foot wingspan), single-engine aircraft with a maximum range of about five hundred miles. This two-seat aircraft was originally designed for Army liaison, towing targets and gliders and artillery spotting. Its slow speed (208 miles per hour, max) and handling characteristics allowed the Lysander to take off from a four-hundred-yard field and land on one even smaller. The short range prevented the Lysander from getting to key places such as Poland, where the local partisans managed to obtain valuable documents and weapons parts from German factories. There was a longer range (thirty-five-hundred-mile) aircraft that could land on rough fields. This was the twin-engine De Havilland D.H. 98 Mosquito. This aircraft was made mostly of wood, but was larger (ten tons, fifty-four-foot wingspan) and not able to use the more numerous small landing areas the Lysander could handle. As a result, many opportunities to obtain valuable items from guerrillas were missed.

The Russians had the Po-2 biplane, a slow but agile aircraft that could land and take off just about anywhere. Its small size (thirty-eight-foot wingspan, 1.35 tons) worked against it in some respects. It could only carry about five hundred pounds of cargo and one or two passengers. Its top speed was a hundred miles an hour, and its maximum range was three hundred miles. The short range was not a major problem, because most of the Soviet guerrillas were just behind the front lines. Landing in enemy territory was not even tried that often, given the danger involved. There were fewer than a thousand of these missions. Most were flown at night, and skillful and experienced pilots were required. But the rewards were great. Guerrilla leaders benefited by a flight back to friendly territory for meetings, and key agents often had to be brought out for thorough debriefings. There was also the morale factor. Guerrillas felt a bit better knowing they had supporters who had the capability to pick them up and fly them out of the precarious situation they were involved in. When guerrillas controlled enough territory to hold a permanent airfield, larger aircraft were brought in. At this point, badly wounded guerrillas could be flown out. This was a major morale booster.

After World War II, helicopters came along, making it easier to support guerrillas. Fixed-wing aircraft also acquired gadgets that could literally grab a cargo container, or fearless passenger, off the ground and haul it into the aircraft. Not for the faint of heart, but it shows you what resourceful people can do.

Even during World War II, the U.S. Army Air Force began forming special aircraft units for high-risk transport flights into enemy territory. Much of this was directed at retrieving shot-down pilots. Eventually this led to the large number of customized transports and helicopters used to support special operations. "Sneaking in by air" has now become a profession.

GERMAN COMMANDOS: THE BRANDENBURGERS

The British and American press played up the exploits of their commandos, leaving most people unaware that the Germans played this game too. The German Army commandos were called "Brandenburgers," after the area where they trained. These men belonged to military intelligence and were not associated with the Nazi Party's Waffen-SS forces. The Brandenburgers didn't get along with the SS anyway, because the man who created them, Admiral Canaris, was a secret anti-Nazi.

The idea of German commandos began after World War I, when Theodore von Hippel, a veteran of von Lettow-Vorbeck's guerrilla operations in Africa, joined the postwar army. Von Hippel advocated a unit of highly trained and resourceful troops who would operate in enemy territory to seize vital bridges and other installations. Von Hippel was thinking of men who spoke the enemy language fluently and wore enemy uniforms. This was illegal according to the laws of war, and such men could be executed if caught. But von Hippel persisted, and a few hundred men were trained for such missions by the time World War II broke out. While von Hippel's men performed well during the invasion of Poland, the army disbanded the unit after the Polish campaign was over. Most German generals did not care for the concept, seeing these troops as a bunch of thugs and criminals. But Admiral Canaris, the head of Abwehr (German military intelligence), did notice, and he gave von Hippel and his troops a home. He set up a training camp for them outside Berlin, in Brandenburg.

While there was some resistance to the commando concept in the Allied armies, the resistance was particularly intense in the German armed forces. Despite this, Canaris backed the Brandenburgers, and several thousand men were trained and deployed. Little has been heard of their activities, mainly because they operated in small units and participated in many clandestine operations. Also, Germany lost the war, so there has been little written about them in Germany, and not much of this translated into other languages. Nevertheless, Brandenburgers participated, with success, in all Germany's invasions during the first two years of the war. They were less successful later on when they tried to apply their skills against guerrillas. By 1944, the Brandenburgers were converted to mechanized infantry (*panzergrenadiers*); at the end of the war there was a Brandenburgers division. When the Abwehr Brandenburgers were shut down, about eighteen hundred of them transferred to an SS commando unit (Otto Skorzeny's Jagdkommando), where they participated in additional spectacular operations until the war ended.

What made the Brandenburgers unique was that they worked for military intelligence, not the combat forces. Most of the Brandenburger's missions had a direct military impact, but their operations were generally more strategic than most other World War II commandos. In this respect, the Brandenburgers were ahead of their time. Many commando units set up after World War II recognized that commandos were more effective not as supersoldiers, but as skilled operators who could take care of important strategic missions.

RUSSIAN COMMANDOS

As obscure as the Brandenburgers are, Russian World War II commandos are even more shrouded in secrecy. There are two reasons for this. First, Russia did not establish any commando units in the Western sense. Second, what commandos the Russians did use either belonged to the NKVD (secret police) or were temporary organizations. The Soviet dictator Stalin was not keen on having any commando units that might threaten his rule. The NKVD's commando units were largely concerned with counterintelligence—catching spies. These were of platoon and company size, and many of them were not commandos in the usual sense; they were not elite combat troops. The temporary commando units usually contained a high proportion of political officers and regular officers selected for their political reliability. These units were trained for a specific mission, and then disbanded (or returned to noncommando status) after the mission was completed. The Russians didn't get into the traditional commando game until the 1960s when they formed Spetsnaz units.

ROYAL MARINE COMMANDOS AFTER WORLD WAR II

Britain, which invented the modern concept of the commando, disbanded its ten Army Commandos at the end of World War II. The Royal Marines, however, saw the commando concepts as a welcome addition to their own doctrine and retained three of their nine Royal Marine Commandos. Since World War II, the Royal Marines have maintained at least three Commando battalions (called Commandos, instead of battalions). Artillery and engineer units are supplied by the Army. Like the U.S. Marines, the Royal Marines realized that assault from the sea always was a commandolike operation requiring special training, bold leadership, and an aggressive spirit. The Royal Marines, like their American counterparts, continued to innovate. In 1956, during the invasion of Egypt, it was a Royal Marine Commando that launched the first helicopter assault from ships against a land target. The Royal Marine Commandos were used extensively to keep the peace in Ireland during the 1970s and 1980s. In 1982, it was two Royal Marine Commandos and one parachute battalion that did most of the fighting to retake the Falkland Islands from Argentina. The Royal Marines have performed peacekeeping duty in the Balkans and Africa, and served as an amphibious fast-reaction force.

While the U.S. Marines made a name for themselves with multidivision amphibious operations in the Pacific during World War II, the Royal Marines stuck with the commando-type operations that characterize what Marines spend most of the time doing between major wars. The last large-scale amphibious operation took place more than half a century ago, at Inchon, Korea, in 1950. Since then, the typical Marine mission has been a quick assault using a small (usually battalion-sized) force.

U.S. RANGER COMPANIES IN KOREA

When the Korean War broke out in June 1950, Ranger veterans immediately saw a need for Rangers. Because the World War II Rangers impressed so many officers who were now, in 1950, working in the Pentagon, the idea of reviving the Rangers for Korea was able to gain traction. In short order—by October, 1950—a Ranger School was established at Fort Benning and volunteers began taking the six-week training course. The 1st Ranger Company was in Korea by December. Meanwhile, two ranger companies had been organized in Korea from volunteers stationed in Japan. These were deactivated in early 1951 as the Ranger companies began to arrive from the United States. Fifteen Ranger companies were organized in the U.S., and eight were sent to Korea. One was sent to West Germany, and the other seven to different bases stateside. But all were demobilized in late 1951. The Ranger proponents in the army had been pushing for the formation of Ranger battalions, but the anti-Ranger factions managed to get the Ranger companies disbanded. The reason was the need for such elite troops in the existing airborne units, and the fact that those units were needed in the event of a Russian invasion of Western Europe. The Ranger companies were drawing a tremendous number of volunteers from the two airborne divisions, which was beginning to hurt the divisions' readiness for combat. Moreover, the Army doctrine was moving towards greater use of nuclear weapons, making elite infantry less essential. This was odd, because the Ranger companies were doing an outstanding job in Korea, and there was no shortage of volunteers to replace losses. While the Ranger companies were gone, the Ranger School was allowed to remain open, to provide Ranger training to officers and NCOs thought to be on the fast track to positions of great responsibility. Between the end of the Korean War (1953) and the arrival of large number of U.S. troops in Vietnam (1965), the usefulness of the Ranger companies and Long Range Reconnaissance Patrols was remembered in the Army. Both would return once Americans found themselves in a major war.

6 THE GOLDEN AGE: ELITE TROOPS

In addition to commandos, World War II also saw the development of specialized elite troops who invented many important skills and tactics now widely used by Special Operations Forces. These elite forces became the prototypes of the armies of Perfect Soldiers that began to appear in the late twentieth century.

PARATROOPERS IN SEARCH OF A MISSION

Paratroopers—infantrymen who use parachutes to arrive on the battlefield—were one of those pre–World War II ideas that were supposed to be the next big thing in warfare. They weren't. But the concept was important, especially for commandos.

Modern parachutes were developed during World War I, and the Italians were the first to use them to put troops on the ground, to drop observers behind enemy lines. The Germans were the only ones to equip their combat pilots with parachutes during World War I. After the war, in the late 1920s, the Italians were the first to experiment with dropping infantry by parachute. The Russians, as we've discussed, were the first to form parachute battalions. They were also the first to use paratroopers in combat, dropping twelve hundred men and eighteen light artillery guns to help stop a 1936 Afghan invasion of Tajikistan. The Germans, French, and Italians noticed this and also formed parachute battalions. Going into World War II, the Germans planned to use a small number of paratroopers (one battalion in 1939) as commandos. They did so when they invaded Norway in early 1940, and Belgium shortly thereafter.

The German technique in Norway was actually ahead of its time. What they did was drop a company of paratroopers on an airfield. After a sharp fight, the paratroopers controlled the airfield, thus allowing many more German infantry to be brought in on transports landed at the captured field. This "air landing" technique has become the standard, and very successful, tactic for using heliborne troops. But in 1940, there were no helicopters. The spectacular commando raid on the formidable Belgium fortress Eban Emael used paratroopers coming in via glider. Again, this recognized that parachutes have severe limitations, and that the heavy explosive charges the Germans needed to blast their way into the fortress were more easily carried on a glider. (Today a helicopter would be used.)

After the British formed their first parachute units in late 1940, they began using the troops in commando raids. The second raid, in 1942, was a spectacular success, with the paratroopers capturing a German radar station (using a new technology) on the French coast, getting away with key equipment and one German radar technician.

The Germans soon revealed the downside of parachute assault, however. In May 1941, the Germans used two thousand paratroopers (plus thousands more glider and air-landed infantry) to attack the British-held island of Crete. The Germans won the battle. This appeared to be a striking victory—forty-two thousand British troops were defeated by twenty-two thousand Germans. Hitler proclaimed that "the German soldier can do anything." But the German generals actually knew better, because Crete was a very costly victory. German casualties were so high, especially among the paratroopers, that many of the airborne battalions were no longer capable of combat once the battle was over. The Germans rebuilt their airborne force to thirty thousand by early 1942, but they never again attempted to pull another desperate battle like Crete.

On Crete, the Germans learned that paratroopers only had a chance to succeed if they were carefully trained and well led. In fact, the most effective paratroopers were commandos dropped from the air. Aside from their better training and the surprise gained from descending out of nowhere, everything else was against a paratrooper. Although they confused the enemy by the suddenness of their descent, the paratroopers themselves were also scattered (by winds or air transports on the wrong course) while landing. No one ever came up with a solution to this problem. Paratroopers also came down with light weapons, although larger and larger gliders were built during the war to carry heavy weapons and even armored vehicles. Still, whatever could be landed from the air was never enough to win without heavy casualties to the paratroopers. In 1943 and 1945, the Allies conducted several large airborne assaults: Sicily, Normandy, southern France, Arnhem, and the Rhine. All of them were more or less successful, but only one of them, Normandy, was a success worth the cost. In virtually every other case the operation was either largely unnecessary or hideously expensive.

Meanwhile, smaller airborne operations actually continued to be quite successful. In late 1942, battalion-sized parachute drops captured important crossroads and airfields. For example, battalion-sized American and British airdrops were used to capture several vital crossroads and airfields during operations in French North Africa in late 1942. A similar-sized operation dropped American reinforcements into the Salerno bridgehead in September 1943, and battalion of paratroopers saved a desperate situation. Another small drop was used to capture the fortified island of Corregidor from the Japanese in early 1945. The Germans' luck with airborne operations went downhill after Crete, even though they only used small drops. One success was a drop on the Aegean island of Leros, after the Italian surrender, in September 1943. Other drops in Russia and North Africa failed, largely due to the poorly trained pilots and a shortage of aircraft. Britain used small-unit drops successfully in Burma.

The larger parachute units (divisions) were less successful. The more paratroopers you put into an operation, the more transport aircraft you needed, and the harder it was to control all the paratroopers who landed where they weren't supposed to. A company was one to two hundred troops and required six to ten transports. Most major drops involved half a dozen or more battalions of paratroopers. Each battalion required twenty to twenty-five transports, and with that many aircraft trying to find the landing zone, often at night, you can see how these major drops quickly turned into a confused mess.

Ironically, the Germans had the right formula for an airborne division in 1940 when they formed the 7th Air Landing Division. This unit used company-sized units of paratroopers, as well as company-sized units landing in gliders. Most of the forty-five hundred troops in the division were infantry whose only special training was to get off transports quickly once they had landed on a recently captured airfield. As successful as the 7th Air Division was early in the war, the Germans were, like everyone else, mesmerized by the idea of parachute divisions. While the Germans never assembled the resources (mainly a lot of transport aircraft and air superiority) for a division-sized drop, the Allies did.

For the Germans, the need for good-quality infantry led to the Luftwaffe raising more parachute units in 1943. In that year, three divisions were created, followed by another six in 1944 and two more in early 1945. Most of these troops did not get parachute training, because the Germans were losing air superiority and couldn't afford to build enough air transports anyway. But since it was prestigious to be a paratrooper, and only volunteers (for the most part) were accepted, the original parachute troops were able to train thousands of additional airborne soldiers. More than a quarter of a million Germans served in the parachute forces. Most of their eight parachute divisions—really excellent motorized infantry outfits—served in the West (Italy and France), and the Allies learned that they were going to have problems whenever they ran into them.

RUSSIA'S PARACHUTE ARMY

The largest (on paper), and second largest (in reality) airborne force of World War II was Russian. In 1941, the nation had five "airborne corps" (each with about ten thousand troops, equivalent to an American airborne division). These units did not all have equipment, and the purges of the late 1930s had eliminated some of the best airborne officers. Then when the Germans invaded in June 1941, the Russian Air Force was quickly destroyed. Lacking air transports, and with the Germans rapidly advancing on the ground, the five airborne corps were sent in as ground troops. Most of these paratroopers were killed before the end of the year, thus destroying the airborne force Russia had spent the last nine years building up. They did not die in vain, however, because the Germans had a tough time whenever they encountered the Russian paratroopers. But by early 1942, only two of the three airborne corps were intact.

Before the Russian paratroopers were destroyed, some of them did get a chance to use their parachuting skills. Between December 1941 and March 1942, thirty-five hundred paratroopers were dropped behind German lines to assist the growing number of guerrilla units being formed. Another seven thousand troops were brought in via gliders, as were supplies for the guerrillas. This activity caught the attention of the Germans, who eventually wiped out nearly all these troops.

Undismayed, the surviving Russian paratroopers were used to train more airborne troops, and five more airborne corps were quickly formed. All ten airborne corps, in fact, saw a lot of combat during the spring of 1942. There were some small parachute drops, but none had much impact on the fighting. In the summer of 1942, the ten airborne corps, and five independent airborne brigades, were turned into regular infantry units and sent south to fight in the battles that led to the German defeat at Stalingrad in early 1943. But even before this campaign was over, paratroopers were pulled out of their infantry jobs at the end of 1942 and used to organize ten guards airborne divisions (basically the same as the previous airborne corps). But again it changed. The Germans began attacking Russia again in the spring of 1943, the paratroopers were once more sent in as ground troops, and most of them were lost.

Still undismayed, the Russians formed another twenty airborne brigades (about fifty thousand troops), which they used to form another six airborne corps. Three of these brigades were used in the first deliberate attempt to use parachutists to support a major operation, the largest Russian airborne operation to date. On September 24th, 1943, three parachute and three air landing brigades hit ground twenty-five miles behind German lines along the Dnieper River near Kanev. Hastily organized, it was a disaster. Most of the parachutists had never jumped out of an airplane before, although many had at least jumped from a training tower in a parachute harness. The inexperienced pilots had to do the drop at night, to avoid the risk of German fighters, and there weren't enough transport aircraft. The Russians also hadn't learned how important it was to move away from their drop zones quickly and form into larger units. The small, scattered Russians were quickly run down and destroyed by the Germans. What can be said is that the distraction took some German combat units away from the front line, and this did allow the oncoming Russian armor units to advance a bit farther than they otherwise would have.

Stalin was not happy with this, the first real test of Russian airborne forces in their designed role. But then, their failure was not surprising. After the Germans threatened to overrun Moscow in 1941, the Russians ruthlessly gathered whatever forces they could to stem the German advance. This meant paratroopers being thrown into ground battles as infantry. Yet the persistent efforts to organize new airborne units recognized that the airborne capability was important. But the Russian Air Force was never able to support airborne operations sufficiently to make them work. For the rest of the war, Soviet airborne forces were kept on the back burner. It wasn't until after the war that the parachute divisions again became well-trained and -equipped forces, with sufficient air transports to move them into combat.

The last major Allied airborne operation occurred in March 1945, when an American and a British airborne division dropped in support of the crossing of the Rhine (at Wesel) by Montgomery's Army group. This took place in daylight, with total air supremacy, and within range of friendly artillery. It wasn't really needed and was never in any danger of failing. There was never to be another like it, for the generals finally realized that large-scale drops were too expensive and confused to work. The future of paratrooper drops was to be in small units for commando-type operations.

THE AMERICAN AIRBORNE ARMY

In the summer of 1940, forty-eight army volunteers formed the U.S. Army Parachute Test Platoon. On August 16, 1940, they made their first mass jump. The exercise was considered a success. America then went on to raise more than one hundred thousand parachute and glider infantry, all of them volunteers. The parachute certainly wasn't anything new to Americans, whose first parachute jump was made from a balloon in 1819 (the earliest such jump was made in France in 1797). The first airplane jump was made by an American in 1912. The basic elements of combat jumps by infantry (using a ripcord) were developed in 1919 and first tested by Americans. Had World War I gone on for an additional year, the first combat jump would have been over

Germany, by American paratroopers. Instead, German paratroopers startled the world in April 1940 when they dropped on a Norwegian airfield and conquered it in hours. The U.S. Army noticed and went on to field the world's largest airborne force—a distinction that has continued to this day. The first American combat jump occurred in North Africa in November, 1942. U.S. paratroopers went on to make a total of ninety-three combat jumps.

There were five airborne divisions formed during the war (11th, 13th, 17th, 82nd, and 101st), plus several independent battalions. Only a third of the airborne troops were trained to use parachutes; the rest came in via gliders. This was a very practical solution to the problem of training a lot of parachutists and finding the aircraft to carry them in. But even with the troops in the gliders, there was a problem with weight. Just like commandos, airborne forces have to travel light. Once they land, the primary means of transport is their own legs. The solution back then was to arm most of the troops with the lighter, five-pound carbine (think of it as an underpowered M-16) and fewer and lighter machine guns. The best-equipped airborne troops actually were the Germans, who by the end of the war had an equivalent to the M-16 (the SG-44, similar in concept to the AK-47) and a light machine gun (the MG-42) that was the model for the first modern American light machine gun (the late-1950s M-60).

The United States managed to raise such a large airborne force by relying heavily on troops and equipment landed by glider (which were basically similar to two engine transports, but without engines and built from wood). When American airborne units were first raised, it was quickly realized that there would not be enough transport aircraft to deliver all the paratroopers who could be trained. Moreover, heavy weapons could not be delivered by parachute. The Germans, of course, had already noted this problem and successfully used gliders (an idea they borrowed from the Russians). So the Allies began creating glider regiments. Only those assigned to the 82nd and 101st Airborne Divisions (and one in British service) saw much action. With sixteen hundred troops, the glider regiments didn't have much more firepower than the parachute regiments. Gliders were able to put the regiment's four 37mm anti-tank guns and eighteen 81mm mortars on the ground quickly. The 37mm guns were too puny to deal with current German tanks, but were useful against bunkers and other vehicles. Some jeeps could also be landed. Since the gliders literally crash-landed, casualties were higher than with the paratroopers. Gliders, for the most part, were lost during the landing process. There was also a spirited debate about what the glider pilots were to do once they had landed. The British formed their glider pilots into companies of infantry. The U.S. glider pilots, being of relatively higher NCO rank, were generally allowed to make themselves useful with the units they landed with.

Only the American 82nd and 101st Divisions were formed early enough to see much action. The other three arrived near the end of the war and served as elite infantry. All five divisions were set to take part in the planned invasion of Japan in late 1945. This actually would have been the largest use of airborne forces ever, although even then it was obvious that using paratroopers in large numbers was wasteful. The problem, as always, was that the transport aircraft often had a hard time finding the intended drop zone. Because it was often necessary to do a drop at night (to avoid enemy fighters or ground fire), navigation was an even larger problem. And then there was the weather. Fog and clouds made navigation difficult, and even if you dropped the paratroopers at the right place, unforeseen winds could scatter them over a wide area. Gliders were also a dicey proposition. Gliders could not make a second pass to make sure they had the right landing zone, so they had to come down wherever they could, often with disastrous results.

Despite all these problems, getting thousands of airborne troops on the ground, behind enemy lines, especially at night, proved disastrous for the enemy—and good for the Allies. This was the commando effect. The airborne troops were trained to operate independently and warned that they might land in some unknown place, apart from other members of their unit. After these drops, therefore, the paratroopers and glider troops went to work on any enemy soldiers they could find. Enemy troops who survived these encounters usually fled and told anyone they ran into that the area was full of vicious enemy paratroopers. But unless the paratroopers linked up with friendly ground forces in a day or two, the enemy would get organized and wipe them out. Yes, they were good, but they weren't bulletproof.

After World War II, most nations maintained some parachute forces, often no more than a battalion or, in larger nations, a brigade. This was because these were elite troops who were trained and equipped to move off by air on short notice. The paratroopers were sort of "commandos lite," and every nation felt a need for a force like this. Just in case.

The World War II experience showed that if you were selective in recruiting—taking only physically fit and highly motivated volunteers—you could turn these young men into effective paratroopers in a few months. Jumping from an airplane loaded down with weapons and equipment separated the warriors from the wannabes. Paratroopers turned out to be useful; large numbers of paratroopers organized into parachute divisions, less so.

THE AMERICAN AMPHIBIOUS ARMY

During the twentieth century, Marines evolved into commandos. This should not be surprising, for soldiers serving on warships have always been somewhat elite. There's not a lot of room on ships, so when you carry soldiers for combat duties you want them to be as competent as possible. When you can't obtain quantity, you rely on quality to prevail. Marines also served as seagoing military police, protecting a ship's officers against mutiny. But at the beginning of the twentieth century, it looked as though the Marines might disappear, the victim of social changes and new technology. Warship crews had become more educated and reliable because of the increased amount of technology on ships. The ancient custom of kidnapping men to serve on ships had also disappeared, as legal systems did away with that and other unfair practices. Army troops became better educated, and faster ships made it possible to move them more quickly to where the fleet might need them. But the Marines of the two foremost naval powers, Britain and the United States, were also very resourceful. During World War I, the Marines of both nations made sure that their troops made it into the fighting on a large scale. The British had a Royal Naval Division on the Western Front, which had a brigade of Royal Marines (plus another brigade's worth elsewhere). American Marines wanted to send a division to Europe, but had to settle for a large brigade.

In the two decades before World War II, American and British Marines made themselves useful in various little wars and developed modern amphibious warfare techniques. But once World War II was under way, the Royal Marines quickly took to the concept of commando operations, renaming and retraining their Marine infantry battalions as Royal Marine Commandos. Given the traditions and normal arduous training of the Royal Marines, this wasn't much of a switch.

American Marines had the same tough attitude toward training. The Marines had always operated in small units aboard warships in distant seas. When the Marines had to be sent ashore, they knew they were going to be outnumbered and that the only way to succeed was to be fast and aggressive. There was no other option. These were the same attitudes and tactics the commandos also found they had to adopt. But the American Marines had another job as America entered World War II. The Japanese had put garrisons on dozens of Pacific islands. While many of these Japanese bases could be smashed by carrier aircraft and bypassed, some had to be captured to become American airfields and fleet bases. This required amphibious assault against fortified beaches.

Traditionally, Marines landed on an undefended beach and then marched to the objective. But many of the Japanese-held islands were so small that all the usable beaches were heavily defended. Still, the Marines felt that their traditionally tough training and newly developed amphibious vehicles and tactics—plus the British-developed amphibious ships like the landing ship tank (LST)—would make these unprecedented attacks possible.

The U.S. Marine Corps proceeded to make a series of hard-fought amphibious assaults from late 1943 to mid-1945. It also became obvious, in battles where Army and Marine divisions served side by side, that the two services had a different approach to ground combat. The Marines were more aggressive; they also organized their troops for a more commando style of fighting. The Army considered this needlessly aggressive, causing more friendly casualties than a slower, more methodic approach. They were having a hard time understanding that the Marines were fighting in support of the Navy. The Navy didn't want to keep its warships and transports sitting still off the island any longer than necessary. The Japanese still had submarines and land-based aircraft in these areas, and the Navy wanted to head for the high seas as soon as the ground combat was concluded.

The U.S. Marines had created commando ("Raider") battalions during World War II, but eventually concluded that there wasn't much difference between the Raider commando units and regular Marine infantry. So the Raiders were used to form more regular Marine units before the war ended. The Marines came out of World War II confident that their high-speed and aggressive style of combat was the way to go. They were right, although it took the Army decades to catch on to why this was so.

While the Royal Marines came out of World War II as a few commando battalions, the U.S. Marine Corps entered the postwar world as three rather large divisions. Although the U.S. Marines had the commando attitudes and practices, it would take several decades before they would reorganize themselves to most effectively operate as commandos.

The U.S. Marines raised six divisions during World War II. Each had nearly twenty thousand troops, once you accounted for all the specialist and support units. The first Marine division (the first-ever U.S. Marine division) was put together between early 1941 and early 1942. It was a high-quality outfit, for the Marines could afford to be selective with recruiting during the 1930s economic depression. Being first had its disadvantages, however, because the 1st Marine Division spent most of its time fighting in disease-ridden jungle islands—first Guadalcanal, and then adjacent islands. Total casualties for the war were 19,284 (28 percent dead, the rest wounded). The 2nd Marine Division began formation at the same time as 1st Division, but had to wait for the 1st Division to get up to strength before it could get enough Marines to reach full strength. This division suffered 8,676 casualties during the war. The 3rd Marine Division was formed in late 1942 and suffered 11,482 casualties during the war. The 4th Marine Division was formed in late 1943 and suffered 16,323 casualties during the war. The 5th Marine Division was formed in early 1944 and suffered 8,563 casualties during this time. The 6th Marine Division was formed in mid-1944 and suffered 8,227 casualties.

The Marines came out of World War II, and the rapid demobilization, in much better shape than the Army. The Marines retained more combat-experienced NCOs and officers, while the Army found many of its troops tied down in occupation duty in Japan and Germany. This did nothing for combat readiness, as the Army discovered when the Korean War broke out in 1950. The Army infantry divisions occupying Japan were the first units sent to Korea, and their lack of training caused them much grief, and many casualties, in combat. The Marines had a much more serious attitude toward getting ready for hard fighting, and they never lost it.

GUERRILLA WARS AND COMMANDOS

World War II was notable for the extent of its "unconventional warfare" operations. During this war, most such unconventional action was guerrillas fighting to free their nations from occupying German or Japanese troops. While previous wars had their share of raiders, commandos, and spies, the guerrilla aspect of warfare was a major element in World War II. This was particularly true for the Allies (mainly Britain and America). To support these many guerrilla wars, America set up the Office of Strategic Services, while the British had the Special Operations Executive. The details of many of these operations are still cloaked in secrecy more than half a century after they took place. After all, some participants are still alive, and in some areas, such as Asia and Europe, passions run generations deep. However, enough information has leaked out over the years to make for some fascinating stories, and lessons for the future.

The OSS evolved into the CIA after World War II. The SOE, which reached a strength of thirteen thousand men and women late in the war, was disbanded in 1946, with many of its key people moving over to Britain's MI6 (their equivalent of the CIA). As you can imagine, MI6 did not like the idea of setting up the SOE in the first place, and taking away one of its key functions (especially in wartime). But the government saw, correctly, that World War II would likely see a lot more guerrilla warfare than any other previous conflict. The resistance movements fighting the occupying enemy troops, more than most people realize, had an impact on the development of commandos and Special Operations troops.

Albania

Albania was invaded and occupied by the Italians in 1939, but an effective resistance movement did not get organized until after the Soviet Union was invaded in June 1941. This was because, as was common with many nations, the best-organized group in the country was the communists. The Soviet Union had written the book on strong organization and aggressive armed resistance at the end of World War I. During that period, the rather small Communist Party in Russia armed itself, got in gear, and took over the country.

In Albania, the local communists formed the core of a politically diverse resistance movement. There were some two to three thousand young men who had gotten an education and some new ideas about how to run their country. The most popular idea was communism, and the discipline and freedom from tribal loyalties enabled this small number of ardent communists to organize an effective guerrilla force. The communist leader was Enver Hoxha (pronounced *hod-ja*). Hoxha was a practical, paranoid, nationalistic, and opportunistic fellow, and when the Germans took over occupation duties in 1943 (after Italy surrendered), Hoxha arranged a truce with the Germans. The Germans were stretched pretty thin during this period, and they noted that Hoxha's people had grabbed most of the Italians' weapons and equipment in return for letting the Italian troops go free. Some left-leaning Italian soldiers even joined the communist guerrillas.

Hoxha didn't want to fight the Germans; he knew they were going to lose the war. Hoxha wanted to go after the Albanian royalist and nationalist guerrillas. In 1944, Hoxha had his rivals on the ropes, and the German military situation was becoming more precarious in Russia and France. Hoxha saw an opportunity and began attacking the Germans, who responded by bringing in a crack mountain infantry division that drove the guerrillas back into the hills.

By early 1945, the best German troops were withdrawn, and most of the remaining Germans were on their way out as well. Hoxha, still with the strongest guerrilla force, soon controlled most of the country. The Allies had recognized Hoxha as the most effective force against the Germans and sent in SOE teams to coordinate arms shipments. At the end of the war, Hoxha disarmed (and often imprisoned or killed) the noncommunist guerrillas. He established a very strict, communist-style police state and died in power in 1986. Although the Albanians had been known as good irregular fighters for centuries, they didn't have to exert themselves too much during World War II. Hoxha demonstrated that good organization and adroit negotiations can obtain a victory a lot more cheaply than hard fighting. The Allies also got a preview of what communist discipline and dedication could do to make illiterate tribesmen effective guerrilla fighters, and would see more of that around the world in the decades after World War II.

Belgium

Belgium contained a lot of Nazi sympathizers during World War II, but the most ardent of them joined the Waffen-SS and went off to fight the Russians. The anti-Nazis, however, stayed home and formed an active armed resistance that fought the Germans throughout the war. The Germans, and their Belgian sympathizers, responded with great brutality, killing more than seventeen thousand Belgian resistance fighters (most of them while involved in sabotage and espionage missions). The resistance was also active in saving Jews, which often led to resistance fighters being sent off to concentration camps along with the people they were trying to protect.

Belgium, like most Western European nations, did not produce as many heavily armed guerrillas as did the movements in Eastern Europe such as Hoxha's in Albania and Tito in the Balkans. Part of this was due to the large number of pro-fascists in Western Europe (where fascism began in the first place). Moreover, Western Europe contained extensive and quite effective government and police institutions. It was a lot more difficult to just "go underground" there. Western Europeans who wanted to fight the Germans often did so by trying to get to Britain. Not surprisingly, many Belgians escaped to Britain and joined the SOE and SAS. One of the five SAS regiments at the end of the war was composed of Belgians. As a result, Belgium has maintained excellent commando units ever since World War II.

Burma

Burma had a lot of resistance groups, but most of them weren't much interested in World War II. The country had been one of the last nations in the region to be turned into a British colony, and many Burmese were rather pleased to see the Japanese arrive and chase the British out. Thus they were willing to collaborate with the Japanese. But let's look a little more in depth at the complexities here. Many Burmese realized that the Japanese might lose the war—and by 1944, many were sure of it. So they officially cooperated with the Japanese while seeking to work for the British (who were fighting in northern Burma throughout the war). Some Burmese genuinely did collaborate with the Japanese; others organized a resistance against them that mainly provided useful intelligence for the British. When the British finally drove the Japanese out of Burma in 1945, the local resistance leaders, many of whom held senior positions in the collaborator government, stepped forward and took over. The British relinquished their Burmese colony in 1947. However, some Burmese did fight, mainly the tribal peoples in north, just as they had fought the Burmese down south before the Japanese or British came along.

The Burmese tribes had gotten a better deal (less interference in their affairs) from the British, and they continued to fight for them. The tribesmen were classic raiders, and were a source of much harassment for the Japanese troops. One British officer, Orde Wingate, noting the ability of the tribesmen to operate deep in the bush, came up with one of the more original ideas of World War II. He organized groups of troops (about three hundred men, basically an infantry company with tribal scouts plus communications and demolitions experts added) that marched deep into the jungle to attack Japanese outposts and supply lines such as railroads, bridges, and truck convoys. The key innovation here was that the Chindits (as these raiders were called) were supplied by air—usually via parachute drop, but sometimes using airfields hacked out of the jungle. This enabled them to keep at it for weeks at a time. These Chindit columns did great damage to the Japanese in 1943 and 1944. The program eventually used gliders to move troops directly into enemy territory, along with building crude but usable airfields in the bush so that the Japanese had to deal with enemy combat bases showing up deep in the enemy rear area. The success of the Chindits led to the formation of a similar American unit, Merrill's Marauders. This experience got many Americans thinking about "airmobile" ground operations, a concept that was used extensively during the Vietnam War and later (as in Afghanistan during the 2001–2002 operations).

Bulgaria

Although the country was controlled by a pro-German government throughout the war, the Bulgarian people had always been very pro-

Russian (especially since the Russians had helped them expel the Turks in the nineteenth century), and the government had to take this into account. So even though Bulgaria was "pro-German," it did not declare war on the Soviet Union until 1944 (after years of pressure from the Germans). Once war was declared, the local communists formed a resistance movement, which became more active as the Soviet armies neared the Bulgarian border. The pro-Nazi government was, of course, anti-communist, and in 1941 and 1942 many of the known Bulgarian communists were rounded up. The Soviet Union landed some agents by air and submarine to help start a partisan movement, but nearly all of these agents were caught and killed. The organization and discipline of the surviving Bulgarian communists, however, enabled them to slowly build a guerrilla organization.

By early 1943 there were about three hundred active guerrillas, and by the summer, nearly seven hundred. The guerrillas operated in groups of ten or twelve men and spent a lot of time taking care of just surviving. Most of their attacks (12 in January 1943, rising to 145 in June) were small scale and included killing a policeman as well as the sabotage of factories, mines, and railroads. The Soviets tried to fly in agents and equipment, but weren't able to accomplish much. More aid came in 1945 from the more numerous Yugoslav communist guerrillas next door, and the larger quantities of weapons and equipment they were getting from the British SOE. By early 1944, the British had liaison officers in Bulgaria, and material assistance began to cross over from Yugoslavia. This was desperately needed, because the Bulgarian guerrillas had only 563 rifles, 314 pistols, thirteen submachine guns, and nine machine guns at the end of 1943—for about two thousand men. Three airdrops (out of fifteen attempted) by the British in early 1944 increased their arsenal.

By early summer 1944, the guerrillas had four thousand men and some three thousand firearms (plus eighteen hundred hand grenades, a favorite guerrilla weapon). At the time, the government thought the guerrillas had twelve thousand men under arms. This is what happens when a disciplined guerrilla force remains active. But the discipline didn't come easy. The army and police were responding to guerrilla actions, and the response was pretty savage, with summary executions of captured guerrillas and reprisals against their families. As a result, the guerrillas maintained discipline by killing any of their number who tried to desert. And there was plenty of reason to desert: Food was often short and guerrillas knew their families were subject to imprisonment if they were identified. The Soviet Army showed up at the end of August, at which point the guerrillas numbered ten thousand men (and some women), all armed. A communist government was installed, which lasted until 1990. The Bulgarian resistance never threatened the existence of the government, but the fact that it was able to survive at all demonstrated what can be done where there is a segment of the population determined to resist. This was one of the things that led to the establishment of the U.S. Special Forces in the 1950s—to better support such resistance movements in the future.

China

China was the scene of the largest guerrilla operations in World War II. There were probably more guerrillas in China than in all the other occupied countries combined—several million of them (most unarmed and performing support roles), who belonged to three different organizations. A number of groups were loyal to Chiang Kai-shek, who ran the Nationalist government (the government recognized by the Allies). Many of these groups were quite independent minded, united only in their hatred of the Japanese invaders.

The most effective guerrillas supported Mao Tse-tung and his Chinese Communist Party. There were also a lot of freelance guerrillas who were basically bandits, except that they would fight the Japanese when they had a chance (or were simply cornered). It was the guerrillas who kept most of the fifty Japanese divisions (including twenty divisions of Chinese troops working for the Japanese) busy during the war. After the Japanese surrendered, the Chinese went back to fighting each other, which was what had enabled the Japanese to do so well in the first place. The fighting in China was not only largely a guerrilla war but also one in which planning and training would win out over numbers and weapons.

The Nationalists always had the advantage in numbers, money, and equipment. But the communists had, as the Chinese like to put it, "virtue." The Nationalists were trying to preserve the feudal remnants of the fallen Chinese empire. The communists represented the future: good government, free of corruption, with fairness for all. The communist were clean-living, honest, true believers, fighting for the people against the corrupt defenders of the old order. Even so, had not the Japanese expanded their war in China (they had already occupied Manchuria for more than thirty years), the Nationalists may well have crushed the communists. "Old China" had defeated many vigorous revolutionary movements in the past.

But the Japanese did advance, and the Nationalist armies took a beating, making them too weak to wipe out the Marxists. Having survived more than a decade of Nationalist attacks, the communists had a hard core of battle-tested veterans out there concentrating on what mattered most: quality manpower. The communists spent more time in ideological training than in military drills and exercises. They correctly understood that it was most important that the individual soldier really believed he was an important and respected part of the organization. Many Westerners (and pro-Nationalist Chinese) missed this point. But in the fighting that continued until 1949 (when the surviving Nationalists fled to Taiwan), it was this quality advantage that made the difference. Many American diplomats and military officers who dealt with the communists during the 1930s and World War II noted this communist attention to motivating the troops. In fact, some of the U.S. Marines who encountered the communists before World War II were so impressed that they used the communist motivational techniques to train Marines who volunteered for the first Raider battalions.

There was nothing particularly sinister about the communist techniques. Basically they preached many of the same principles other twentieth-century motivational and organization-building programs did: Pay attention to your people, listen to your people, make sure your people know what the organization's goals are and that they agree with these goals. These are the principles that are the foundation of any successful commando unit. While the communists had flawed economic ideas, and were rather quick to identify "enemies of the people" and apply the death penalty, their core concepts worked. The communists ultimately became corrupt themselves and unpopular within a generation, but during World War II the communist guerrillas were still a force to fear on the battlefield. Hundreds of American officers and NCOs were able to observe communist guerrillas during World War II, and that experience played a major role in the formation of the U.S. Special Forces in the early 1950s: Clearly, America would need something like the Special Forces to deal with similar movements elsewhere.

Czechoslovakia

Czechoslovakia was occupied by the Germans a year before World War II began, but they never were entirely successful in creating a strong resistance movement. Hitler sent one of his favorite SS officers, Reinhard Heydrich, to run things in the country, and the Czech government in exile, upset at the low level of guerrilla activity back home, convinced the British SOE to assassinate the new leader. It was thought that this would provoke a savage German retaliation, which would in turn spur Czechs to increase their resistance to the German occupation. A hit team was therefore trained and sent into Czechoslovakia in 1942, and Heydrich was killed while riding down a country road in his staff car. As expected, the Nazis were decidedly poor losers. Two nearby villages, suspected of providing assistance for the assassins, were destroyed. All the men were shot, while the women and children were sent to concentration camps where most of them died as well. It was only the beginning. The Germans began a massive and brutal campaign to stamp out whatever resistance there was, real or imagined. More than 350,000 Czechs were sent to concentration camps, and 250,000 of them died there. Many others died during the anti-resistance campaign. Even this, however, did not encourage the Czechs to increase their armed resistance to the Germans. For the rest of the war, what was left of the Czech resistance operated primarily as an information-gathering organization for the Allies. Still, the Czech guerrillas did receive weapons from SOE, and at the very end of the war they rose up against the Germans. Before the Russian and Allied troops arrived, several thousand more Czechs were killed. As a result of the Heydrich backlash, SOE developed "invisible sabotage" and untraceable assassination techniques. In other words, a lot of deaths were made to seem like accidents. The untraceable assassinations were rather more difficult, however, and the result was that Nazi big shots were not as likely to be assassinated for the rest of the war. While killing a Nazi Golden Boy like Heydrich had great propaganda value, it also angered the Nazis and it drove the Germans to more effective and brutal anti-guerrilla operations. This was not in the Allies' interests. So the lesson is: always look beyond accomplishing the mission and measure the aftereffects.

Denmark

Despite their Viking ancestry, the Danes had lost most of their warlike ways over the centuries. This was obvious in the opening days of World War II when in 1940, it took the Germans exactly one day to occupy the country. There were other reasons for this rapid conquest: Denmark is not very large, not very defensible, and had largely disarmed itself before the war anyway by declaring itself neutral. The Germans didn't respect that neutrality, but to show their appreciation for not putting up a fight, the Danish government was left in place. At first, the Germans controlled everything, but with a light touch. Nevertheless, Germany was still at war, and it began milking the Danish economy to support the Nazi war effort. After a year, this caused severe shortages for the Danish population. This in turn led to the organization of a resistance movement. By 1943, sabotage against the Germans and espionage for the Allies became common. The Germans began to crack down, even though the Danes were careful not to do anything too obvious. The Germans, believing their anti-Semitic propaganda, decided that any problems were the fault of the small Jewish population. So they tried to round up the nation's Jews. Fortunately, the Danish resistance managed to get most of them out of the country to Sweden, a novel feat for European resistance movements. The Germans were quite angry about this and squeezed the Danes economically even further. So the guerrillas made plans for an armed uprising. Then the war ended before these could be carried out. The lesson learned here was that if overt violence could be avoided, a resistance movement could achieve quite a lot against occupiers lulled into letting their guard down.

Ethiopia

Ethiopia was occupied by the Italians in 1936, and the resistance in this country was widespread and active from the very beginning. By the time the British were poised to retake Ethiopia in 1941, the Italians were dismayed by the wrath of local partisans. The Italians had suffered a major defeat by the Ethiopians in the nineteenth century, and a certain amount of fear remained among Italian soldiers, who thus preferred to make deals with the locals to keep the peace. This was a rare situation during World War II, except where the Italians were involved. Most Italians were not very enthusiastic about the war, and whenever they had occupation duty, they tended to make deals with the local guerrillas. During the war, however, the local Ethiopian guerrillas were not in a mood to make deals—the Italians had used chemical weapons during their invasion. Most Italians were glad to let the British take over in 1941.

European Jews

Europe's Jewish population was not, as most people think, uninvolved in guerrilla warfare. Resistance to the German extermination policy actually developed rapidly among them. Many Jews fled their homes when it became clear what the Germans were up to—and these fugitives took refuge in forests all over Europe and formed guerrilla bands. But the Jewish guerrillas had a harder time that most others. Although the Jews usually fought against German and other Axis troops, they sometimes found themselves fighting non-Jewish guerrillas. The Germans didn't have a monopoly on anti-Semitism.

Actually, fighting among guerrillas was not restricted to Jewish and non-Jewish groups. In most cases, the guerrillas cooperated against the common German enemy, but politics and ethnicity often caused them to fight each other. Jews who were stuck in ghettos often armed themselves for self-defense. In the case of the Warsaw ghetto, the Jews conducted a heroic uprising that was crushed with great brutality by the Germans. Resistance groups were even formed inside concentration camps, in which there were occasional uprisings, including one in the Sobibor, Poland, extermination camp. The Germans went to great lengths to keep this particular incident secret, lest other doomed Jews be encouraged to try it themselves. Most Jewish guerrillas, however, belonged to nationalist resistance groups, such as the Yugoslav partisans.

One major reason why there wasn't more Jewish armed resistance was the gradual, and clever, way in which the Nazis introduced the "Final Solution." This extermination campaign itself was the result the Wansee conference in early 1942. And even then it was kept a secret—as much as these things can be kept secret. The Germans carried on, as before, persecuting the Jews, leaving their victims to keep a low profile and wait for the war to end. Since the Jews were under constant pressure from the Nazis and local anti-Semites, there was less opportunity to sneak away and join the partisans or otherwise organize armed resistance. Nevertheless, the degree of Jewish resistance was substantial, if generally unrecognized.

France

France was conquered in 1940, and some armed resistance was active from the beginning. The southern part of the country was left independent until early 1943, when the Germans took control of the entire country. The south did not provide much resistance until the Germans moved in, but it was different in the north. There were several different resistance organizations, including a communist one that only became active after the Soviet Union was invaded in June 1941. Before the Germans invaded Russia, the French communists collaborated with the Nazi occupiers and the Vichy government in the south.

By 1943, the resistance was more united, or at least better coordinated. The U.S. OSS and British SOE supplied weapons and technical assistance. The French government in exile, led by General Charles de Gaulle, had a lot to say about whom the OSS and SOE supported. This caused some problems, because de Gaulle was quite the anti-communist and, naturally, tried to get more support for guerrilla groups that supported him; they would also be loyal to him when Allied armies returned to France and de Gaulle tried to reestablish a French government. Many of the more effective guerrilla groups were communist and, naturally, anti–de Gaulle. About a third of the French "Maquis" (guerrillas) were in communist-led groups. The OSS and SOE wanted to get the guerrillas to fight the Germans in the short term, and avoid a post-D-Day civil war in France in the long term. De Gaulle eventually came out on top, but the infighting among different guerrilla groups did not help matters. Moreover, the Germans were energetic in anti-partisan operations, particularly because the resistance was the principal espionage operation in the country and was responsible for getting many downed Allied pilots back to Britain.

The resistance didn't begin active military operations (as opposed to sabotage, espionage, and assassinations) until after the Allied invasion of Normandy in June 1944. This aided the Allies in driving the Germans out of France by the end of the year. The Allies wanted the Maquis to build up their manpower and weapons stockpiles, so that they could make a maximum effort when the Allied invasion of France came "sometime in 1944." But many Maquis were not willing to wait. In early 1943, there were one hundred "serious" sabotage attacks on the railroads: derailment or significant damage to tracks or bridges. By the end of the year, the attacks were up to six hundred a month. It got so bad that the Germans had to bring in twenty thousand German railway repair men (the French repair crews were suspect).

The Maquis' attacks on the railroads increased further in 1944, where in the first three months of that year 808 locomotives were destroyed (compared to 387 destroyed by Allied air attacks). The Allies increased arms shipments to the Maquis in early 1944, delivering seventy-five thousand rifles and submachine guns, three hundred bazookas, and 143 mortars. By D-Day (June 6, 1944), it was estimated that twenty thousand Maquis were armed with military weapons, while another twenty thousand were less well armed (hunting rifles, shotguns, a grenade, or a pistol).

However, there was never as much assistance from the French resistance as popular legend (especially in France) would have it. The political clashes among the guerrillas (especially the communist ones and all the others) often got in the way. And many French resistance fighters did not join until D-Day. The real resistance heroes were the ones who put their lives on the line (and often lost) between 1940 and 1943. In those early days, there were a lot of collaborators, and many guerrillas were betrayed to the Nazis (who generally interrogated, using torture, before executing any guerrillas they captured). After D-Day, however, the Maquis were a major factor in making it difficult for the Germans to move around, and thousands of German soldiers were killed or wounded by the Maquis. But the French fighters also took a lot of casualties. Some 12 percent of the two hundred thousand men and women who served in the Maquis throughout the war were killed. The Germans killed another two hundred thousand real or suspected Maquis. The Maquis also executed some eleven thousand collaborators (the postwar government executed seven hundred, and put forty thousand in prison). Many future CIA and Special Forces member first encountered guerrilla warfare while serving with the OSS in France. Valuable lessons were learned.

Germany

Germany saw resistance to the Nazis begin as soon as Hitler took over in 1933. Many attempts on his life were made, the most famous one being the bomb blast on June 20, 1944, that Der Führer miraculously survived. Before the war began in 1939, many senior German Army officers were active in trying to get rid of the Nazis. But the British and French, not keen about assassinating heads of state, were hesitant to cooperate, and the Army became less of a source of resistance activity after the war began. The major problems were communications, and the inability to get British agents inside Germany. While the resistance was widespread, it was never organized on a large scale. The Nazi secret police was very effective, and paranoid, inside Germany. The Gestapo was constantly arresting actual or suspected resistance members. But aside from trying to get rid of Hitler, the resistance did provide espionage services for the Allies, especially the communist agents working for the Soviet Union. When the war ended, many of the surviving resistance participants took part in the rebuilding of the German government, despite the fact that most Germans considered them traitors.

Greece

Greece was invaded by Germany in 1941, and, because of the country's political divisions, many resistance movements promptly began. As a result, the competing guerrillas spent more time fighting each other than they did going after the Germans or otherwise supporting the Allies. The OSS and SOE tried to get the various resistance groups to cooperate, but they had little success. Naturally, the Germans took advantage of the situation by playing one guerrilla faction against the other. This was made easier because the better-organized, and more ruthless, guerrillas were communists. The Germans had little trouble encouraging the noncommunist guerrillas to go after the communists. When the Germans withdrew from Greece in 1944 to avoid being cut off by the Red Army advancing out of Ukraine, the partisans continued to fight each other. British troops then arrived to try to restore order, and the guerrillas promptly responded by fighting the British. This civil war continued until the late 1940s, ending only when a deal was made with Yugoslavia to cut off aid to the communist guerrillas. The situation in Greece was one of the worst the Allies had to face. Yugoslavia was a close second, except there the communists won their war with the noncommunist guerrillas before the war ended and, ultimately, there was only one guerrilla organization to contend with. Both these situations drove home the lesson that just because a foreign invader occupies a country does not mean the locals are going to form a "united front" to resist. If anything, the various political factions will blame each other for failing to keep the enemy out in the first place, and begin thinking about who will run the country when the war is over.

Hungary

Hungary had a pro-fascist government when World War II broke out, and thus became an active ally of Germany. Initially (after Germany invaded Russia in 1941), the only resistance came from the communists, but they were ruthlessly hunted down by the secret police. Things began to change in early 1943 when a Hungarian Army force was destroyed at the Battle of Stalingrad. This caused popular enthusiasm for the war, and the Germans, to decline. Strikes, anti-government demonstrations, and increasing anti-German attitudes, often encouraged by the communists, eventually led to the Germans moving in to occupy the country in March 1944. The Germans were afraid of Hungary making a separate peace with the Russians and cutting off a major supply route to German troops in Russia. This assessment was correct, because once the Germans took over, armed guerrillas became active. Anti-German feelings became so intense that parts of the Hungarian Army went over to the Russians. The effect was similar to a civil war, and the country was in chaos until the Red Army arrived in late 1944. The guerrillas had been largely apolitical, but once the Russians showed up the noncommunist elements were purged from the resistance and a communist government established. The lesson from this was that even a nation that is an active ally of an enemy may have a population that is against that policy and, under the right conditions, will be willing to rise up against the government. But to make this work, you need agents inside the country who can get a good sense of who really thinks what.

Indonesia

Known as the Netherlands East Indies back then, Indonesia was a Dutch colony when the Japanese invaded in early 1942. There already existed a guerrilla movement dedicated to getting the Dutch out, and the guerrillas weren't sure the Japanese were any better than the Dutch, or that the Japanese would last long. So the resistance movement developed a clever approach and agreed among themselves to bet on both sides. Some of the Indonesian resistance leaders actively collaborated with the Japanese, even helping enlist Indonesians in pro-Japanese military units. Meanwhile, other resistance leaders, as part of the plan, took to the hills and, with some Allied assistance, organized a moderately successful guerrilla movement. When the Dutch returned in 1945, they discovered that both the pro-Allied guerrillas and the pro-Japanese collaborationists were lined up against them, aided by the fact that the surrendering Japanese abandoned a lot of equipment (which the guerrillas seized). The result was a fairly bloody war for independence that the Dutch lost (in 1950). This showed that both invaders and anyone trying to help the guerrillas have to be careful about the loyalties of the locals. The Indonesians weren't the only ones to pull off this "playing both sides of the fence" routine; they just did it better than anyone else.

Italy

Italy began to see armed resistance groups in 1940 once many Italians realized that Mussolini and the fascist government had dragged them into World War II as a German ally. Italy had been anti-German for centuries and had fought against them during World War I. Many Italians really wanted no part of fighting their former World War I allies. Mussolini's fascists weren't quite as much a dictatorship as the German Nazis were, and a lot of open opposition was tolerated. The Italian Fascists also weren't as efficient or bloody minded as the Nazis. And the anti-Fascist groups had a lot of friends in government, which led to Mussolini being forced out of office in July 1943 in a coup engineered by the king (helped along by an Allied invasion of southern Italy). The Germans saw this coming and occupied Italy north of Naples. The Germans were a lot more ruthless dealing with opposition to fascist rule. As a result, armed resistance to the German occupation began. However, many Italian fascists, backing the Germans, fought as well, and this led to nearly two years of savage fighting between Italian anti-fascist partisans and German troops and pro-fascist armed groups assisting the Germans. Mussolini himself was rescued by German commandos shortly after he was overthrown. Later in 1945, Mussolini was caught by some pro-communist partisans and executed on the spot. The communist guerrillas were such a powerful force during the last two years of the war that the Italian Communist Party became the most powerful such party in Europe after it was over. The OSS and SOE had no choice but to support the communist guerrillas, even though the communists were not very cooperative.

The Netherlands

The Netherlands was conquered by the Germans in five days during early 1940. This was party because many of the Dutch either sympathized with the Germans or, more often, considered the war over and the Germans the victors. So for the first year or so of occupation, there wasn't much resistance. Then the Dutch began to notice increasing Allied success—a lot of British, and then American, bombers flew over the Netherlands on their way to German targets. This caused many Netherlanders to change their minds, and a resistance movement grew. The Germans had a lot of troops in the Netherlands, because the country is on the coast and there was always fear of British commando raids. There were also a lot of German sympathizers among the population, which made the German secret police more effective. The similarity of the Dutch and German languages made it easier for German police to operate in the Netherlands. So large-scale guerrilla operations never became a major factor. But sabotage and espionage were common, coordinated by the government in exile in London. Prince Bernard, the husband of Queen Juliana, by birth a German, actually ran the resistance from inside the Netherlands for a while. Nevertheless, 23 percent of the country's Jews were saved from Nazi death camps, and the Germans were always under observation by pro-Allied Dutch spies through most of the war. The Netherlands was also a small country and there weren't many places for guerrillas to hide out. The OSS and SOE had to make a decision to concentrate on sabotage and espionage in the Netherlands; otherwise they would have wasted a lot of effort, agents, and Dutch guerrillas trying to organize and use larger guerrilla units.

Norway

Norway was invaded and occupied by the Germans in early 1940, but a resistance movement was quickly organized. The Norwegians decided to avoid sabotage and armed attacks, however, because they knew the Germans would just retaliate and kill a lot of innocent people. What the Norwegian resistance did do was set up a large spy network that observed what the Germans were up to, reporting this to the Allies. The resistance also assisted British commando operations within the country, especially against heavy-water production facilities in Norway that the Germans needed for their nuclear weapons research. The British conducted a lot of commando operations in Norway, partly because the country was a distance from other German forces in Europe. This meant German ships and warplanes could not be quickly shifted to Norway to deal with suspected commando raids. Also, the use of commandos meant the Germans had no excuse to inflict reprisals on Norwegians. The commando raids caused the Germans to suspect that one of the Allied 1944 invasions would be in Norway. As a result, seventeen German divisions (about three hundred thousand troops) were stationed in Norway during most of 1944, thus tying up considerable forces in an area the Allies in fact had no intention of invading. This larger number of German troops also made it even more difficult for the Norwegian guerrillas to operate, which didn't matter since the Norwegian guerrilla units just waited for the end of the war. Here was a situation in which the OSS and SOE didn't press the Norwegians on undertaking aggressive guerrilla operations, as long as the guerrillas provided support for Allied raids on German military and economic installations. The Norwegians were okay with that, and that's all OSS/SOE needed.

The Philippines

Guerrilla units were being formed in the Philippines even before the last regular U.S. and Philippine units surrendered on Bataan and Corregidor in mid-1942. Many troops, especially those not in contact with Japanese troops, fled to the mountains of the numerous Philippine islands. With limited supplies of weapons and ammunition, they formed resistance units and harassed Japanese garrisons for the next two years. The Philippine people generally supported the resistance, especially if the guerrillas didn't hit the Japanese in such a way that reprisals would cause widespread death and destruction to the local civilians. Some 30 percent of the Filipinos were inclined to collaborate with the Japanese, but this percentage was steadily reduced during 1943 and 1944 as the guerrillas learned to just kill collaborators.

Cut off from resupply because of the long distance to the nearest Allied bases, it wasn't until late 1943 that regular contact was established. Actually, it was more than a year before the United States realized that there was an extensive guerrilla war going on in the Philippines. The guerrillas hadn't been able to take much radio equipment with them to the hills. But once it was realized that the guerrillas were there, U.S. submarines and aircraft began to land weapons and agents. Most of the partisans were Philippine citizens, along with some U.S. officers and troops. The leadership was provided by Filipino and American Army officers who refused to surrender. Two exceptions were the communist and Moro (Islamic tribes in the south) guerrillas, who used party and tribal leaders, respectively.

Some radio contact was always maintained with the Allies, and as more radios were sent in during 1944, the guerrillas became an invaluable source of information on the Japanese garrison. When the Allies invaded the Philippines in late 1944, nearly one hundred thousand armed partisans were a major asset in quickly defeating the Japanese ground forces. After World War II, the communist and Moro guerrillas continued to fight the newly independent Philippine government into the 1950s. While major resistance by these groups subsided by the 1960s, both communists and Moros revived their guerrilla operations again in the 1980s—and it continues to this day. The Philippine experience was another source of inspiration for the formation of the U.S. Special Forces in the 1950s.

Poland

Poland was invaded and carved up by Germany and the Soviets in 1939. Despite the presence of the two most ruthless secret police organizations in history—the NKVD and Gestapo—a Polish resistance movement quickly developed. At first, the local communists collaborated in both the German and Russian occupation zones. As a result, the resistance was always hostile to the communists, even after Germany invaded Russia in 1941, and the communists formed their own guerrilla units. At first, only Britain offered assistance, but after 1941 some aid came from the Russians (mostly for the communist-controlled units).

The Germans were ruthless in their suppression of the Polish guerrillas, and millions of Poles were killed in the process. The resistance was initially known as the Home Army. This organization was loyal to the government in exile in London, which was set up after the 1939 German/Soviet invasion. The Home Army and communist guerrillas didn't fight each other, at least not much, but the Soviets weren't subtle about how much they wanted the communist guerrillas to be in charge once the war was over. Toward the end of the war, the communist guerrillas often refused to participate in operations that might make Home Army forces stronger—say, attacking and seizing a German supply dump. When the Soviet Army drove out the Germans in 1945, the Home Army ended up at war with Soviet troops (who wanted to disarm the Home Army).

By the late 1940s, the Home Army was destroyed, militarily and politically, and a communist government was established. Poland was a good example of a guerrilla war in which the guerrillas are being supported by two different foreign nations, each with a different view of what the postwar government should be like. The majority of Poles wanted nothing to do with the Soviet Union in particular, and communism in general. But the Red Army was in Poland at the end of the war, and it took another forty-five years before the Russians could be sent home. The good guys may win in the end, but you can spend a long time waiting for that.

Siam (Thailand)

Siam was the only independent nation in Southeast Asia at the start of World War II. Rather than invade, the Japanese applied diplomatic pressure on the Thais to allow Japanese troops passage on their way to the invasions of British-held Malaya and Burma. Most Thais wanted to stay completely out of World War II, but the government did not want to risk Japanese invasion and domination. The Japanese occupied the country with fifty thousand troops anyway, and forced the government to declare war on the United States (the Thai ambassador in Washington never got around to formally delivering the declaration, so the U.S. never declared war on Siam). This attitude extended to a well-organized and widely supported resistance movement. The partisans were led by senior government officials. It wasn't until 1944 that the OSS was able to get teams into Thailand, and by early 1945, much valuable information was being sent to the Allies about Japanese operations in the area. After the war, Thailand's real loyalties were recognized and the country was not treated as an enemy nation.

This was an example of how careful a conqueror has to be. The Japanese thought they controlled Thailand, and in many respects they did. In actuality, the Thais considered them arrogant foreigners. Because Thailand was an "ally" of Japan, however, there was no reason for the usual Japanese reprisals against local civilians. The lesson here is that passive resistance can be effective if done right.

USSR

The USSR saw partisan (the term Russians preferred, rather than guerrilla) groups form right from the start of the German invasion in June 1941. While many of the people in western Russia were not Russian, and didn't much like Russians or communists, there were many local communist officials who used their organizational skills to form guerrilla bands. These "commissars" (as communist officials were called) soon discovered that the Germans had a policy of immediate execution for people such as themselves. This forced the commissars to either head for the forests or get picked up by the Germans and shot.

The German tanks advanced so swiftly in 1941 that millions of Russian soldiers were bypassed. Many of these were not immediately surrounded by the slower German infantry that came behind the tanks. While most of these bypassed Russian troops dug in to fight and be killed or captured, thousands fled like the commissars. Through 1941 and early 1942, partisan activity was largely uncoordinated and sometimes nationalist. Especially in Ukraine and the Baltic states, many partisans were either nationalist, anti-communist, or Jewish (or a combination). In the Baltic states and western Ukraine, the anti-Russian locals often refused to support the guerrillas, or turned them in. By the end of 1942, most of the partisans realized that their chances of surviving were better if they played along with the Soviets. During 1943 and 1944, the Germans found themselves with a growing number of active guerrilla units operating in their rear area. At first, the guerrillas attacked to obtain weapons and food.

When the Red Army went over to the offensive in late 1943, the guerrillas were called on to coordinate their attacks with them. The guerrillas would shut down the railroad system with coordinated attacks, and ambush unescorted truck convoys. Maintenance units, airfields, hospitals, and rest areas were all subject to attack. These partisans became a major problem by late 1944, and the Germans had to stations dozen of divisions of older or infirm troops to protect their rear-area installations. The Germans also tried to wipe out the larger and more troublesome guerrilla units, with some success. But the guerrillas were so numerous and widespread that eliminating them completely was impossible.

Eventually, the Soviets sent in enough radios and commissars to gain a measure of control over most of them. Soviet guerrillas killed some forty thousand Nazi troops and did enormous damage to German railroads, trucks, and roads. In 1944, the guerrillas, numbering several hundred thousand, were a major asset for the advancing Red Army. When the war ended, the Russians tried to disarm and interrogate all the guerrillas, suspecting that some of them were anti-communist. This assessment proved to be correct, as thousands of guerrillas stayed in the forests when the Red Army showed up and began fighting Russians. This partisan war did not end until the early 1950s, when the last Ukrainian guerrillas were killed or captured. The dogged persistence of the Ukrainian guerrillas, and the inability of the United States to assist them, was another of the events that led to the forming of the U.S. Army Special Forces.

Vietnam

Vietnam had became a French colony in the late nineteenth century after the French intervened in one of the frequent Vietnamese civil wars. Because the Vietnamese were used to fighting each other so often, it took a while for them to get organized and get a guerrilla war going. There were actually several resistance movements, which was typical of Vietnam's fractious nature. A growing Communist Party was becoming more of a factor in the resistance to the French, but nothing that really threatened French rule. What changed the situation dramatically was the defeat of France by Germany in 1940. Vichy France (the part unoccupied by the Germans—southern France) was allowed to retain control of its colonies.

Actually the Germans couldn't do much about this, because Britain (and later the United States) maintained control of the ocean areas around German-occupied Europe, making it impossible for the Vichy French or Germans to get to France's overseas colonies. But the Japanese did have some use for Vietnam—as a land route for their planned invasions of British colonies to the south and west. So the country was taken over by the Japanese in late 1941, more or less peacefully. Then the anti-French guerrillas promptly shifted their operations to resist them. The Vietnamese didn't fall for the Japanese idea of "Asia for the Asians." As in most other Japanese-occupied nations, it was soon obvious that the Japanese were really thinking of "Asia for the Japanese."

The most effective guerrillas were communist led by Ho Chi Minh, but included noncommunist groups as well. Armed attacks were made on the Japanese and espionage conducted for the Allies. In return, the Allies supplied weapons and supplies. This was the same resistance organization—the Vietminh—that ultimately took over all of Vietnam in 1975. The Vietnam guerrillas also received help from the Russians and Chinese (both communist and noncommunist), but it was the Chinese communists who provided the most effective assistance when the French returned (in force) after World War II to reestablish control. The Japanese involuntarily provided much support also, because the Vietminh grabbed Japanese weapons (despite the arrival of British troops to take the Japanese surrender). With the Japanese out of the way, the Vietminh went back to fighting the French. This was the most extreme example of a World War II guerrilla movement that continued fighting after World War II was over. The lesson is that many of these wartime guerrilla movements will keep going until the guerrillas' aims are achieved. So no matter who is supplying outside assistance, the guerrillas always are the ones who decide when their struggle is over.

Yugoslavia

Yugoslavia was invaded by the Germans in early 1941, but Italians (who had been fighting in Albania since 1939) were given the job of occupying the country until 1943 (when Italy switched sides). The Italians were not bloody minded enough to do the rough work of terrorizing, and killing, civilians, so Croat and Bosnian units were raised for this. The Croats had long been pro-German and were set up (by the Germans) as an independent nation. In response, more Croats (as a percentage of the population) took up arms and fought for the Germans than was true of any other German ally. Croats were particularly enthusiastic about fighting the largely Serb Yugoslav partisans. Bosnians (Yugoslav Muslims) were also eager about fighting the Serbs, who had been rough on the Bosnians ever since the Muslim Turks lost control of the region earlier in the century.

The Yugoslav partisans themselves were split into two main groups, monarchists (who wanted to bring back the monarchy) and nationalists (who simply wanted to restore the government that the Germans had defeated). The smaller group of communist guerrillas wanted to set up a communist dictatorship after the war. Naturally, the Allies favored the monarchists, until they noted that they were collaborating with the Germans in order to weaken the communist partisans. The Yugoslav resistance was more of a civil war (guerrillas killed more Yugoslavs than the Germans or Italians did), but the Allies were fighting the Germans and so ended by supporting the communist guerrillas (who also collaborated with the Germans, but a lot less than the monarchists). The monarchists, who were largely Croat, thought they could play the communist partisans (who were largely Serb) off against Germans, but it backfired.

For all the fighting that went on among Yugoslavs, the local partisans were the only ones in World War II who liberated themselves. When the Red Army showed up at the Yugoslav border in early 1945, the communist guerrillas (who now controlled the entire country) told them, "Thank you, now go away." And the Russians did. Savvy observers of World War II guerrilla wars warned that it was only a matter of time before the various factions in Yugoslavia went at it again. In the 1990s they did. This time the Bosnians and Croats played the Western Allies against the Serbs. Remember, many guerrilla wars are like locusts; they reoccur at intervals.

7 SHADOW WARS AND THE THREAT

The Golden Age for commandos during World War II was followed by a Dark Age as the generals asserted their anti-commando attitude. Most generals saw commandos as elitist troublemakers and never really felt comfortable having them around. Most commando units were disbanded at the end of World War II. Actually, this began to happen even before the war ended. But the pro-commando officers did not go away, and the spirit of the commando survived in such places as the newly formed CIA (in 1947) and any Army base where you could find more than a few Ranger or OSS veterans. Commando operations were gone, but not forgotten. And those with World War II commando experience had long and vivid memories.

Ironically, the one outfit that gets the most credit in the popular press and literature for commando operations, the CIA, has had the least to do with it. The CIA *has* been involved in this sort of thing, but not nearly as much as adventure novels would lead you to believe.

While the CIA turned into a pretty good intelligence agency, it found itself stymied by the new kinds of guerrilla wars that were breaking out in the wake of World War II. This led to the creation of the U.S. Army Special Forces, and a new form of special operations.

COVERT COMMANDOS

The World War II American Office of Strategic Services was not actually a commando operation, but it contained many of the people who got involved in commando missions and worked with guerrilla forces.

By 1947, it was converted into what we know as the CIA. Seeing it as competition, the Department of Defense and State Department were none too happy with its creation. What ensued was a classic bureaucratic turf battle. By stressing their wartime accomplishments, however, and the need to avoid "another Pearl Harbor" through better intelligence, the CIA won the argument and became America's "Central" Intelligence Agency. The argument may not have been valid: The presence of a CIA-type organization in the 1930s probably would not have prevented the Pearl Harbor attack. Penetrating Japanese society was difficult, and getting inside the military government that was running Japan would have been near impossible.

Nevertheless, "no more Pearl Harbors" bothered American politicians, and the CIA became another tool for the executive branch—the president and his staff—to use. And use it they did. They had to catch up with the Russian KGB, which had been operating in the United States since the 1930s. By the late 1950s, it was obvious that for the Russians World War II was not over. KGB agents were supporting communist guerrilla operations wherever they could find local support. Welcome to the beginning of the Cold War.

There were never any CIA commandos, although small groups of CIA agents sometimes found themselves temporarily operating like commandos, usually in life-or-death situations that could also be described as "self-defense." What the CIA did do was contact opposition groups in nations hostile to the United States and help those rebels operate more effectively. In this sense, the CIA was operating much like the OSS did with anti-Nazi and anti-Japanese guerrillas during World War II.

The CIA soon discovered that energizing anti-Nazi and anti-Japanese guerrillas was a lot easier than getting behind anti-communist groups. The Russian communists had created a police state that even the Nazis admired for its brutal efficiency. The Russians had also put together a counterintelligence system that was remarkable in its ability to keep secrets and catch spies. The Russians exported this knowledge to their allies and communist guerrilla movements.

Moreover, communist propaganda had deluded many journalists and commentators in the West into believing that the Soviet Union and other communist states were the future in terms of humane and socially progressive government. This was a startling achievement, for there was a steady stream of refugees from communist countries (where getting out was extremely difficult) who told a quite different story. Until the late 1980s, when the communist empire fell apart, no CIA-backed guerrilla operation was able to topple a communist government. Noncommunist governments, or nations seemingly likely to go communist, were another story. But once a communist-style police state was set up, the only way to topple it was a spontaneous uprising by nearly the entire population. That's what happened in the Soviet Union and Eastern Europe between 1989 and 1991. Who knew?

In reality, most of what CIA field agents did was pretty mundane—largely collecting information in foreign countries using local contacts and agents, or even via such simple acts as reading the local newspapers. They also carried out unwarlike acts like giving money to pro-U.S. political parties and bribing the local media (a common custom in many nations) to run more pro-American material.

Backing groups with guns in foreign countries was tricky, and the older agents, with World War II experience, knew this. Any OSS agent who had worked with guerrillas during the war knew how divided, unpredictable, and even untrustworthy they could be. In the first decade of the CIA's existence, it learned the hard way that backing guerrillas trying to take down a communist government was a losing proposition. And since the Department of Defense was not about to let the CIA form its own little army, or even commando unit, it would have to pick its fights carefully.

The idea of supporting armed groups in countries you don't get along with is an ancient one. Genghis Khan, the great Mongol conqueror, spent some time exiled in China, where the Chinese assisted him in going back to defeat his enemies. In this way, the Chinese kept the Mongols from invading because they were so busy fighting each other. It didn't ultimately work with Genghis, but the ploy did work most of the time for centuries.

The CIA, like the U.S. Army, studied both ancient and twentieth-century experiences with guerrilla war. What it discovered was sobering, although not sobering enough to keep us out of Vietnam. And the reason for that was because we did not fully appreciate the new communist approach to guerrilla wars—both running them and fighting them—until it was too late.

Finally, the CIA was eased out of the paramilitary business in 1961, when the Bay of Pigs Cuban invasion failed. This program was put together by the CIA, using fifteen hundred anti-communist Cuban exiles trained and equipped for this purpose. But the newly inaugurated president Kennedy inherited this plan from his predecessor, Dwight D. Eisenhower, and didn't really believe it would work. He was right, because it was subsequently learned that most Cubans were hostile to the invasion. Still, Kennedy was already taken with the spirit, competence, and enthusiasm demonstrated by the Army Special Forces.

After the April 1961 Bay of Pigs fiasco, Kennedy declared the Special Forces to be the guerrilla war specialists. This was not a major disaster for the CIA, which had plenty of other intelligence work to do. In effect, letting the Army Special Forces handle most of the counterguerrilla and commando operations helped the CIA by providing it with better-trained, and more numerous, people it could work with in this area. Many of the key people in the CIA and the Special Forces had worked together in the OSS during World War II, and were already developing a working relationship that endures to the present.

HOW TO CREATE A SUCCESSFUL GUERRILLA MOVEMENT

The Chinese communists were the most energetic twentieth-century guerrillas and were the ones to literally "write a book" on how to run a guerrilla war. There was nothing the Chinese communists did with guerrilla war that was particularly unique, except that they wrote it all down and ran a formal educational program to produce more well-trained guerrillas. Actually, they wrote and distributed a number of pamphlets and books on the subject. This was a typical twentieth-century development: Procedures that had been reinvented, and then forgotten, many times in the past were finally recorded and preserved for easy reuse. This makes a difference. In the past, an exceptionally sharp leader could reinvent the many steps needed for successful guerrilla warfare, but many of his subordinates would not have as many of the details right, and that can cause fatal problems.

An example of this was seen among the Philippine guerrillas during World War II. Most of the guerrilla bands that formed after the

Japanese conquered the islands in early 1942 were led by U.S. or Filipino officers who refused to surrender. Some of them were more successful than others, and those differences can be traced directly to how well the guerrilla leaders reinvented the practice of guerrilla warfare. Some of these officers were very good at it, and they survived and thrived. Others missed important details and were less successful, often being caught and killed by the Japanese.

The "Book of Guerrilla Warfare" that the Chinese communists created was based on much trial and error. The Chinese had observed the success of the Russian Revolution of 1917, and quickly realized that the Marxist belief that urban workers were the vanguard of the revolution was flawed. Karl Marx failed to understand that in some countries the "peasants," or poor farmers, were the ones more likely to get behind an armed revolution. The Chinese communists made many mistakes as they pursued their guerrilla war—but they took notes. The basic drill the Chinese communists developed involved a three-phase, long-term operation.

The Organization Phase. The guerrilla leaders had to first find each other and determine who had the smarts, skills, and dedication to get such a war started. These key people were generally referred to as the "cadres" (professional revolutionaries). Then they concentrated on developing local support. The cadres organized themselves into small cells, got themselves educated on guerrilla procedures, and proceeded to convert as many people (usually poor farmers) to the virtue of the revolutionary cause (in this case, communism) as they could. This was often accompanied by combat operations such as killing corrupt, and unpopular, local government officials, landlords, police informers, and businessmen, which made the local government control weaker, and helped with recruiting the awe inspired. The terror was also meant to show the locals that the communists meant business and were not to be messed with. During this phase, the government usually considered the communist rebels "criminal elements." There was something to this, as the communists did not shy away from bank robbery or stealing money and goods from government organizations. It was the terror campaign against government officials, however, that did the most damage.

The Guerrilla Phase. Once local areas were effectively under communist control (either openly, as in "liberated zones" run by commu-

nists, or covertly, when the local officials were terrorized into cooperating with the communists), you moved on to the Guerrilla Phase.
Here the cadres created combat units (usually small ones with twenty
to thirty men and women each) and started attacking local police with
bought or stolen guns. Doing this provided more weapons (taken from
dead policemen). Ambushes are, in this phase, the favored form of
fighting. The idea is to expand the size of liberated zones. With larger
areas under guerrilla control, the cadres can establish more popular
forms of government ("sharing the wealth") as well as taxing the people to keep the war effort going. Popularity is the key here, because it
helps recruit new fighters and cadres. One of the ways to be popular is
is to terrorize "enemies of the people"—government officials, wealthy
people, and anyone who doesn't agree with you. At this point (if not
earlier), the government is likely to send in the army and more police.
So the idea is to wear the government forces down with constant small
attacks. Avoid any battles that cannot be won. Remember, you won't
survive this phase if you haven't got most of the population on your
side. If the government shapes up and wins back the allegiance of
most of the population, you're toast.

   The Mobile Phase. If you do go from success to success during the
Guerrilla Phase, eventually you'll switch over to the Mobile Phase.
Here you create larger military units (battalions of several hundred
men and women, brigades of two to five battalions, and divisions of
two to five brigades). At this point, you're fighting a civil war. You
drive the government forces out of the countryside and into the cities.
Once you have the cities surrounded, you starve them out—and victory is yours.

   This is the playbook used by all post–World War II communist
guerrilla wars. It didn't always work, but it made guerrilla movements
more formidable threats to the governments that were fighting them.

   Hundreds of American military personnel and OSS agents came
into contact with the Chinese communist guerrillas during World War
II. Many understood that they were observing something special. Once
the Cold War began in the late 1940s and it became apparent that
the Chinese communist guerrilla playbook was going to be applied
worldwide, there was considerable thought given to how this threat
could be countered. This was one of the reasons the U.S. Special
Forces were created: to help governments beat communist guerrilla

U.S. Army soldiers from the 1st Special Forces Group, Fort Lewis, Washington, receive hand-to-hand combat training from members of the Royal Thai Army during Exercise CG 2001.

An air warfare instructor points to a target downrange for a British Special Forces member from the 22nd Special Air Service (SAS) at Nevada Station in Hereford, England.

In Afghanistan, small pilotless aircraft become the perfect guards for an air base by flying just outside the base and transmitting back live video.

All photos: Department of Defense

Smoke rises in the background as members of Navy Sea-Air-Land (SEAL) Team Five sight in on a target with their M-4 carbines. The rifles are equipped with M-203 grenade launchers.

Setting up a favorite commando weapon, the Claymore mine, which will kill troops or wreck unarmored vehicles 109 yards away with a fan-shaped pattern of steel balls.

Commandos of the 41st Royal British Marines plant demolition charges along railroad tracks of an enemy supply line that they demolished during a commando raid, eight miles south of Songjin, Korea, on April 10, 1951.

One U.S. Army soldier armed with a Beretta runs across an opening while another covers him. The soldiers are participating in a joint United States and United Kingdom Special Forces exercise.

Bomb equipped with a JDAM guidance kit on a Navy fighter ready to take off.

Marines attached to the Military Operations in an Urbanized Terrain (MOUT) training facility demonstrate a quick method of securing a building.

AN/GVS-5 laser range finder.

AN/PVS-7B night vision system
for an individual soldier lets you
see in the dark.

AN/GVS-5 laser
range finder.

A Zodiac inflatable raft
departs U.S.S. *Tucson* (SSN
770) while off the coast
of Chile.

U.S. Air Force MH-53 departs for a mission.

A Navy Mark V special operations craft, a 50-ton, 82-foot-long speedboat used to insert and extract SEAL combat swimmers in high-threat areas, is squeezed into a C-5 Galaxy aircraft from the 349th Air Mobility Wing, Travis Air Force Base, California, with only inches to spare.

Members of a Navy SEAL team fast-rope from a 20th Special Operations Squadron MH-53J Pave Low III helicopter to the bridge of the vehicle cargo ship *Cape Mohican* (T-AKR-5065) during the joint service Exercise Ocean Venture, 1982. The SEALs are practicing shipboard insertion and exfiltration techniques.

A search party made up of Turkish commandos. Air Force volunteers and Army Special Forces prepare to search for USAF Lieutenant Colonel (LTC) Michael R. Couillard and his son Matthew, both of whom survived after being lost for nine days in the mountains of Turkey.

A boat from the Navy Special Boat Unit 22, Sacramento, California, carries members from Navy SEAL Team Five, San Diego, California, as they practice beach incursions during Exercise NE 2001, in Alaska.

During the Urban Warrior Exercise, a British Royal Marine Commando fills out a casualty card to document and research the overall success of the exercise.

Special Forces Group at Fort Bragg, North Carolina, calculate the time-fuse length to an explosive charge for unexploded ordinances (UXO) disposal during Operation Focus Relief II (OFR II) in Thies, Senegal.

Members of the 75th Rangers (Airborne), Fort Benning, Georgia, perform weapons training in the desert of Egypt. The soldiers are armed with M-16 rifles and M-60 machine guns.

Three Greek Army Special Forces Commando Squadron soldiers stand guard, two with rifles and the third standing behind a machine gun mounted in the back of an IFOR-marked Mercedes-Benz four-by-four.

A United States Air Force C-17A Globemaster III
deployed from the 437th Airlift Wing, Charleston
Air Force Base, South Carolina, drops an international
mix of paratroopers.

U.S. Marine with a 12-gauge shotgun aboard a cargo ship.

U.S. Navy SEALs search the passage-
ways of the USNS *Leroy Grumman*
for an intruder during a search-and-
seizure exercise.

Standard weapon for U.S. commandos, the 5.56mm M-4
carbine (an M-16 with a shorter barrel), with M-203
40mm grenade launcher attached.

methods). About the same time, Britain confronted similar guerrilla movements and developed its own methods for dealing with the problem.

In the end, the Chinese guerrilla "how-to" books didn't unleash worldwide revolution. But the wide distribution of this knowledge has resulted in more guerrilla movements, and more of them are having more success. Which reminds us that education does not always have to be a good thing.

HOW TO DEFEAT A SUCCESSFUL GUERRILLA MOVEMENT

We tend to forget one very important aspect of the Vietnam War. Before Vietnam, the United States and its allies had defeated nearly all of the communist guerrilla movements it fought against.

Prior to the Vietnam War, the U.S. armed forces had amassed considerable experience in the conduct of insurgency and counterinsurgency warfare. Lessons were learned, but when the Vietnam War came along they were either forgotten or misapplied.

The idea that a communist insurgency was unbeatable was rather firmly established by the Vietnam War, particularly in leftist circles. This is hardly the case. Indeed, in the two decades prior to the insertion of massive American forces into Vietnam, communist guerrillas had not done very well overall.

As the United States faced communist guerrillas in Vietnam in the early 1960s, the historical record was on America's side. All the pundits intoned this wisdom; after all, it was part of the historical record, and you could look it up. What few observers or participants bothered to focus on, however, was the key factor that had led to all those guerrilla defeats: the lack of nearby safe havens and sources of supply.

Winning "hearts and minds" was important, but not as important as logistics: steady supplies of food, ammunition, and weapons. As in conventional warfare, these are more important than anything else. Even guerrillas have to eat, and you need safe areas where you can train and rest your troops. This factor was consistently played down during the Vietnam War. Many knowledgeable observers at the time pointed out the presence of communist sanctuaries and illegal supply lines, such as the Ho Chi Minh Trail through "neutral" Laos. But

COMMUNIST GUERRILLA CAMPAIGNS, 1942–1965*

GUERRILLA WAR	WHEN	WINNER
Greek Civil War	1944–1949	Government
Spanish Republican Insurgency	1944–1952	Government
Chinese Civil War	1945–1949	Guerrillas
Indochina War	1945–1954	Guerrillas
Iranian Communist Uprising	1945–1946	Government
Philippine Huk War	1946–1954	Government
Madagascan Nationalist Revolt	1947–1949	Government
South Korean Guerrilla War	1948–1953	Government
Malayan Emergency	1948–1960	Government
Kenyan Mau-Mau Rebellion	1952–1955	Government
Cuban Revolution	1956–1958	Guerrillas
Sarawak/Sabah "Confrontation"	1960–1966	Government

*Left out are noncommunist guerrilla wars such as the Ukrainian National Army insurgency of 1942–1953 and those in Burma, India, and South America; World War II partisan campaigns that ended when World War II did; and guerrilla wars that were still going on in 1965 (several in Africa, Asia, Latin America, and elsewhere).

such was the political situation during the Vietnam War that it was not possible to give the guerrilla sanctuaries and supply lines the importance and attention they deserved. North Vietnam and the United States had agreed to observe the neutrality of Laos in 1962, and North Vietnam would never admit it was in Laos and using that nation as a base for fighting in South Vietnam. Russia blocked efforts by the United Nations to press the matter. A similar situation existed in Cambodia, with North Vietnam denying it was there. Richard Nixon is still vilified for going after communist sanctuaries and supply lines in Laos and Cambodia. The hearts and minds that counted most, it turned out, were the ones in the United States. But most important for future wars, it's absolutely critical for anti-guerrilla operations to understand the weaknesses of the guerrillas themselves.

The United States went into Vietnam with long experience with guerrilla wars. The American Revolution saw widespread guerrilla operations by American rebels and pro-British irregulars. The Indian wars, which did not end until around 1900, were guerrilla wars, and the guerrillas lost. But in the twentieth century, America gained considerable, very practical experience in defeating guerrilla opponents.

The Philippine Insurrection, 1899–1902

When the Spanish took over the Philippines in the sixteenth century, they found a collection of islands occupied by a disunited population composed of dozens of warring tribes. After centuries of Spanish rule, Filipinos were never able to get a successful revolution going so that they could rule themselves free of foreign domination. In 1896, rebels tried again, but the Spanish knew the rebels were not very disciplined and some of the factions didn't like each other. Taking advantage of that, plus some bribes, led to the collapse of the rebellion. Then Spain had the misfortune to get into a war with the United States, and in 1898 the U.S. Navy showed up in the Philippines, sank the Spanish warships present, and promptly took over the country. Thus ended the Spanish-American War, and the beginning of America's first guerrilla war of the twentieth century.

The leaders of the rebel groups—especially Emilio Aguinaldo, the most popular—quickly realized that the Americans were not going home right away. So the rebels declared a "Republic of the Philippines," and in early 1899 fighting commenced. They had grabbed many weapons from the Spanish and thought they could fight a regular war with the Americans. Against an army leavened with many experienced American Civil War and Indian war officers and NCO veterans, however, the Filipinos didn't stand a chance.

By the end of 1899, the rebels were back to guerrilla war. While it had worked against the Spanish, it was less successful now against the Americans. The U.S. Army had their several decades of recent experience chasing hostile Indians, and those lessons were promptly applied to the Filipino guerrillas. Just as in the American West, some of the U.S. troops garrisoned towns and fortified camps, while others went into the bush to pursue the guerrillas. Moreover, Americans loved to build and improve things, so many public works projects (roads, bridges, schools) were undertaken. These projects were very popular with most Filipinos, many of whom were hired to do the work.

Because America also had a reputation as a fair-minded and generous nation, a large minority of Filipinos were willing to wait and see how the Americans would act toward them. Further aid projects, doing good works the Spanish had previously done on a much smaller scale, caused more Filipinos to switch their allegiance. The Americans admittedly made it worthwhile for rebels to surrender. Senior rebels were rewarded with government jobs and other goodies if they surrendered and swore loyalty to the United States. One senior guerrilla leader who surrendered was made a provincial governor. Gaining the loyalty of more Filipinos brought forth more information on where the guerrillas were and what they were up to. Taking advantage of this, Brigadier General Frederick Funston devised and led a daring commando raid, using loyal Filipinos pretending to be guerrillas, to capture Aguinaldo. Once this was done, and realizing that the Americans were not as inept or as cruel as the Spanish, the rebel leader took the loyalty oath and became a professional politician. After another year, the remaining rebels (except for some Moro tribes in the south) surrendered. A century later, the Moros are still fighting.

The Philippine Insurrection left four thousand Americans dead (three thousand of them by disease). Perhaps as many as twenty thousand Filipinos died. For decades it was claimed that hundreds of thousands died, but that was due to propaganda as divisive in the United States as the later Vietnam War. Despite the hostile press back home, however, and because of a much more practical approach to fighting the war, and without outside support for the rebels, the conflict was over in four years. Another factor in the American victory was the failure of the rebels to unite. This was a common problem in guerrilla wars, where widespread unrest does not eliminate local loyalties. The United States took advantage of these divisions and never lost sight of the fact that "all politics is local." Despite the fact that the Philippine operations were the first major American war of the twentieth century, and the successful suppression of a guerrilla movement as well, the U.S. Army didn't add this hard-won knowledge to its institutional memory. This was particularly strange when you remember America's long experience with guerrilla operations, and the fact that after the Spanish-American War, the army founded a War College and instituted an extensive program for educating officers and studying war.

American officers, however, like officers in most nations, didn't consider guerrilla operations to be "real" war. As a result of this conceit, the American Army (but not the Marines) was forced, at great cost, to start from scratch each time it confronted guerrilla warfare over the next century.

The "Banana Wars," 1912–1934

During this period, as discussed earlier, the Marines established a reputation as resourceful peacekeepers throughout Central America and the Caribbean, particularly in Nicaragua (1912–1913, 1927–1933), Haiti (1915–1934), and the Dominican Republic (1916–1922). These conflicts were called the "Banana Wars," because some of them were undertaken to restore peace in tropical nations where American companies were growing bananas for sale in the United States. Unlike the Army's experience in the Philippines, the Marines were faced with civil wars. While the rebels usually claimed they were fighting for the oppressed majority, in fact these conflicts were more often brawls fought between different wealthy clans that had taken turns running the country for generations. In the Caribbean, the Marines used the same approach as the Army in the Philippines and with the same results. Unlike the Army, the Marines did take note of their success, and how they did it, and wrote it all down. Two Marine majors, Samuel M. Harrington and Harold H. Utley, captured the Marine Corps' counterinsurgency warfare experience into the *Small Wars Manual*. No one outside the Marine Corps, however, paid much attention. This was especially true during America's next big experience with guerrilla warfare, in Vietnam.

There the Marines actually did try to apply the lessons of their prior experiences, but were discouraged by the Army. Since World War II, the Marines had been convinced to modify their thinking about guerrilla operations. For example, the "new thinking" played down the techniques that had worked in the past. In hindsight, it was foolish for the Army to ignore what the Marines knew or even their own experience. But at the time it was thought that the past was obsolete. It wasn't.

Philippine-American Guerrilla Operations in World War II

This was one of the more successful guerrilla wars during World War II. It was even more so because for the first year, the Filipino guerrillas were cut off from any outside support, and didn't begin to get significant aid until early 1944. By the time the American fleet invaded in late 1944, there were some 150,000 organized guerrillas operating on the islands. Two years earlier, when American commanders had first found out about the movement, it had come as a complete surprise. Prewar planning had not taken this into account, despite the Army's experience with Filipino guerrillas four decades earlier. But General MacArthur, the commander of American forces in the area, quickly realized the possibilities. He formalized the organizations the guerrillas had put together, promoted many of their leaders, and encouraged the Filipinos to prepare for the return of American troops. When the American invasion did take place, the guerrillas proved invaluable. Actually, they proved their worth even before the invasion, providing information on where the Japanese troops were and the state of Japanese defenses. Just before, and after, the landings, the guerrillas sabotaged Japanese transportation (destroying bridges and roads) and ambushed Japanese convoys. Downed American pilots were rescued from capture (and often execution) by the Japanese. Once the American troops were ashore, the guerrillas served as scouts and prevented the Japanese from using their infiltration tactics to attack American bases. The Japanese soon took to the hills and jungles themselves. The guerrillas were then used to hunt down and kill small groups of Japanese troops trying to operate like guerrillas. Years of brutal occupation by the Japanese gave them a certain enthusiasm for this work. But as valuable as the Filipino guerrillas were in the fighting, this contribution was played down after the war. Even the official U.S. Army history of the Philippines campaign hardly mentioned their substantial contribution. At this point, an astute observer could conclude that the Army had an institutional prejudice against guerrilla operations. And such an astute observer would be right.

HOW TO FIGHT GUERRILLAS AND WIN

As we've discussed, many American military men and OSS (later CIA) agents obtained extensive guerrilla war experience during and after World War II. Despite the ready availability of all this experience on dealing with guerrillas, the military establishment played down the importance of guerrilla wars and, more dangerously, any realistic study of how to win them. You got the impression that because American troops had always been able to defeat guerrillas, there was no point in studying how they pulled it off. As was learned in Vietnam, however, life is not that simple. But there were always small numbers of military men who did study guerrilla operations, and they developed some basic rules. Many of these World War II guerrilla war vets ended up in the U.S. Army Special Forces when that organization was formed in 1953. Unfortunately, the Special Forces were not called upon to help run the war in Vietnam. If they had been allowed to stipulate how American forces would fight, there might have been a different outcome. Without knowing that, however, they most likely would have provided the following basic rules (gained from more than half a century of American experience in such conflicts).

Travel Light

Although the introduction of helicopters in Vietnam gave American troops great mobility, it was not the kind of mobility they needed to actually defeat the guerrillas. The experience of American troops has shown that the best anti-guerrilla troops travel light, carrying as little weight as possible. But even in Vietnam, where troops moved to the combat zone in helicopters and were supplied by them as well, American soldiers still carried twenty to thirty pounds more weight than the communist troops they were chasing through the jungle. The problem, however, was more than the extra poundage; it was the mind-set of moving fast and light. In Vietnam, commanders paid more attention to their fears of being caught short than to their desire to get the job done. Although some American troops were able to operate light, as with the LRRPs and SOG patrols, these men were considered elite, and kind of weird. Most commanders preferred to stick with excessive weight, and failure.

This changed, to an extent, in Afghanistan. The commandos and Special Forces traveled light and fast; the regular infantry came more heavily equipped. It had to do with training. The commandos and Special Forces practiced fighting while lightly equipped, and were much better trained than regular troops anyway. Earlier in the twentieth century, there was not as much essential heavy equipment (like body armor) to be had; it was easier for troops to dump the bedrolls, rations, and other equipment and just take off after guerrillas. That particular style of combat has not yet been recaptured.

Keep to the Bush and Boondocks

Time and again in the past, it had been shown that the best way to defeat guerrillas was to pursue them relentlessly in their own element. When this was done, as SEALs and Special Forces often did in Vietnam, their prey were either caught and destroyed, or persuaded to return to civilian life and stop fighting. Guerrillas cannot afford to be constantly on the run; they haven't got the resources (food, bases, medical facilities) to keep at it. American troops do have such resources, but in Vietnam, cautious commanders tended to avoid sending their troops into the bush for extended periods of time. Part of this had to do with poor training and leadership, but there was also the feeling that "real soldiers" didn't spend most of their time chasing irregulars through the wilderness. Every time U.S. troops have been successful smashing guerrillas, however, this is exactly what they have done.

In Afghanistan, American troops did go out and chase enemy troops. But this was done in two ways, with two different kinds of troops. The commandos and Special Forces traveled light and were trained for this kind of backwoods grab-ass. The regular troops, trained for more intense combat, went out loaded down with body armor and equipment. As a result, these troops were less agile in keeping up with the lightly equipped Taliban and al-Qaeda fighters. Nevertheless, the policy in Afghanistan has been to keep troops operating in the backcountry whenever it was suspected that enemy troops were operating there.

Know Your Enemy

Gathering intelligence has, for centuries, been recognized as the most effective way to get a handle on the depredations of irregular (guerrilla) troops. Basically, this means collecting information (via bribes, paid informers, prisoners, and vigorous scouting) and keeping it well organized. Identify the key people on the other side and go after them, with money, bullets, or less savory tactics. Knowing about the guerrilla leaders you are fighting can be extremely valuable. Such knowledge reveals which leaders are sloppy and thus easier to catch. You can also become familiar with disputes and rivalries within the guerrilla organization (such divisions always exist) and then take advantage of them.

Information on the enemy was collected during the Vietnam and Afghanistan wars, but it was used more wisely in Afghanistan. During Vietnam, there were constant problems with communist spies operating in South Vietnamese military headquarters; there was also a reluctance to negotiate with communist units in the field (as hard as that was, it was possible).

Offer Generous Terms

Never underestimate the usefulness of bribes. In particular, you want to make guerrilla leaders offers they cannot refuse. And when you do get these guys to switch sides, don't keep it a secret. The guerrillas are fighting for economic reasons, and you want as many of them as possible to know that you have a solution to their money problems. But money isn't enough; there are also political needs. Many guerrillas will be enticed to switch sides with offers of jobs in the loyalist government, green cards, or whatever it takes. Because this is always cheaper than getting American troops killed, it's an option that should always be considered. Money and goods can also motivate rank-and-file guerrillas and the civilians who support them.

The Vietnam War saw the use of the Chieu Hoi program, but this went after low-ranking guerrillas and rewarded them with jobs such as scouting for American troops. This was not enough. Timidity is always a prelude to failure. Such was not the case in Afghanistan, where money and other aid were offered in abundance to warlords and tribal chiefs to obtain their cooperation. Groups that had supported the Taliban were regularly convinced that the Northern Alliance (backed by the Americans) was a better deal, and eventually nearly all Taliban supporters switched sides. You could make the argument that Afghan politics was prone to frequent switching of sides. But this had historically been the case in Vietnam as well. The major difference was the better discipline of the communists. Among the many useful tools the Vietnamese communists obtained from their Russian and Chinese mentors was the use of political officers in all military units (to monitor and enforce loyalty) and extensive informer networks among the troops. This made it more difficult—but not impossible—to offer terms when fighting the communist guerrillas. In other communist insurgencies, the use of generous terms had worked, and it could have worked in Vietnam as well.

Offer a Viable Alternative Political Solution

To defeat guerrillas once and for all, you have to address the basic problems that caused people to take up arms in the first place. It's important that American troops have enough authority to undertake needed political reforms, or enough clout (political, diplomatic, and military) to get the local government to do it. Reforms usually involve fair taxation and administration of justice. Landownership and economic laws are also important issues. Ignore them, and you'll find that the popular anger just keeps producing more guerrillas for you to fight. Address these issues—even if you don't resolve all or any of them—and you'll gain more popular support and have fewer people shooting at you.

In the Philippines and the Banana Republics, the political problems were addressed (although never completely), while in Vietnam there was a reluctance to "interfere in the internal affairs of a sovereign nation." As if half a million American troops in Vietnam wasn't already "interference." Doing more to get the South Vietnamese government's political affairs in order would have more quickly led to victory and an American withdrawal. Afghanistan was a war in which offering the population a political alternative was a major weapon. And it worked—just as such a pitch had worked in the past in the Philippines.

Protect the People

The easiest way to beat guerrillas is to cut them off from the support of the population. The easiest way to do that is to convince the people that you are more likely to protect them than the guerrillas. Most civilians don't want to be part of any war. The guerrillas and their core supporters are always a minority of the population, so there is ample opportunity to win the loyalty and gratitude of neutral civilians. If you don't, the guerrillas will. Doing this is much easier in theory than in practice.

In Vietnam, Americans failed in this regard because of the reluctance to get U.S. troops in the bush to keep the guerrillas on the run. Thus unhindered, the guerrillas could make their rounds at night, making sure those civilians who might lean toward supporting the government were sufficiently terrorized to change their minds. The U.S. Marines, remembering their Banana Wars experience, put troops in villages on a full-time basis to keep the guerrillas out, and it worked. But the Army was in charge, and the Marine approach was discouraged and eventually stopped. The Army made the situation worse by regularly using artillery and bombing against guerrillas fighting in villages and towns. This killed civilians and, as the guerrillas expected, made them more hostile to Americans and the South Vietnamese government.

In Afghanistan, the older American experience was recalled and applied. Civilian casualties were kept low, and efforts were made to protect them; it was also made known that the Americans were doing this.

Negotiate

In all the pre-Vietnam insurgencies America was involved in, the negotiation approach was used early and often. Vietnam should have been no different, but the U.S. government saw this war as a quasi-religious crusade against "Godless communism," and no negotiation was allowed at the troop level. This didn't stop contacts and negotiation, especially between the South Vietnamese army and the South Vietnamese guerrillas. The North Vietnamese were another matter; they were more hard core and, like American troops, ordered not to negotiate with the enemy. The South Vietnamese guerrillas (the Vietcong) were never fully trusted by the North Vietnamese, largely became many of the Vietcong were not communists. But even with these barriers to negotiation, the opportunities were still there, and on occasion more entrepreneurial and opportunistic Americans did it anyway. Often the result was simply a local truce, but frequently the talks led to the guerrillas changing sides.

In earlier American guerrilla wars, negotiation was a powerful tool for ending guerrilla activity. In Afghanistan, the situation was quite different, with negotiation seen, from the beginning, as a valuable tool. And it was.

When All Else Fails . . .

If aggressive patrols, negotiation, generous terms, and bribes aren't working against your most troublesome guerrilla foes, there are other options. A century ago, as we've seen, Britain invented concentration camps to deprive Boer guerrillas of support from friendly farmers. Relocating civilians from out in the bush to better-secured locations, to prevent them from supplying guerrillas with food and information, is still a viable tactic. Many anti-guerrilla operations still make use of the ancient practice of taking (and sometimes killing) hostages. The hostages are usually relatives of the guerrillas, especially those who are known to be particularly close to their families (some guerrilla leaders couldn't care less what you do with their kinfolk, so you have to choose your hostages carefully). Torture is also considered a useful tool in some cases, although the real solution here is to simply get more skillful interrogators to entice the captured guerrillas to talk. Some of these tactics, such as taking hostages, are frowned upon in most Western nations but still used widely in places like South Asia and the Middle East. In Pakistan, the chief suspect in the murder of American journalist Daniel Pearl was convinced to surrender after some of his kin were taken hostage by the Pakistani government. If you are fighting a movement that is threatening to use nuclear or chemical weapons against you, unpalatable measures become less so.

The biggest asset most guerrilla movements have is the reluctance of professional soldiers to pay attention to the tactics that work with them. Professional soldiers tend to feel that guerrillas are a nuisance, at worst, and not a threat to regular troops. These attitudes tend to be remarkably persistent, and once the guerrillas become a major threat it's often too late to do anything about it. Too bad, because the solutions have never been much of a secret.

8 SPECIAL FORCES AND VIETNAM

The excellence of America's Perfect Soldiers—Special Forces, SEALs, Delta, LRRPs, and Rangers—can be traced back to the Vietnam War. While that conflict is commonly seen as an American military defeat, it wasn't. Vietnam was a political and leadership failure, but U.S. troops were unbeatable on the battlefield. Particularly feared by communist troops were America's Perfect Soldiers. Unable to win a political victory, American armed forces remembered what they had done right, leading to a growing number of Perfect Soldiers in the U.S. armed forces.

But first, the elite troops that performed so well in Vietnam had to be created. This took place a decade before America entered the Vietnam War, as new ideas developed during the 1950s. As a result of the new thinking, the U.S. Army created the Special Forces (commandos used to train resistance fighters in enemy territory) and Long Range Reconnaissance Patrols. The search for new ways to fight continued into the 1960s. Even as America was fighting in Vietnam, the Russians developed their concept of large-scale commando (Spetsnaz) assaults to tear up the enemy rear area. Meanwhile, as the Vietnam War ended, America had revived the elite Ranger infantry and the use of purely commando-type raids. Going into the 1970s, an explosive growth in terrorism brought back the concept of small commando units for dealing with hijacked aircraft or some bad guys who are who are barricaded somewhere and refusing to give up. Most nations created a supercommando force (the U.S. Delta Force, German SGS, and so on), while many localities fielded a Special Weapons and Tactics (SWAT) team. Here is where training and equipment became exotic, much to the delight of people who wrote adventure novels.

But the most numerous, and most important, Perfect Soldiers to come out of this post–World War II ferment were the U.S. Army Special Forces.

THE SPECIAL FORCES

Nicknamed the "Green Berets," the Special Forces were created in the early 1950s to organize guerrilla forces behind enemy lines. Or, as the Pentagon officially put it: "to infiltrate by land, sea or air, deep into enemy-occupied territory and organize the resistance/guerrilla potential to conduct Special Forces operations, with emphasis on guerrilla warfare." This is what the Special Forces did in Afghanistan in 2001, so you can see that their primary mission has not changed in half a century.

As a natural corollary to this mission, they also began to develop ways to fight guerrillas, especially communist guerrillas. But this was not all that straightforward. Professional soldiers didn't want to be bothered with guerrillas, who were considered unreliable, unpredictable, and more of a nuisance than a threat. But there were a lot of officers and NCOs in the post–World War II Army who had experience with guerrillas and knew that, like it or not, the Army would eventually have to deal with these irregular fighters. Still, the brass was having none of it in the late 1940s. So the men who would create the American Special Forces had to first settle for a psychological warfare operation in the late 1940s. Because guerrilla wars always seemed to be in the news during that period (Greece, Malaya, Kenya, Cyprus, and more), and the communists were calling for guerrilla wars all over the world, the psychological warfare operation was allowed to gradually morph into the Special Forces by 1956, when the Psychological Warfare Center at Fort Bragg, North Carolina, was renamed the U.S. Army Special Warfare School.

Once the Korean War began in 1950, the Special Forces advocates in the Pentagon received some attention. New ideas are not much wanted in peacetime, but once a war starts, anyone doing something different can expect some support. In September 1950, a Psychological Warfare Division was established within the Army General Staff (in G-3). While most American generals still did not consider guerrilla operations "real soldiering," they increasingly realized that they'd have to deal with them. The communists were successfully using propaganda and political organization to sway public opinion and foment guerrilla warfare throughout the world. The compromise solution was more emphasis on psychological warfare. In the late 1940s, this was a hot topic. The Cold War was new at the time, and people were searching for ways to counter communist tactics. The Special Forces advocates used the psychological warfare angle to get themselves resources, and the Pentagon was as susceptible as anyone else. The Army needed Special Forces; it just weren't ready to admit this quite yet.

In early 1951, the Psychological Warfare operation got more power, money, and autonomy when it became the Office of the Chief of Psychological Warfare (OCPW). This was a first for the Pentagon, as OCPW was an autonomous Special Staff Division working directly for the chief of staff. Keep in mind that the uniformed Special Forces advocates in the Pentagon were practicing what they preached—guerrilla warfare—in getting the OCPW established. The OCPW contained many World War II veterans who had worked on commando, guerrilla, and psychological warfare operations against the Germans and Japanese. Here they were using those skills against communists, and the Pentagon bureaucracy.

The Special Forces advocates had managed to get an Army field manual on guerrilla warfare published (FM 31–21, *The Organization and Conduct of Guerrilla Warfare,* 1951). This manual contained practical advice on how to deal with starting guerrilla wars, although little on recognizing how the communists had updated and improved this form of warfare. Moreover, the OCPW did not ignore its primary job: psychological warfare. Throughout the 1950s, much of OCPW's effort was devoted to studies on psychological warfare and developing new techniques.

Even before North Korea invaded South Korea in 1950, there had been an active communist guerrilla movement going in the south. This put guerrilla warfare on the front pages, and American veterans of World War II guerrilla operations managed to interest enough people in Congress to get Public Law 597 passed. This allowed the Army to get into the "unconventional (guerrilla) warfare" business, even if many Army generals were not interested.

Brigadier General Robert McClure, the chief Special Forces advocate and head of OCPW, moved quickly to take advantage of Public Law 597. In May 1952, he opened the Psychological Warfare Center at Fort Bragg. Because of Public Law 597, this soon became the Special Warfare School (which, to this day, has a large psychological warfare component). The law stipulated twenty-three hundred troops for the new Special Forces units. McClure sent the word out throughout the Army for any men with guerrilla war experience to consider moving over to the Fort Bragg operations. This bought in more operators, many with recent experience in places like Korea and other post–World War II guerrilla wars. McClure also went looking for experienced operators (as Special Forces troops came to be called). He was granted access to World War II OSS personnel records. There he found thirty-five hundred individuals with experience in guerrilla operations. Some fifteen hundred of these men were found to be "available," and most were induced (or, if in the reserves, ordered) to return to active duty. Also recruited were men from Eastern Europe who could speak the local languages and were eager to evict the communist governments being imposed by the Soviet Union. The name of this first unit was the 10th Special Forces Group.

The Psychological Warfare field operatives were called Special Forces, a term used by the OSS for men and women who operated in enemy territory during World War II. Some of those first Special Forces troops had served in the OSS version ten years earlier. The Special Forces in the early days, therefore, established several practices that persist to the present. First, the Special Forces soldier had to be older, more experienced. In those early days, combat veterans and those who had served with the OSS were given preference. Everyone had to be a volunteer and willing to operate in extremely dangerous situations. This included the possibility of spending months, or years, deep in enemy territory, or operating in civilian clothes, which could get you executed as a spy if captured. It was a new kind of war for professional soldiers, and all sorts of eager volunteers clamored to get in. Within months, hundreds of experienced volunteers arrived at Fort Bragg to train. Officially, the Special Forces were being trained (as the Army put it) "to infiltrate by land, sea or air, deep into enemy-occupied territory and organize the resistance/guerrilla potential to conduct Special Forces operations, with emphasis on guerrilla warfare." But those first Special Forces volunteers trained for other missions as well, including deep-penetration raids, intelligence gathering, and counterinsurgency—defeating guerrilla movements.

The Army now had a splendid tool, but the Korean War stalemated after 1951 and ended in 1953. In late 1953, however, there was a workers' uprising in communist East Germany. The demonstrations and riots were put down swiftly and brutally by the Army and police. Nevertheless, it reminded everyone that there were a lot of unhappy people behind the Iron Curtain. These were perfect candidates for anticommunist guerrillas. So the 10th Special Forces Group was split in half. One part went to West Germany as the 10th Special Forces Group, while the remainder stayed in Fort Bragg as the 77th Special Forces Group. Fort Bragg would continue to train Special Forces recruits and form new groups for other parts of the world. In 1957, the 1st Special Forces group was established in Okinawa, providing Special Forces troopers for Asian operations.

Although the Special Forces started as a part of Psychological Warfare operations, that gradually changed. At first, stirring up guerrilla movements in enemy territory was considered a useful psychological warfare tool. But by the end of the 1950s, Special Forces field operations were increasingly seen as more critical than psychological warfare. The tail was wagging the dog.

In the early 1960s, the Special Forces came to the notice of President John F. Kennedy. After a 1961 visit to Fort Bragg, Kennedy decided Special Forces were the future of warfare in this age of nuclear weapons (that everyone was afraid to use), and he began to pour a lot of resources into the program. Kennedy also made their unofficial green berets official. The Special Forces increased from fifteen hundred men to nine thousand because of the president's enthusiasm for special operations. He saw them as a solution to the increasing problem of communist-sponsored "wars of national liberation." As a direct result of Kennedy's enthusiasm, the 5th Special Forces Group was activated in late 1961, and the 8th, 6th, and 3rd in 1963. Psychological warfare was now in the back, with Special Forces firmly in control of what was coming to be called special operations.

THE GREEN BERETS GO TO VIETNAM

This expansion came none too soon, for the Vietnam War was looming. American advisers had been in South Vietnam since the mid-1950s. Despite the efforts of the Special Forces, the corrupt and inept South Vietnamese government was making its own people increasingly angry. There were communist (and noncommunist) guerrillas out in the bush fighting the South Vietnamese government. Even with American advisers who had been in South Vietnam since the 1950s, the country was becoming increasingly embroiled in a war of national unification (something most Vietnamese favored). By 1961, about half of the eleven hundred American troops in Vietnam were Special Forces. In 1962, a special headquarters was activated to oversee Special Forces activities in Vietnam, a task that was taken over by the 5th Special Forces Group when it arrived in October 1965. The 5th Special Forces Group consisted of five companies. Each had a headquarters, known as a "C-Detachment," and several subordinate commands, known as "B-Detachments." Each B-Detachment oversaw the operations of several A-Teams.

An A-Team was the normal operational unit of the Special Forces. First formalized in 1958, each had twelve men. It consisted of two officers, two operations and intelligence sergeants, two weapons sergeants, two communications sergeants, two medics, and two engineers. Each man was cross-trained in at least one other skill and spoke at least one foreign language. The ability to speak French came in handy in Vietnam, because it had been a French colony for nearly a century. The Special Forces teams trained Vietnamese Army soldiers, as well as tribesmen in the Central Highlands. At the peak of the war, nearly one hundred A-Teams were operating as part of the 5th Special Forces Group, plus a few teams from the 1st and 7th Special Forces Groups.

As American involvement in the Vietnam War increased, the Special Forces activities concentrated in two main areas. First, they ran their own war in the mountain forests of the Central Highlands. Second, there was another secret (and, technically, illegal) operation that the Special Forces ran in Laos. In support of both of these operations, U.S. Special Forces also trained South Vietnam Special Forces (who were pretty good).

When the Vietnam War began accelerating in 1964, there were only 951 Special Forces troops in Vietnam. Already, however, they had been organizing the tribes in the Central Highlands and had nineteen thousand tribesmen armed and on the payroll as Civilian Irregular Defense Groups (CIDG). These units not only defended their villages from South Vietnamese guerrillas (the Vietcong) and North Vietnamese troops, but would also ambush them. By 1965, there were 1,828 Special Forces soldiers in Vietnam, who were training and advising 30,400 CIDG, plus 28,800 Regional Forces (villagers armed and trained just to defend their own villages from Vietcong and North Vietnamese). In that year, Special Forces teams also organized and trained and the first Mobile Strike Force, or "Mike Force," battalions (eighteen hundred men in that year) from among the tribal warriors. These units were basically better-trained, more mobile, and better-paid CIDG. When Special Forces patrols detected Vietcong or North Vietnamese units small enough for a Mike Force battalion (a few hundred tribesmen) to handle, they could send the Mike Force units out after the enemy troops. Since the tribesmen knew the mountains and forests better than any Vietnamese, they usually won the battles.

In 1966, Special Forces strength in Vietnam was up to 2,589. These Americans had organized 66,000 local forces (34,800 CIDG, 28,000 Regional Forces, and 3,200 Mike Force troops) in South Vietnam and Laos. In 1967, there were 2,762 Special Forces troops in Vietnam supervising 58,200 local forces (34,300 CIDG, 18,200 Regional Forces, and 5,700 Mike Force troops). In 1968, 3,581 Special Forces troops were running 41,300 local forces (27,000 CIDG, 7,300 Regional Forces, and 7,000 Mike Force troops). In 1969, 3,741 Special Forces troops were running 38,100 local forces (28,100 CIDG, 700 Regional Forces, and 9,300 Mike Force troops). In 1970, 2,940 Special Forces troops were running 8,100 local forces (6,300 CIDG and 1,800 Mike Force troops). After 1970, Special Forces rapidly shut down operations in Vietnam and were gone from the region by the end of 1972 (except for some teams in Thailand).

Most of the work in Vietnam was done by Special Forces troopers of the 5th Special Forces Group, and, of course, they saw fighting as well. Members of the 5th received 16 Medals of Honor, one Distinguished Service Medal, 90 Distinguished Service Crosses, 814 Silver Stars, 13,234 Bronze Stars, 235 Legions of Merit, 46 Distinguished

Flying Crosses, 232 Soldier's Medals, 4,891 Air Medals, 6,908 Army Commendation Medals, and 2,658 Purple Hearts.

Not all the Special Forces' time was spent fighting and training local troops. They also participated in thousands of rural development projects. During the twelve years the Special Forces were in Vietnam (officially and unofficially), they built 670 bridges, 130 churches, more than 1,000 classrooms, 400 dispensaries, 110 hospitals, 275 marketplaces, over 1,200 miles of roads, 6,500 wells, and thousands of other projects. Most of this was done in the Central Highlands, to secure the support of the tribes in the area.

During the Vietnam War, the U.S. Army and the Special Forces were operating by different rules. The Army was always up against the South Vietnamese government, which could veto many of the essential policies needed to gain the support of the civilian population. Not so the Special Forces, who operated in the Central Highlands, an area where the Vietnamese didn't have much control. In effect, the Special Forces became the government in much of the Central Highlands. Compared to the corrupt and trigger-happy Vietnamese, the Special Forces were generous and considerate. So it's no surprise that the Special Forces gained the support (often quite enthusiastically) of the mountain tribes.

In all previous guerrilla wars the United States participated in (and won), America had control of the local government and was able to provide honest and efficient administration. This gained American troops the support of local civilians and made it possible to defeat the guerrillas. Nevertheless, even if the Special Forces had been allowed to operate in all of South Vietnam, there still would have been the problem of dealing with the corrupt South Vietnamese government.

This was the vital difference between the situation in Vietnam and other guerrilla wars involving Americans. A less corrupt and more efficient government in South Vietnam would have made the Vietnam War more like other American encounters with guerrillas. The South Vietnamese guerrillas would also have been less of a problem and the war could have been fought with conventional armies. In the end, that's how North Vietnam conquered South Vietnam—with a conventional invasion of armored and infantry units across the Vietnamese DMZ (demilitarized zone).

THE SPECIAL FORCES AND THE MOUNTAIN TRIBES OF VIETNAM

It was 1956 when the Special Forces first arrived in Vietnam, and their first job was to train South Vietnamese Special Forces troops. Over the next five years, the Americans created a credible South Vietnamese Special Forces organization. This was a frustrating mission, however, because the South Vietnamese government and armed forces were quite corrupt. Everything was for sale. If communist guerrillas had the money, they could buy information and weapons from South Vietnamese soldiers. The Vietnamese Special Forces troops trained by the Americans were better soldiers and more reliable, but they were always subject to the whims of South Vietnamese politics. While the Special Forces were training their Vietnamese counterparts, the CIA was looking for some help in its various operations up in the mountains of Central Vietnam and across the border in Laos. The CIA and Special Forces shared a common ancestor, the World War II OSS, and there were still many former OSS men in both the CIA and the Special Forces. So in 1959, small numbers of Special Forces troops began to work with the CIA.

The CIA had arrived in South Vietnam in 1954, right after the country was created (at the end of the war between France and the Vietnamese communist Vietminh guerrillas). While all Vietnamese wanted the French out, all Vietnamese did not want to be ruled by communists. So Vietnam was divided as part of the deal that had France giving up control and the Vietnamese governing themselves.

North Vietnam was a communist police state, although it was run by people who were considered national heroes for resisting the Japanese and French. South Vietnam, on the other hand, was run by people who had worked for the French. While South Vietnam was a democracy, the various religious, financial, and political interests were willing to cheat when it came to elections. There was popular dissatisfaction with the government in the south, but at the same time, many South Vietnamese wanted nothing to do with a communist government. The CIA walked right into the middle of this and found itself dealing with a nation full of feuding political parties, religious groups, mountain tribes, and huge criminal organizations. Plus the communists, and they were trying to get an insurgency going. The CIA soon realized that the communists, supported by the North Vietnamese, were not a major threat unless the North Vietnamese could send weapons and men down into the south. This wasn't easy, because there was a heavily defended DMZ between South Vietnam and North Vietnam. But in the late 1950s, the North Vietnamese decided to build a system of trails through Laos, to the west, and into the most heavily populated part of South Vietnam: the Mekong delta. The CIA, with agents operating in Laos, caught wind of this, and in 1959 arranged to obtain the services of some Special Forces troops to help them keep an eye on what would eventually be known as the Ho Chi Minh Trail.

From this modest start, it wasn't long before the Special Forces began working with the CIA to do something about the situation with the mountain tribes in the Central Highlands of South Vietnam. The corrupt South Vietnamese government was practically at war with these tribes, and the CIA wanted to prevent the situation from getting any worse.

There are several distinct ethnic and cultural groups in Indochina. In the lowland river valleys, deltas, and coastal plains, there are the more numerous Vietnamese and Khmer (Cambodians); about 90 percent of the Indochinese population lives in the lowlands. The mountainous interior, however, is inhabited by numerous non-Vietnamese tribes whom the French dubbed the "Montagnards" (mountaineers). These people are a combination of Malay tribes who had lived in the area for centuries, with more recent arrivals of Chinese (of Han extraction) from the north, as well as some Polynesians and even some Mongols. Montagnards numbered from 750,000 to 1,000,000 people thinly spread across the Central Highlands of South Vietnam, plus several hundred thousand more in the mountainous regions of North Vietnam, about 300,000 in Laos, and another 200,000 in Cambodia. Like mountain people everywhere, the Montagnards did not get along with the flatlanders (the Vietnamese living along the coastal plain and river valleys).

In South Vietnam, there were some thirty different Montagnard communities, numbering from a relative handful up to 100,000 or 120,000 people in the case of the Rhadé tribe. Although some of the Montagnard tribes are racially akin to the Vietnamese, and most have many cultural ties with them, the Montagnards were, at the time, generally despised by the Vietnamese, who called the tribes *moi* or "savages." Yet this was not true. While the Montagnards led a simple existence, based on hunting and primitive agriculture, they had a rich cultural life.

To make matters worse, the Vietnamese tended to exploit and discriminate against the tribal peoples. This included a late-1950s program to send thousands of Vietnamese settlers into the Central Highlands. As a result of this, and the huge cultural differences, the tribal peoples tended to hate Vietnamese in turn.

During the First Indochina War (1945–1954), the Vietnamese communists had competed with the French for the allegiance of the mountain people. The communists won that one, especially in North Vietnam. After the partition of Vietnam in 1954, the North Vietnamese trained some ten thousand Montagnards in medical, educational, and other technical skills, and some of the hatred between the two groups was eliminated. Also, communist economic control was less strict in the bush where the Montagnards lived, so the North Vietnam Montagnards remained loyal during the American phase of the Vietnam War. Later the enmity returned when the communists attempted to assert more control in Montagnard areas.

It was different in South Vietnam, where the traditional animosities were not reduced, and there were no offers of education and economic aid to the mountain people. Instead, South Vietnam began settling Vietnamese in traditionally Montagnard territory. Often abuse of the local people came into play, although it often was no more than a Vietnamese making a joke about the Montagnards' often darker skin or inability to speak Vietnamese well. Thus, no matter what the official policy in North Vietnam or South Vietnam, the Montagnards were treated with contempt and disdain by the average Vietnamese. From their perspective, the Montagnards returned the feeling, considering the Vietnamese pompous snobs who wouldn't last a day in the bush.

In the late 1950s, because of increasing persecution by the South Vietnamese, the Montagnards had begun to develop a political movement. The Montagnards wanted a return to the hands-off approach the French had adopted; they were nostalgic for the days of French rule. The French had not allowed the Vietnamese to interfere in Montagnard affairs, and this was seen as a much better arrangement. The Montagnards tried to take over Pleiku, the major town in the Central Highlands, in 1958. The South Vietnamese reacted violently to this, putting down the uprising with great brutality. Many Montagnard leaders were arrested and jailed for many years. This caused some of the Montagnards in South Vietnam to join the communist guerrillas.

It was during all this that the Montagnards first came to the attention of the United States. American missionaries, anthropologists, and aid workers had been moving into the Central Highlands since the 1954 partition of Vietnam. At the time, the CIA kept in touch with many Americans working in out-of-the-way places, as a cheap means of getting firsthand information. By the late 1950s, the CIA concluded that although there was some Vietcong or South Vietnamese activity among the Montagnards, the Montagnards were not getting along with the South Vietnamese, and the Montagnards were very capable fighters. There were reports of Montagnards armed with spears and bows defeating Vietcong and South Vietnamese soldiers. If the communists gained the loyalty of the Montagnards, South Vietnam would be cut in half by a communist-controlled Central Highlands. In October 1961, a delegation from the CIA and the Special Forces visited the Rhadé tribesmen to see if they could convince them to support the Saigon government. The CIA offered money, arms, and aid, all provided by Special Forces troops, to the Montagnards to prevent them from joining the communists.

The Americans had several advantages working with the Montagnards. First of all, the Americans were obviously not Vietnamese. In fact, the Special Forces, with their berets, reminded the Montagnards of the French (who now represented the "good old days"). The Montagnards were also willing to overlook the fact that America was backing South Vietnam. Second, the Americans had lots of goodies and were generous. The Special Forces knew from World War II experience that goodwill and lots of presents were often all that was needed to gain the loyalty of tribal peoples. Most important, the Special Forces had been trained throughout the 1950s to handle this kind of situation; they immediately recognized the opportunity the mountain tribes presented. Moreover, the CIA and Special Forces were the kind of adventurers and macho guys the tribal warriors could relate to. These tall, mostly pasty-faced "flatlanders" arrive with loot and are generous with it—and all they want us to do is kill Vietnamese? Hey, what a deal. The Special Forces troopers affectionately dubbed tribesmen "Yards" and developed close relationships with them (including several Special Forces soldiers marrying Montagnard women).

The relationship was similar to what the British established with the Nepalese Gurkhas and other troops from what they called "warrior races." By providing these troops with modern equipment, weapons, training, and the services of first-rate officers, combat units of exceptional quality could be turned out. The Montagnards had significant advantages when operating out in the bush. They had grown up there and knew their way around the forests, mountains, and jungles of up-country Indochina. They could listen to the surroundings and know who was where. They knew the sounds of different insects and animals—or whether they made no sounds at all—depending on where people or other creatures were. Smells also provided a lot of information. Yards, Americans, and Vietnamese all smelled differently because of their diets. Anytime someone pissed in the bush, he was leaving his ID behind for any passing Yard.

Warriors by inclination, the tribes were constantly feuding with their neighbors and particularly with non-Montagnards. With proper training and leadership, they could be outstanding soldiers, especially when operating in the environment they grew up in. Being largely illiterate, they were taught skills that could be shown by instructors and memorized. This was the kind of training and combat leadership that U.S. Special Forces were able to provide.

By the end of 1963, the Special Forces replaced the CIA as the American presence in the Central Highlands. Some 674 Green Berets, plus—surprisingly—some South Vietnamese Special Forces personnel, were working with the Montagnards, of whom some forty to sixty thousand were equipped with modern weapons. Since most Montagnards were not interested in getting involved in a major war outside their own home area, the Special Forces set up several military programs that gave Montagnard villagers a choice. For Montagnards just looking for self-defense against Vietcong attacks, there were the Regional Forces programs. The Special Forces supplied weapons and training to villagers. While the Regional Forces were staunch in defending their villages, they were not often interested in going out looking for communist troops.

For more warlike activities, the CIDGs were set up. This protected the Montagnards from communists and communist influence and helped prevent the passage of Ho Chi Minh Trail cargo into South Vietnam. In 1965, Special Forces also began organizing Mike Force battalions using Montagnard mercenaries to provide more effective reaction forces for the protection of isolated camps: The idea was that if the VC hit a camp, a Mike Force battalion would immediately be sent in pursuit. These forces proved very effective throughout the Central Highlands. There were five Mike Forces. Each consisted of a Special Forces A-Team, one or more CIDG battalions, a recon company, and a Montagnard mercenary parachute company. In the Central Highlands and border areas, the Mike Forces got a real workout. These Forces were disbanded when the Special Forces left in 1971.

Not all Montagnard groups had the same military potential. Several tribes were outstanding soldiers, however. These included the Hre (110,000 people), Renago (10,000), Rhadé (120,000), Sedang (70,000), and, arguably the best of all, the Nung (15,000, with more in North Vietnam). All were originally from South China, except the Rhadé, who were Malay-Polynesian (Pacific islander). Rarely did more than 10 percent of a tribe join Special Forces–organized units. But the Nung, who qualified for the most difficult assignments, established a reputation much larger than the few thousand of them who served in combat.

Many of the Montagnards were in it for the money as much as for the adventure. Their own jungle economy had little use for money, so the Special Forces sometimes had to pay them in gold or goods. But this was still cheap. The highest-paid Montagnard warrior made less than the lowest-ranking U.S. soldier. In other words, you could put ten Montagnards in the field for what it cost to send one American out to fight. However, the Montagnards were comparing themselves not to Americans, but to Vietnamese, and they couldn't help but notice that Uncle Sam paid them more than what South Vietnam paid its Army officers. The Montagnards thought this was a most accurate and fair pay scale. The South Vietnamese generally kept their mouths shut.

Many of the Montagnards were warriors in the classic sense. Like the Gurkhas and similar groups, they literally laughed at death and got on very well with the warrior types attracted to U.S. Army Special Forces duty. Indeed, it was the bond of trust, mutual dependence, and fighting spirit between the Special Forces troopers and the Montagnards that produced a unique military organization. Many Special

Forces soldiers voluntarily went back to Vietnam for tour after tour so as to keep close to "their Yards." Some of the Special Forces folks went native, moving in with the Montagnards, learning the language and customs and, as noted, sometimes even marrying Montagnard women. The Yards reciprocated, becoming expert in the use of much U.S. military technology and creating some amazingly lethal combat units. The best Yard soldiers were young men in their late teens or early twenties. Like males their age the world over, they were fascinated by American technology and Americans in general.

The Yards knew the bush. They could track anything over any kind of terrain and could generally detect other troops in the forest long before Americans or Vietnamese could. But the Americans brought with them useful technology. The Americans had the radios and the skills needed to call in airpower and artillery. American medical technology not only went to war but also made life a lot more secure for the Montagnard families. The Yards appreciated the medical care, especially if it saved the life of a family member. The Montagnard religion saw spirits in everything they dealt with (animals, inanimate objects, and people). The Special Forces' use of modern medicine was, as the Yards saw it, the sign of mighty spirits working for these Americans.

The Montagnards were not always ideal soldiers. There is an ancient difference between warriors and soldiers. The former are eager and possess considerable combat skills, but lack discipline. Moreover, the Montagnards often served under their own leaders, which made it more difficult to turn the warrior habits into more disciplined behavior. Although the Special Forces worked to change the warrior mentality, it was slow going. Over the years, by trial, error, and determined instructions, more and more of the Montagnard fighters became disciplined soldiers, and many of these were promoted to elite positions like paratroopers and long-range scouts. Meanwhile, the Special Forces were careful regarding how they used their Montagnard warriors. The Montagnards were stalwart in the defense, but could be difficult to control in an attack and had a hard time coordinating their actions in large-scale operations.

In 1970, as U.S. involvement began to "wind down," administrative control of Montagnard CIDG and Mike Force units was transferred to South Vietnam, which converted most of them into South

Vietnamese Ranger battalions. Although desertions rose, the Montagnard units remained very effective. Only late in the war did the communists make any serious inroads into the Montagnard community. During their final 1975 offensive, the communists made promises and payments to key Montagnard groups, whereupon the South Vietnamese found that some of the Montagnard support they had long taken for granted was no longer available. After the war, however, the communists engaged in payback against the Montagnards. Not exactly genocide, but if your name was on "the list" you were in big trouble. The Vietnamese also went back to dumping on the Yards. As the population of lowlanders continued to increase, more Vietnamese moved into traditional Montagnard territory, increasing friction and, ultimately, displacing the Yards.

The Special Forces learned some valuable lessons in the Central Highlands. They confirmed that their training techniques and methods of dealing with tribal peoples were effective. But they also learned that outside forces—in this case the corrupt South Vietnamese government—could easily undo all their work. The Special Forces are trying to avoid this in Afghanistan, but as with the Vietnam experience, it's a struggle dealing with political corruption and a local government that doesn't work too well.

THE SECRET WAR IN LAOS

The Special Forces also fought a secret war in Laos throughout the 1960s. North Vietnam had more than a hundred thousand labor troops and thirty to fifty thousand combat troops in Laos at the time. Facing them were some two thousand American (mostly Special Forces) and as many as eight thousand Montagnard, Laotian, and Cambodian mercenary troops. This American-led force proved to be the deadliest troops the North Vietnamese (by their own admission) faced. This story is still largely unknown. The main objective of this operation was to keep an eye on the North Vietnamese supply operation in Laos, and attack it whenever the opportunity presented itself.

Studies and Observation Group (SOG) was the top-secret U.S. Army organization that ran this war. Before SOG received that name, it was called the Special Operations Group, a name that was quickly changed to provide a little more cover. SOG was run by Military

Assistance Command—Vietnam (MACV), the headquarters for all U.S. forces in Vietnam.

What eventually became the SOG operation started in 1958 as a South Vietnamese version of the U.S. Special Forces (the CIA was providing assistance in this area). The SOG took over the CIA operation in 1964. The SOG reported directly to the Pentagon, via MACV, and could appeal that high if someone in Vietnam didn't give them what they wanted. SOG had its own air and naval forces, and that included U.S. Army, Navy, and Air Force units. There was also a South Vietnamese helicopter unit flying CH-34s and a C-123 transport aircraft unit with Nationalist Chinese pilots. These were needed to fly SOG teams into areas where, by treaty, U.S. forces were not supposed to be.

SOG's mandate covered a wide area. It was an intelligence organization, able to collect information where U.S. troops could not officially do so. Squad-sized SOG recon teams (RTs) were dropped by parachute or landed from helicopters in areas adjacent to South Vietnam. Each RT contained Americans and Montagnards. The Americans provided the leadership and radio operators; the Montagnards provided their lifelong knowledge of the bush.

The secrecy of this operation arose from a 1962 treaty in which the United States and North Vietnam agreed to respect the neutrality of Laos and Cambodia. The CIA soon discovered that seven thousand North Vietnamese troops had not left Laos, and those troops were preparing well-hidden camps in which North Vietnamese could station themselves in that country. But because of the treaty, the CIA only had a few operatives in Laos (as part of the U.S. embassy staff), and for two years these CIA agents and a pro-American Hmong tribal Army tried to keep an eye on the Ho Chi Minh Trail, which ran through Laos. Finally, in 1964, it was decided that some experienced American troops would be needed, and SOG was formed. SOG was needed not only for keeping an eye on Laos, but also for similar operations in North Vietnam, the more remote regions of South Vietnam, and Cambodia. Most of the action was in Laos.

Ground operations were run by OPS-35 (a subunit of SOG) and used (eventually) seventy-nine RTs that proved to be some of the most effective combat units ever fielded by the United States. This was so because RTs did not just collect information regarding the enemy;

they also called in air or artillery strikes to do something about it. The SOG RTs were meant to be very efficient. When an RT spotted something while deep in enemy territory, the three U.S. members of the team knew what was a worthwhile target and what wasn't. These experienced Special Forces troops also knew how to call in available artillery or (more usually) air strikes to destroy North Vietnamese bases or supply dumps.

Between September 1965 and April 1972, OPS-35 conducted 1,579 reconnaissance patrols (RT), 216 platoon-sized patrols, and three multiplatoon-sized operations in Laos. From 1967 through April 1972, OPS-35 conducted 1,398 reconnaissance missions, thirty-eight platoon-sized patrols, and twelve multiplatoon operations in Cambodia. Technically, the SOG wasn't part of Special Forces, but most of its key personnel came from Special Forces.

Most SOG combat units were squads (the recon teams of three U.S. and four to nine Montagnard soldiers). The RTs were in constant action throughout the late 1960s. For platoon-sized operations, there were Hatchet Forces: one or more platoons, each with four or five U.S. troops and twenty to thirty Montagnards. These were used when muscle was needed on the ground, for raids and the destruction of large enemy installations. Larger operations used Search, Location, and Annihilation Mission (SLAM) companies, which were larger versions of the Hatchet Forces, being company-sized units with three or four platoons organized like the Hatchet Force platoons. This use of locally organized units was classic Special Forces work, just the sort of work that is still being done in Afghanistan. SOG also had call on CIDG battalions.

Ultimately, SOG could call on any U.S.-controlled military unit. Because it reported directly to the Pentagon and often carried out missions specifically requested by the president, the Pentagon let everyone know that when SOG asked for something, it was to be delivered immediately.

The RT organization (imposed by the need to respect Laotian "neutrality") turned out to be a good idea. The SOG RTs were organized with three Americans and six to nine Montagnard (usually Nung) mercenaries. The team leader was an American, and he was referred to as the 1–0 ("one oh"). His second in command was an American and was called the 1–1 ("one one"). The third American was the radio operator and was called the 1–2. Sometimes a South Vietnamese Special Forces officer or NCO accompanied the team to gain some tactical experience or to help with some technical matter, such as translating captured documents or interrogations of North Vietnamese prisoners. The SOG teams were named in a similar fashion depending on which area [CCN, CCC, or CCS (Command Control North Center or South)] they belonged to. Each area would use one type of names—say, tools or states.

The 1–0 had to be very, very good, for the survival of an RT depended on his skill and leadership. Naturally, anyone who was an SOG 1–0 was considered a very superior soldier (most were senior NCOs). The Nung tribesmen in an RT were carefully selected from volunteers and trained for months before going on their first mission. Nung volunteers with combat experience were preferred. The RTs went out on patrol about once a month, so they had plenty of time to train, practice, and rehearse, and this they did a lot of.

SOG was also the chief means of rescuing POWs and downed pilots in enemy territory, especially in North Vietnam, Laos, and Cambodia. The U.S. Air Force had its search-and-rescue (SAR) helicopters, but often needed some knowledgeable people on the ground. That's where one or more SOG RTs came in, to go in and fight off enemy troops who were closing in on the downed pilot. Less successful were attempts to grab American prisoners of war (POWs) from the communists. Part of this was due to the fact that the communists didn't take many prisoners in the first place. And those who were taken were moved around regularly to different jungle camps, just as all the communist troops did.

SOG also trained all its own non-U.S. personnel. This meant many training camps for Montagnards (who did not all speak the same language) and Cambodians. South Vietnamese were also trained, especially those who were sent into North Vietnam. Most of the training was combat related, including parachute training for some of the Montagnards, but some of it was technical as well.

SOG was heavily involved in many of the psychological warfare operations conducted during the war. This was especially the case with what were called "black" operations—those that required secrecy, such as planting booby-trapped ammunition in communist ammo dumps. Finally, the SOG was the last resort for any really, really important job that had to be done right away and was very risky. A typical example of this was getting back sensitive documents—codebooks, lists of secret agents, or the like. Going into North Vietnam to rescue downed pilots (and fight off North Vietnamese ground troops in the process) was something else SOG did, because no one else dared to.

In the spring of 1972, the Americans left and SOG operations were handed over to the South Vietnamese.

THE NORTH VIETNAMESE STRIKE BACK

By 1966, the North Vietnamese were aware that something going on in their Laos, and they didn't like it at all. It was bad enough that they could not catch these American patrols, but the Americans were calling in air strikes on stockpiled supplies and troop concentrations along the Ho Chi Minh Trail. The North Vietnamese decided to do something drastic to stamp out this American patrolling activity. So they took their only parachute unit, the 305th Brigade, disbanded it, and used many of these elite troops to form three counter-recon battalions. These troops were volunteers and true believers in the North Vietnam cause. They were good, they were capable, they were dedicated, and now they were out to kill SOG patrols. These efforts hurt SOG, causing hundreds of casualties, but were not able to stop the patrols or the damage they were doing.

The North Vietnamese were never able to eliminate the SOG patrols, and they had to keep three divisions in Laos, plus special counter-recon units, to keep the SOG from shutting down the Ho Chi Minh Trail. But the price paid by the SOG troopers was high. Like many battles, it was hard to tell who was the winner and who was the loser.

PSYCHOLOGICAL WARFARE

The Special Forces, who began with them, still knew techniques from the Psychological Warfare organization. The 6th Psychological Operations Battalion went to Vietnam in 1966, and in 1967 it was expanded to the 4th Psychological Operations Group. While a lot of their work was with leaflets and more traditional media, the Psyops soldiers also worked with Special Forces to perform some more exotic feats.

While the Vietnamese communists (north and south) had the edge in spies and double agents, the Special Forces also knew that the communists tended to be more than a little paranoid and fanatic about security. So the Special Forces took advantage of these characteristics. The tricks used are found in police work today. For example, cops catch a member of a criminal gang and get information out of the gangster by threatening to put the word out on the street that the guy talked. This could easily be a death sentence. The same thing worked in Vietnam with members of the communist "mob." Playing mind games was always an important component of psychological warfare, and the Special Forces made the most of it.

For example, communist prisoners were sometimes allowed to escape. But in the backpack the prisoner was allowed to "steal" on his way out, there was hidden a transponder. The movement of the fleeing prisoner could be tracked from the air. When it appeared that the prisoner had returned to one of the well-hidden bases on the Ho Chi Minh Trail (or within South Vietnam), the bombers were called in to devastate the place. In another scheme, the Special Forces took some real North Vietnamese defectors, put them in uniforms indicating a higher rank, worked up a cover story, and then moved them by helicopter to the Ho Chi Minh Trail, where they were dropped off to wander down the trail for a few days collecting information firsthand. Then they were picked up at a prearranged spot.

The Special Forces psychological warfare troops in Vietnam learned a lot about what works, and what doesn't. The bag of tricks the Special Forces took into Afghanistan contained a lot of items first tried out in Vietnam.

THE SECRET WAR IN CAMBODIA

When the French lost their struggle to the Vietnamese communists in 1953, they relinquished control of Laos and Cambodia as well as Vietnam. While the communists took over in North Vietnam, the old royal families returned to control in Laos and Cambodia.

During the Vietnam War, neither country was able to remain neutral while the North Vietnamese fought to take over South Vietnam. The North Vietnamese simply moved into Laos to set up their Ho Chi Minh Trail. Cambodia was another story. There were several groups of communists in Cambodia, including the Khmer Rouge (Red Cambodians). The Cambodian royalists, however, had managed to maintain the allegiance of most of the people.

The Viet cong had long used the thinly populated Cambodian border areas for establishing bases immune from American or South Vietnamese attack. The president (formerly king, and in the 1990s king once more) of Cambodia, Norodom Sihanouk, sought to play off America, China, and both Vietnams to keep Cambodia out of the war and the communists out of Cambodian politics. He allowed the communists to operate in those South Vietnamese border areas as long as they did not provide support for the Cambodian communists. This worked for a while, even as Sihanouk saw, in the early 1960s, that the North Vietnamese were likely to win their war. Sihanouk reduced his support for South Vietnam and America accordingly. The North Vietnamese also noted Sihanouk's changing attitude and pressed for more leeway to expand their supply operations in Cambodia. By the late 1960s, the North Vietnamese were hiring Cambodian firms to truck food and munitions from Cambodian ports to supply dumps three miles from the South Vietnamese border. At first, there was some attempt to hide this traffic. But by early 1969, ships from communist countries were regularly unloading food and ammunition at the Cambodian ports. From them, the North Vietnamese were supporting two hundred thousand Vietcong and North Vietnamese troops, including three divisions of troops in Cambodia itself. In effect, all of their operations in the Mekong delta (most of southern South Vietnam) were supported by material brought in via Cambodian depots.

The Cambodian government insisted that these depots, and the supply arrangements, did not exist. This was done with a straight face because the Cambodians had no official arrangement with the North Vietnamese; everything was done with a nod and a wink. The North Vietnamese bribed key Cambodians (mainly members of the royal family). The Cambodian royals then set up front companies to hire Cambodians to unload the ships and truck the military supplies (labeled as something legal) to areas in rural Cambodia where North Vietnamese drivers would take over and move the supplies to the North Vietnamese camps near the South Vietnamese border.

SOG patrols into Cambodia began in 1967, and ample evidence was found. But President Johnson did not want the diplomatic and political problem involved in questioning Cambodian neutrality, even though the SOG clearly demonstrated that the Cambodians were anything but neutral. The official U.S. line was that these rumored North Vietnamese supply arrangements didn't exist. Thousands of South Vietnamese and American soldiers were killed because the North Vietnamese units using the Cambodian supply line were able to receive ammunition and other supplies.

When President Nixon succeeded Johnson, this proved to be a major embarrassment. The "Cambodian cover-up" became headline news in 1969, and Nixon ordered the Cambodian bases attacked. SOG had been raiding North Vietnamese bases in Cambodia for two years, but there were a lot more enemy soldiers there, per square mile, than in Laos, and SOG was unable to stop the enemy activity by itself. This was another important lesson for the Special Forces: A small number of Perfect Soldiers can only do so much.

THE OTHER COMMANDOS OF VIETNAM

The Special Forces weren't the only special operations and commando-type troops in Vietnam. Navy SEALs and UDT swimmers were there for most of the war. British and Australian SAS commandos also spent time in Vietnam, and Army infantry units in the form of LRRP units developed their own commando capabilities. This had been done twelve years earlier in Korea, but the idea barely survived in the peacetime Army. In 1958, two LRRP companies were formed in Europe. In addition to being sent deep into communist-held territory, these LRRPs were also equipped with backpack nuclear weapons. This, however, barely kept the LRRP concept alive.

The value of LRRPs was quickly rediscovered in Vietnam. When the Special Forces began training for long-range patrols in 1964, they realized that these were skills that could be useful for any Army or Marine unit in Vietnam. By 1966, the Special Forces were operating the MACV-Recondo (LRRP) School in Nha Trang. The course lasted three weeks, and only 62 percent of those who entered (3,357 out of 5,395) passed. There were more than 3,357 LRRPS. Many combat-experienced men were able to join teams directly, and many LRRPs came back for a second or third tour in Vietnam.

Commanders of some divisions and brigades organized their own

LRRP units early on, but by late 1967, the Army formalized the LRRP operations. Each division and corps was authorized a LRRP company (118 men, organized into sixteen 6-man patrol units). Brigades usually managed to put together a LRRP platoon (eight six-man patrol units).

Combat was not a primary objective for the LRRP, and there was no direct contact with the enemy in 38 percent of the twenty-three thousand LRRP missions. When LRRPs did run into the enemy, they killed nearly ten thousand of them. This should not be surprising, because the LRRPs were well-trained, experienced troops who were deliberately trying to stay out of sight. In addition, there were far more enemy casualties resulting from information provided by LRRPs. A common LRRP mission was to go quietly into the bush and find out where the enemy was. Then artillery, bombers, and sometimes ground troops would be sent in to attack.

Like the SOG RTs (which recruited some men from the LRRP ranks), the LRRPs were elite troops. All volunteers, they had plenty of time to train, and the LRRP patrol teams were tight. Despite the dangerous missions, there were only 450 LRRPs killed in action (out of some 5,000 men who served). Put another way, only one in fifty-one LRRP patrols resulted in a LRRP getting killed. Actually, the odds were better than that because when a LRRP patrol got into trouble, it was usually big trouble. There were several cases of entire LRRP patrols being wiped out. So each time a LRRP went out on patrol, he had about a 1 percent chance of running into a deadly situation. These were better odds than the troops in regular infantry units faced. But it wasn't a cushy job; it was extremely dangerous. What kept the LRRPs alive was lots of training and experience. The Recondo School also screened out guys who would do the wrong thing at the wrong time. All of this made a big difference on the battlefield.

There were never more than sixteen hundred men serving as LRRPs at any one time (about 8 percent of all Army infantry in Vietnam). The peak strength was probably in early 1969, when there were fifteen LRRP companies in Vietnam (including one from the Indiana National Guard). About this time, the Army finally accepted the fact that LRRPs were useful and should be a permanent part of the organization. So the Rangers were revived. The 75th Infantry Regiment became the Ranger outfit, and each of the LRRP companies became a company in that regiment. After U.S. forces left Vietnam in 1972, however, all but two Ranger companies were disbanded. In 1974, those two Ranger companies were used to form the 1st Battalion of the 75th Infantry Regiment (later to become the 75th Ranger Regiment). LRRPs were now to be formed in divisions when the commanders saw the need. But, as with the Special Forces, most generals didn't want to be bothered with trying to maintain specialized units of Perfect Soldiers.

The Navy SEALs were organized in 1962 when the Navy realized that the new president, John Kennedy, was enthusiastic about special operations, and got their first combat experience in Vietnam. Even as the SEAL teams were training and organizing in the United States, some SEALs were sent to Vietnam to help train SEALs for the South Vietnamese Navy. American SEALs began Vietnam combat operations in 1962, and kept sending more men until seven platoons of SEAL Team One were all in Vietnam. The SEALs operated like the LRRPs, except that they worked mostly in the Mekong River delta and along rivers and coastlines in South Vietnam. Some SEALs operated inland, in Laos and Cambodia (for the SOG) and North Vietnam (for the CIA). But the SEALs were most useful where there was water, mainly because that's how they were trained and also because they had special boat units that could get them into a good location for starting a mission, and pick them up later. There were also Navy helicopter units operating along the rivers.

About a thousand SEALs served in Vietnam, and only forty-six were killed in action. None was ever captured. Three SEALs won our nation's highest award for bravery in combat, the Medal of Honor. The SEALs were classic commandos, like the British SAS, and generally operated as such in Vietnam.

LRRP RULES

Another legacy of the nearly ten thousand Perfect Soldiers (LRRPs, SOG RTs, and Special Forces) in Vietnam was a shared belief in basic combat practices, ones that are often forgotten in peacetime. Because of the large number of practitioners who came out of Vietnam after having used these rules to survive, they have become much more institutionalized in the services. That's important, because a lot of what an Army does it does because "it's always been done that way." This is the way of the LRRP (or Special Forces, or SEAL or any Perfect Soldier):

- **Plan carefully.** Just running off in a hurry to perform a patrol, or attack, or defense of a hill doesn't work if you don't plan. There's not always time for this, but often there is. LRRPs would spend a week or more planning each mission. Collecting information, examining and analyzing it, they discussed the options with the rest of the unit: All this often makes the difference between life and death.
- **Practice.** Training is one thing, but practice is for a specific mission. LRRPs were always seen practicing new moves, or old ones. These were often seemingly complicated drills that, in an emergency, would provide an edge. When a mission was planned, the LRRPs would practice specific maneuvers they might use (like getting up, or down, cliffs). Maintaining proficiency with special types of mines also took a lot of time. Going over maps to make sure everyone knew the "playbook" for the next mission was another effort that paid off in the field. Practice was also the best way to integrate (and check out) a new member of the team. A LRRP unit was like a sports team. Everyone had to know how the other guy would react in different situations.
- **Dress for success.** LRRPs paid close attention to what they wore in the field and how they wore it. Before the went off on a mission, everyone jumped up and down to pinpoint and eliminate "battle rattle" (things that made noise when the man moved). Equipment was worn so that it could be grabbed quickly in an emergency. It was put into rucksacks in the order that it would be needed. LRRPs also reminded everyone that you have a better chance of living if you travel light. This is something armies, especially during peacetime, have a hard time remembering. Even on long patrols, LRRPs generally carried no more than fifty pounds, and most of that was weapons and munitions. LRRPs wore floppy-brim bush hats, not helmets, because this saved weight and made less noise. LRRPs also went without flak jackets, which just slowed them down. The LRRP experience also made the Army pay more attention to the infantryman's equipment. The LRRPs took it upon themselves to experiment with new equipment and weapons, and this spurred the Army to let them try new equipment that was being developed. The cur-

rent MREs (Meals, Ready to Eat—freeze-dried meals), for example, were first used by the LRRPs (and called "LRRP rations"). The current shorter-barreled M-16 (the M-4) was first adopted by LRRPs who got their hands on the CAR-15 (a commercially developed weapon by the same guy who designed the M-16). Camouflage uniforms, new load-carrying gear, and special jungle boots were all innovations championed by the LRRPs.

- **Silent night.** The LRRPs knew the advantages of operating at night (or at least in the shadows) and keeping quiet. In the field, LRRPs communicated mostly by hand signals. Like the Montagnards they often operated with, LRRPs learned to read the sounds and smells of their surroundings. LRRPs also learned the value of deception and the importance of fading into the background. They regularly used face paint to complete the cover-up. Silence comes in many forms, and LRRPs used all of them. Those lessons stayed with the rest of the Army, such was the reputation of LRRP success, and survival.
- **Speed counts.** Doing everything faster than the enemy was another factor in the relatively low casualty rate among LRRPs. When helicopters dropped them off in enemy territory, they moved out of the area quickly (to avoid any enemy troops attracted by the sight and sound of the helicopter). When on patrol, LRRPs were always ready to execute maneuvers and, in general, move faster than any foe. Speed was life, especially in little things. This was another lesson that lingered on in the Army after Vietnam.

Many officers noted that the LRRPs, Special Forces, and SOG troops could fight outnumbered and win, and generally controlled any battle they got into. While these troops were seen as elite infantry, it was understood that their techniques and training methods could be applied to any troops. Indeed, some battalion commanders in the Army, for example, did train their troops up to this new standard and got the same exceptional results. The Army infantry was never the same after being exposed to LRRP rules.

LESSONS OF VIETNAM

In Vietnam, the Special Forces learned that the lessons gained from their World War II experiences were still valid. A few hundred well-trained Special Forces troops could still have a tremendous effect on a war, a lesson that was repeated in Afghanistan. Vietnam also reinforced the importance of Special Forces as an essential intelligence-collection operation. This was proved again and again in the decades after Vietnam, and again in Afghanistan and Iraq. While World War II indicated what an organization of Perfect Soldiers like the Special Forces might be, Vietnam proved it.

The Special Forces, in particular, learned that it was not enough to do a good job. You had to have the ear of the people at the top. You had to convince the people in charge that you knew what you were doing and, if given a chance, would do it right. Along these lines, the Special Forces maintained their close relations with the CIA. When the CIA and Special Forces first encountered each other in Vietnam during the late 1950s, they realized they had a lot in common. Indeed, some men in both organizations had worked together in the OSS during World War II. A little-noticed development after Vietnam was the regular cooperation by the Special Forces and CIA. Just as the Marines became known as "State Department Troops" because of all their peacekeeping missions before World War II, the Special Forces have increasingly become the "CIA Troops." During the Vietnam War, the CIA and Special Forces generally agreed about what the true situation was in South Vietnam. The CIA took the heat for this when it delivered its reports to the White House, but the Special Forces paid in blood when the U.S. government consistently refused to recognize the true nature of the Vietnam War.

The Special Forces not only learned their lessons from Vietnam but have made sure anyone they work with shares in this wisdom and understands. Thirty years after Vietnam, in Afghanistan, the Special Forces were allowed to do their job. They were allowed to do what works. They were allowed to be Perfect Soldiers.

NEW THINKING AFTER VIETNAM

When the Vietnam War was over, so was the way the armed forces did business. The draft was gone. The Army would have to concentrate more on quality, because there was going to be a lot less quantity. Thus the revived interest in Ranger units. But the veterans of Vietnam noted some other important things. They realized that the old thinking, about elite units taking good leaders away from regular units, was not true. They had observed that, in Vietnam, the LRRP and SOG units attracted a particular kind of soldier who would not necessarily make a good NCO in a regular infantry unit. Many of the LRRP/SOG guys tend to be natural-born warriors, not natural-born leaders. This means that the warriors are in it for the thrills and the challenge. These are not the majority in elite units, but are always a noticeable minority.

Soldiers did not spend all their time in elite units, and would usually go back to a regular unit with a lot of valuable experience. For example, an NCO or officer who had served in an elite unit had proved that he had special leadership qualities. And he needed them. Elite units were full of very capable people trained to do very dangerous work. They also didn't suffer fools gladly, especially if the fool was in charge. An officer or NCO successfully completing a few years in an elite unit has proved that he can run with the best. But getting along with elite troopers means developing a tolerance for erratic and eccentric behavior. LRRPs in particular are not big on snappy uniforms or saluting. Special Forces are notorious for getting out of uniform and into the local threads at the first opportunity. But the Special Forces are so elite that officers don't come and go. They stay for their entire career. The Rangers and paratroopers do have officers who don't make Ranger or paratrooper duty their career, but are there to hone their leadership skills in the very demanding atmosphere of a unit full of Perfect Soldiers.

The big lesson seems to be that if you don't try to create huge (more than 10 percent of your total manpower) elite units, you won't be siphoning away too many good leaders. If your elite units are really elite (and not just a bunch of pampered thugs who are politically loyal), you have a crack unit and a place to test and train exceptional leaders for your regular leaders. The Army apparently realized this after the Korean War, when it kept the Ranger School open even though there were no Ranger units. It did the same thing with paratrooper training, encouraging young officers and NCOs to go through jump school to prove they had the right stuff.

In the decades after Vietnam, the Army accepted the usefulness of Perfect Soldiers, and developed ways to train and use them efficiently.

SPETSNAZ AND SAPPERS

The communist nations, for all their fierce militarism, were not enthusiastic about commandos and Special Forces–type troops. There was probably the fear that these hotshots might prove politically unreliable and cause problems by providing the muscle for a coup. Despite this, there were two formidable commando forces to come out of communist nations after World War II. One was a copy of the British Commandos and SAS (the Russian Spetsnaz) and the other a response to a battlefield need (the communist Vietnamese sappers).

SPETSNAZ

After World War II, it took the Soviet Union a decade or so to note the success of commandos in Western armies during that conflict and attempt to emulate their success. In the 1960s, the Red Army began to organize "troops of special purpose" (*Spetsialnoye nazranie,* or Spetsnaz for short) units. The Soviet Union had always had some form of commandos, but these were special units of the secret police (KGB), and were used more as a special police squad than what we usually think of as commandos. Also, for special operations, the army would form temporary units consisting entirely of officers. The Russians wanted their commandos, above all else, politically reliable. The Spetsnaz were permanent units.

The Spetsnaz, however, were organized, trained, and to be used somewhat differently than the other commandos. The Russians did not have many career soldiers, so most of their Spetsnaz were carefully selected conscripts. These men were put through an intense training program and organized into slightly larger teams than their Western counterparts. The Russians also planned to use more teams for their command operations than Western nations would (hundreds of teams versus dozens in the Western nations). This was the typical, "quantity has a quality all its own" approach the Russians had long favored. In the 1980s, the Russians had a chance to use their Spetsnaz in combat, and found them the most effective force they sent into the Afghanistan war.

The Spetsnaz were originally organized to provide the equivalent of a horde of SAS-type raiding teams. A Spetsnaz brigade of thirteen hundred men could field about one hundred eight- to ten-man teams. A Spetsnaz company had 135 men, further divided into fifteen independent teams. The actual organization of these brigades was four parachute battalions, an assassin company, a headquarters, and support troops (mainly communications). A naval Spetsnaz brigade had two battalions of "combat swimmers" (comparable to U.S. SEALs), a parachute battalion, a submarine company (using small, stealthy subs carrying a few men each), and other units the Army Spetsnaz brigades had. There were also many independent Spetsnaz companies assigned to armies or smaller units.

In wartime, each team would be given an objective to destroy deep inside enemy territory. If not destroying military targets (airfields, missile launchers, headquarters), teams would go deep and find out what was happening in the enemy rear. Put simply, the job of the Spetsnaz was reconnaissance and sabotage. The Spetsnaz teams would get to the target by parachute, ship, submarine, or as "tourists" before the war began. At the height of the Cold War, the Soviet Union had about thirty thousand Spetsnaz in service.

There was one flaw with this system: Most of the Spetsnaz troopers were conscripts, in the Army for two years. The Russians made this work by being selective in whom they chose to be in the Spetsnaz, and putting the recruits through a rigorous, and violent, training program. Think of them as paratroopers with additional training in demolitions, infiltration, foreign languages (which many Russian conscripts had studied in high school), and reconnaissance. Perhaps most important, the Spetsnaz recruits were taught to think for themselves. This was a rare directive in the Soviet (or Russian) armed forces. But for commandos to be effective, they had to think independently, and the Soviets realized this when they set up the Spetsnaz and the Spetsnaz training program.

During the Soviet period, the Spetsnaz were seen as an elite organization and a career-enhancing qualification to have on your resumé. Here's how the selection worked: Because the Army had more volunteers than it needed, the Spetsnaz would take the top graduates from the training program. A favorite method was to send volunteers to the six-month NCO course (normally used to turn bright recruits into junior sergeants). This course had a high washout rate, but those who made it through were competent leaders and just the kind of people the Spetsnaz were looking for. Even after the Soviet Union fell, the Spetsnaz were still seen as an elite. It did not go unnoticed that veterans of the unit were always in demand as well-paid bodyguards and security experts during the 1990s.

The Soviets knew they were getting a lot of eager, motivated, and not thoroughly trained or experienced Spetsnaz troopers. But they had so many of them that it was felt they'd do enough damage to make it all worthwhile. We'll never know if the original idea of using massive numbers of Spetsnaz would have worked, but the Spetsnaz were effective during the 1980s Afghanistan war. The main reason wasn't the superior Spetsnaz combat skills, but their initiative and independent thinking. The Afghans they were fighting noted this, and learned to clear out of the area if Spetsnaz were found to be operating there.

The Spetsnaz recognized the need for career troops for some jobs, such as assassins. Therefore, each Spetsnaz brigade was staffed with seventy to eighty career soldiers, whose job was to find, identify, and kill key enemy political and military leaders.

When the Soviet Union fell in 1991, the Spetsnaz didn't disappear. The new nations formed from parts of the Soviet Union inherited any Spetsnaz units stationed in their territory. Many of these non-Russian Spetsnaz still exist, although most are not of the same quality as they were when the Soviet Union still existed. Although there are fewer Spetsnaz today, there are about ten thousand of them in Russian service. And more of them are career soldiers (more than half, versus 20 to 30 percent during the Soviet period).

Many of the current Spetsnaz are specialists, with specific skills needed for underwater operations (comparable to the U.S. SEALs) and anti-terrorist operations (like the U.S. Delta Force). But there are still eight brigades—seven Army and one Navy. The post–Soviet Union Russian government maintained the strength of its commandos because it knew it would need some skilled and dependable troops for emergencies. Unfortunately, the corruption that swept the rest of the armed forces hit the Spetsnaz as well. Officers stole and took bribes, as did NCOs, while the lower-ranking troops developed a bad attitude toward military service. During the 1990s, the government raised the pay of and tried to improve the living conditions for the Spetsnaz, lest they lose the loyalty of the most effective troops available to them.

SPETSNAZ IN AFGHANISTAN

The Russians also carefully studied the experience of their Spetsnaz in Afghanistan, and have shared much of this knowledge with the United States and its Special Forces. The Russians admit that they did not expect what happened to them in Afghanistan. This was not the first time they had invaded a neighbor to ensure that the local communists didn't lose control. In 1956, the Soviets went into Hungary, and despite stiff resistance (2,300 Russian casualties, including 669 dead), they quickly subdued the population. In 1968, they did the same thing in Czechoslovakia, but because of less resistance, only suffered ninety-six troops killed before restoring the local communists to power. But in Afghanistan they ran into a warrior society, and a poverty-stricken one at that.

The lack of roads and railroads, and the presence of so much disease, limited the number of troops the Russians could support with food and other supplies. Thus there were never more than 104,000 Russian troops in Afghanistan at any one time. And for the ten years the Russian army was in Afghanistan, only 642,000 troops served there—most for one year, because keeping these conscript soldiers there longer led to serious morale problems. Combat losses were fifty-four thousand wounded and fifteen thousand killed (or missing) in combat. But another 416,000 troops were out of action for varying lengths of time because of disease (including 115,308 soldiers with infectious hepatitis and 31,080 with typhoid fever, plus differing occurrences of malaria, amebic dysentery, and meningitis). That's 73 percent of the men sent to Afghanistan getting sick, wounded, or killed. On average, units saw 30 percent of their troops out of action at any time because of sickness. After several years, it became obvious that the most effective troops in Afghanistan were the paratroopers and Spetsnaz (both usually moved by helicopter). Nearly all the Spetsnaz and paratroopers in service at the time got a tour of duty in Afghanistan.

The Spetsnaz and paratroopers could take the fight to the enemy, and for this reason the Afghans feared these Russian commandos. The Russian ground and support troops served mainly as targets for the frequent Afghan ambushes. The Russians lost about 120 trucks (mostly) and armored vehicles a month. But the Air Force only lost, on average, three or four aircraft (mostly helicopters) a month. After the Russians left Afghanistan and analyzed their experience, they realized that they should have put more emphasis on their elite units—not just Spetsnaz, but also paratroopers, air assault troops, and mountain infantry. The senior commanders in Afghanistan did not always use their elite forces to best effect and, besides Spetsnaz, there weren't enough of them. The Russians also had some support among Afghans, but they never exploited this. Russian soldiers abused civilians (rape and robbery were common) and were rarely punished.

It's no accident that U.S. Special Forces in Afghanistan did what worked for the Russians, and avoided what didn't. The U.S. put few troops into Afghanistan, and most of them were commandos. Most movement was by helicopter, and road traffic was kept to a minimum to deny hostile Afghans any targets. Thus the American operations in Afghanistan were much more successful than the Russian ones.

RUSSIAN SPECIAL ASSAULT UNITS

After the Spetsnaz had been around for about ten years, various organizations in the Soviet government decided that they could use similar troops for their own special needs. Thus in the 1970s and 1980s, there appeared Spetsnaz clones called Spetsgruppa. Used most was Spetsgruppa Alfa (Special Group A), which was established in 1974 to do the same peacetime work as the U.S. Delta Force or British SAS. In other words, anti-terrorist assignments or special raids. It was Spetsgruppa Alfa that was sent to Kabul, Afghanistan, in 1980 to make sure the troublesome Afghan president Amin and his family were eliminated from the scene and killed. Survivors (members of the presidential palace staff) of the Spetsgruppa Alfa assault reported that the Spetsnaz troopers systematically hunted down and killed their targets with a minimum of fuss. Very professional. The surviving Afghans were suitably impressed. Spetsgruppa Alfa now belongs to the FSB (the successor to the KGB) and numbers about three hundred men (and a few women).

At the same time Spetsgruppa Alfa was established, another section of the KGB organized Spetsgruppa Vympel. This group was trained to perform wartime assassination and kidnapping jobs for the KGB. The FSB also inherited Spetsgruppa Vympel, which is slightly smaller (less than a hundred men) than Spetsgruppa Alfa and is used mainly for hostage rescue.

In the late 1970s, the Interior Ministry formed its own Spetsnaz-type units (called "Omon," or Black Berets) for hostage rescue and special raids. Not quite as good as the Spetsnaz or Spetsgruppa, the Omon still exists as sort of a super-SWAT team for the national police.

The Ministry of Justice has its own Spetsgruppa, called Spetsnaz UIN (Group for Special Assignment). Spetsnaz UIN is used to deal with revolts or hostage situations in prisons.

There is even a private company, GROM Security Company, that employs former Spetsnaz and Spetsgruppa troopers and provides bodyguards and security services for those who can afford it. Actually, GROM is a semi-official organization, because its largest customer is the Russian government. By providing higher pay for Spetsnaz personnel, GROM can provide the highest level of security. The government connection ensures that GROM maintains good relationships with the Spetsnaz and ministries that have Spetsgruppa.

NORTH VIETNAMESE SAPPERS

As an example of how commandos operate in wartime after World War II, let's take a look at one of most combat-experienced, and little-known, commando outfits of the twentieth century: the communist Vietnamese sappers. These troops operated against French, American, and South Vietnamese troops from the early 1950s to the 1970s.

The sappers were a special type of commando, and their specialty was sneaking into heavily defended enemy bases and destroying things. This is where *sapper* comes from. Americans call sappers combat engineers, and they do things like blow up enemy fortifications and clear minefields. They often do this under fire. That's how the North Vietnamese sappers started out. But they soon realized that if they operated at night, and very carefully, they could do the job without getting shot at.

The typical operation had a dozen or so sappers attacking a fortified American base containing more than a hundred troops. The sappers would sneak through all the minefields and barbed wire, blow up much of the American base, kill and wound many of the American troops, and then get away without taking any casualties. The main job of the sappers was to destroy things, not people. And they did so with remarkable success. Not just enemy bases, but also aircraft on the ground and ships anchored in South Vietnamese ports. At one point, naval sappers even sank a small American aircraft carrier.

The sappers were well-trained, carefully selected troops engaging in thoroughly planned assaults. This was a classic approach to commando operations. The sapper concept was developed by the Vietnamese communists during the war with the French (1945–1954). The first communist troops sent to fight in South Vietnam, in 1957, were also sappers. By 1975, there were nearly twenty thousand men (and some women) in sapper units. Throughout the entire American phase of the Vietnam War, more than fifty thousand North Vietnamese served in sapper units. But as careful as the sappers were, they took a lot of casualties.

Sappers were organized into 100- to 150-man battalions. Each battalion had three thirty-six-man companies, each company had two eighteen-man platoons, each platoon had three six-man squads, and each squad had two three-man cells. Sapper battalions also had some support troops: radio operators, medical and technical specialists.

Initially, all sappers were volunteers. Veteran sappers would decide which volunteers to accept for training. As the war with the Americans intensified during the 1960s, there were a lot of semivolunteers. Experienced sappers would examine new draftees who had completed their basic training and offer them a chance to be sappers. Since they were the elite of the North Vietnamese army, most accepted. Those who didn't were sent to sapper school anyway, where the training staff would try to convince them to get with it. You could still wash out of sapper school, as many did. So the sappers were always basically volunteers.

Like American Special Forces A-Teams, each man in a sapper unit had a specialty. The basic sapper training was six to twelve months long, depending on what specialty a man was being prepared for. But there were subjects all trainees were taught:

- **Assault techniques.** This included drills on how to quickly carry out basic attack maneuvers quietly and at night. The key to such attacks was coordination and precision. Once learned, sappers spent time continuing to practice these drills.
- **Breaching obstacles.** Experience had given the sappers useful techniques for getting through minefields and barbed wire quietly and in the dark. For the defender, this was the scariest sapper skill. To do this right required practice and strong nerves. Those who showed the most talent for it were usually allowed to specialize in this area. People who were good at this were *very* good. American Vietnam veterans who experienced sapper attacks are often most amazed at how the lead sapper was able to work his way through the obstacles surrounding the American camp.
- **Camouflage.** Sappers were taught that if the enemy couldn't see you, he couldn't hurt you. The highly disciplined sapper candidates were expected to take the camouflage techniques taught all North Vietnamese soldiers and simply use them better. Because sappers worked close to the enemy more often than most North Vietnamese troops, they either became very good at camouflage, or they died.
- **Infiltration.** These were the basic skills of moving in enemy territory and figuring out how to get into an enemy base. This training was based on years of experience and was constantly updated as the enemy changed his defensive techniques. The training taught how the enemy set up his defenses and what was the best way to move without being detected. Some of the advice was eminently practical. For example, members of the breaching team (the first sappers through the defenders minefields and barbed wire) wore only shorts, or went naked, so that they had more skin exposed to feel things such as wire, mines, or booby traps.
- **Exfiltration.** These are the special techniques used to get away safely after a raid. Sappers were too valuable to lose needlessly. When planning an operation, much attention was paid to getting everyone out. This training was not only practical, in that sense, but also good for morale.

- **Explosives.** The weapons sappers used most were explosives. Every sapper was taught the basics of handling different types of explosives and building various types of bombs. A favorite sapper explosive was dud American shells and bombs. Sappers were taught how to safely disarm these and "harvest" the explosives. Some sappers were given advanced training in this area and would operate at improvised "explosives factories" where American shells (and small bombs) would be brought for harvesting. Most often, though, the harvesting was done on the spot because the dud might go off if a defective fuse suddenly got well. The explosives factories were mainly for repackaging the explosives for new uses (mortar shells, land mines, and so on).

- **Navigation.** Getting around in the jungle at night, especially if you didn't have local guides, required training. Time was spent training how to do this. Most of the sappers came from towns or farming villages and didn't have much experience moving long distances through the bush (naturally, they preferred to use well-marked roads, rivers, or canals).

- **Reconnaissance.** This is what sappers actually spent most of their time doing. Information on the enemy was one of their most powerful weapons. Recruits were taught the tricks of the trade, and the importance of improvising in the field. At this point, recruits were also tested to see who had a real talent for picking up information quickly.

- **Small-unit tactics.** This built on the basic training all Vietnamese soldiers received. The sapper were considered light infantry and could also be used as infantry if needed.

- **Special equipment training.** Some sappers learned how to use scuba gear, drive trucks, operate radios, and operate any special gear needed to accomplish a mission.

- **Weapons training.** In addition to becoming proficient with their own Russian-made weapons, sappers were taught the basics of American weapons. There was also instruction on the use of specialized sapper weapons, like flame throwers.

- **Planning.** Sappers were taught how the planning process worked, for it was the key to success for any commando operation. This included how to determine what information was needed for a mission, as well as how to plan and rehearse an attack and assign men to the different tasks.

Sappers were assigned to larger units (infantry regiments or divisions), and that unit commander would select targets he wanted attacked. The sappers were also considered a recon and intelligence unit, so a commander might order his sappers to check out an area for likely targets to hit and then make a decision based on what the sappers reported.

Once a target was selected, it would be more carefully scouted. A model of the enemy base would be built out of sand, rocks, and twigs and a plan developed, and practiced. During the planning, it might be determined that the task was too dangerous or that more resources were needed. Unless it was a critical target, the operation would often be canceled. Indeed, dozens of operations were planned for each one that was carried out. The sappers believed success came most often when they were confident that their plan would work. In most cases, they were right. And that's what made sappers so scary. Once you were under attack, you knew you were probably toast.

Sappers also destroyed unguarded (or less guarded) targets such as bridges, railroads, roads, piers, and so on.

Sapper assaults were fast—usually they were in and out in less than an hour. What the sappers did is what any successful commando unit does. They were unique, however, in that they were commandos who specialized in attacking the fortified bases of a better-armed and more numerous enemy. Initially, the sappers were basically elite guerrillas. But once the North Vietnamese started their sapper school, the sappers became an elite organization.

After Vietnam was united, however, it was not possible to maintain the sapper force. Vietnam is a poor country (at least with the communists running the economy) and could not afford to have several thousand soldiers doing nothing but sapper training. The deadliest commando force of the twentieth century, therefore, slowly faded away. Sappers still exist in the Vietnamese Army, but they work more traditionally as engineers. There is still a tradition of elite assault sappers, but the commando capability is largely gone.

All commando units today follow the same basic selection and training routines of the Vietnamese sappers. It's what works. Always has and always will.

10 AFGHANISTAN: THE FIRST COMMANDO WAR

Sixty years after Japanese aircraft bombed Pearl Harbor and killed more than two thousand Americans, terrorists hijacked four airliners and, ultimately, two rammed them into the two World Trade Towers in New York City and one the Pentagon in Washington. The death toll was higher than Pearl Harbor. Within hours of the Japanese attack, Japan declared war. In the style of twenty-first-century terrorism, however, no one immediately took credit for the September 11, 2001, attacks. Throughout the 1990s, there had been terrorist attacks against American targets, but never anything large enough to constitute an act of war. Now it was different. It was war. It was known which terrorist organizations were making the 2001 attacks, and in the months following September 11, American armed forces went after the most likely suspect: the al-Qaeda organization and its bases in Afghanistan.

This presented a unique set of problems. Afghanistan has no access to the sea. And political turmoil there had broken out years earlier, when the king was deposed in 1974. There followed a struggle between royalists, reformers, and communists. In 1979, Russia intervened to support the pro-Russian communist faction. The Russians fought a savage war to suppress the more conservative (religiously and politically) Afghans who continued to oppose the pro-communist government that only had support in the major cities. More than a million Afghans were killed and more than three million fled to Pakistan, where they lived miserable lives in squalid refugee camps. But in 1989, the Russians gave up trying to pacify the country and just left. Even though the Russians were gone, the Afghan communist government still existed and continued to fight until 1992. Then the various mujahideen (guerrilla "holy warriors") factions in Afghanistan began fighting each other.

In 1994, something unexpected arrived on the scene—a militia composed of religious students, or Talibs. The Taliban had enormous popular appeal, because people knew its members were pious and honest and only wanted to bring order to Afghanistan. Since nearly every Afghan had a gun, the Taliban provided a worthy cause for many Afghans to get behind. By 1996, most of warring mujahideen militias had been destroyed, won over, or chased away. The Taliban was left controlling 80 percent of the country.

Five years later the Taliban was still unable to conquer the last 10 percent, mostly in the north. Moreover, the Taliban members had made themselves increasingly unpopular by imposing a particularly oppressive and conservative version of Islam. This problem went back to the origins of the Taliban in the Pakistan refugee camps. Pakistan Army intelligence (ISI) got behind the Taliban movement early on, feeling that it was Pakistan's only chance to have some control over the chaotic situation in neighboring Afghanistan. The religious schools that trained the young Taliban warriors were originally backed by pious Muslims from Saudi Arabia. Afghan clerics exiled in Pakistani refugee camps took the money and ran the schools. There, a lot of young men and boys among the refugee population saw life as a Talib as an attractive alternative to drab and pointless camp life. Parents also approved, feeling that it was a choice between the kid being a Talib, or a drug addict or bandit. When the Russians left and the refugees saw Afghanistan slip into violent anarchy, it didn't take too much encouragement for the Talibs to get behind the idea of a religious government in their homeland. The ISI approved, providing weapons and transport, and the Taliban went to war with the Afghan warlords who were tearing the country apart in a struggle for power.

Quite by chance, most of the key leaders of the Taliban were from the southern Kandahar region of Afghanistan. This was no problem at first. But once the Taliban was in control of most of the country, and the fighting continued, resentment began to appear. This was made worse by the insistence of the Kandaharis that their local customs, such as mandatory beards, no entertainments, and shutting up the women at home, become the accepted interpretation of Islamic law throughout the country. No one, however, wanted another civil war either. And the Taliban wisely called for foreign volunteers (Pakistani religious students preferred, but a lot of Arabs showed up) to fill out their armies when Afghans grew reluctant to serve. Actually, Afghanistan wasn't engaged in major fighting during the last few years before September 11, 2001. The average military units were a few hundred guys rolling along the few roads in a motley collection of trucks, cars, and armored vehicles. Casualties had also been low.

But losses among civilians, because of a record-breaking drought, were much larger than from the fighting. And the Taliban's insistence on providing sanctuary to terrorist kingpin Osama bin Laden, and harassment of foreign aid agencies, did not win it any points among the Afghan population: The foreign aid was desperately needed, and the Taliban appeared to be getting in the way. There are also ethnic considerations. The largest minority in the country, the Pushtuns, are not a majority—they're about 40 percent of the population. The opposition Northern Alliance is mostly Tajik (25 percent of the population), Hazara (19 percent), and the much-persecuted Shia Muslims (15 percent, spread among several ethnic groups).

While the Taliban's use of foreigners (Pakistanis and Arabs, for the most part) to do the fighting against the Northern Alliance was appreciated by Afghans, there was also resentment about all those armed foreigners running around and giving orders in the name of the Taliban.

On September 11, 2001, the only friends the United States had in Afghanistan were the Northern Alliance. But this outfit was in bad shape. On September 9th, al-Qaeda assassins killed the capable and charismatic Northern Alliance military leader Ahmad Shah Masood. The Taliban followed this up with another major attack on the Northern Alliance. Still, the Taliban was now a spent force, militarily and politically.

In 1999, it had been able to amass twenty thousand fighters against the Northern Alliance for a summer offensive. About a quarter of these men were foreigners (mostly Pakistani Pushtun volunteers from religious schools in Pakistan). The main areas of Northern Alliance control were in the north, in the provinces on the Tajik border, and northeast of Kabul in the roomy Panjir Valley (the home of Northern Alliance leader Masood). The 1999 fighting was brutal by Afghan standards, with nearly seven thousand dead and wounded (mostly Taliban). Afghans on both sides of the fighting began to lose their enthusiasm for fighting after that bloody summer. The offensives in the summers of 2000 and 2001 were much more modest affairs, featuring fewer fighters and a higher proportion of non-Afghans fighting for the Taliban. By 2001, the Taliban was lucky to get a few thousand men into action, and most of them were not Afghans. The Taliban was now more feared than respected among Afghans, something the United States quickly realized once American commandos, CIA agents, and Special Forces were inside the country.

The Northern Alliance, however, was discouraged as well. Many more Northern Alliance warlords were making deals with the Taliban and switching sides. But the Taliban couldn't do much with this, because the majority of Afghans were content to stay in their villages and pretend to be ruled by the Taliban. The Northern Alliance had, however, lost most of its territory in northern Afghanistan, meaning that its main source of arms and ammunition was in danger of being cut off. Russia had been selling, and giving, weapons to the Northern Alliance for years, and the freebies had increased as Russia became aware that the Taliban and al-Qaeda were supporting the Chechen rebels Russia was fighting in the Caucasus. But the Northern Alliance was fading fast on September 11, 2001, and the Taliban refused American demands to turn over Osama bin Laden and other al-Qaeda leaders.

The United States quickly obtained overflight and basing arrangements from Afghanistan's neighbors (Pakistan, Tajikistan, and Uzbekistan at first). On October 7, 2001, U.S. warplanes, operating from carriers off the Pakistani coast, began bombing Taliban military targets.

But before the U.S. war in Afghanistan got much farther than bombing, certain myths and realities about fighting there had to be understood.

MYTHS AND REALITIES OF THE AFGHAN WAR

American ground troops were needed to win. Up to a point. But there were two problems with this. For one, there was logistics—getting supplies of food and ammunition to the troops. There are no railroads in Afghanistan, so all supplies must move by truck over a poor road network. The Russians ran into this problem and, as a result, were never able to maintain more than one hundred thousand troops in the country. American soldiers require more supplies per man, thus even fewer (perhaps fifty thousand) troops could be brought into the country. But that's not the worst problem. If American troops had entered Afghanistan, more Afghans would have resisted. Afghans don't like armed foreigners. That's a national custom we didn't want to trigger. Many Pushtuns were dodging service in the Taliban armed forces in September 2001. This would have changed if most of the soldiers on the other side were American. From the beginning, many American generals believed that the war could be won mainly with Perfect Soldiers—Special Forces and commandos working with whatever Afghan allies we could round up.

The Taliban had an army. Sort of. But most of the best Taliban troops were foreigners (on September 11, 2001, about fourteen thousand Pakistanis, mostly Pushtuns, and six thousand bin Laden troops, who were largely Arabs). The Taliban Afghan troops were reluctant warriors, weary from twenty years of war. There was resentment among Afghans against the foreign troops. As long as the enemy on the ground were Northern Alliance Afghans, most Taliban Afghans would be tempted to switch sides. Once that started, soon the only fighters left in the Taliban army would be foreigners. Afghans traditionally fight fiercely against foreigners. This ferocity could be seen in the way Northern Alliance fighters treated foreign Taliban troops. Often no prisoners were taken, no deals were made.

The Northern Alliance had an army. Not an army in the traditional sense. The Northern Alliance was truly an alliance. But the various factions contributed bands of warriors, not soldiers. American Special Forces troops trained some Northern Alliance warriors as soldiers, yet American generals had to get used to working with warriors rather than better-disciplined and more reliable soldiers. The U.S. Special Forces were experts in making this sort of arrangement work. Moreover, the Afghan way of war put great emphasis on fighting that produced low casualties. If they are in the mood, warriors can be fierce. But you can't order them around like soldiers. So the Northern Alliance had what can best be called a collection of tribal contingents, more loyal to the warrior chief leading them than anyone else. American commanders had to brush up on how tribal warlords used their troops (carefully and with a lot of persuasion and promises of loot). **This was a military operation.** In part, the war in Afghanistan was military, but mostly it was diplomatic. The road to victory was marked by the number of pro-Taliban tribes who could be convinced to switch sides and work with the United States, as well as with the Northern Alliance. This involved a lot of talk and well-placed gifts. Some of the booty was in cash, but much of the loot desired was political and, more immediately, things like food and weapons. The political goodies included things like a place in a future government, assurances of future support (as was already being offered to Uzbekistan and Tajikistan), and maybe a few green cards. There's also the information war. Crafting a convincing message about why we were there and what we were doing went a long way toward attracting popular, political, and military support.

We're fighting Afghanistan. We were actually fighting one faction of a nine-year-old civil war. Much of Afghanistan was inclined to be on our side. Winning more of that support was not a matter of fighting; it was more saying the right things and doing favors for people (food and medical care were popular). Victory came to whoever ended up with the support of the most Afghans.

A Northern Alliance victory will end terrorism in Afghanistan. This was not guaranteed. A Northern Alliance victory was expected to leave many parts of Afghanistan out of its control. Moreover, the Pushtuns, who were the main support of the Taliban, have most of their population in Pakistan. Many bin Laden terrorists operated out of northern Pakistan. When the Taliban lost control of Afghanistan, it was known to still have support in Pakistan. Crushing the Taliban in Afghanistan was a plus, but few thought it would totally eliminate terrorist operations in the region.

Russia lost the war in Afghanistan. No, the Russians simply got tired of the losses as well as the expense and just went home. The Russians lost fifteen thousand troops, while a million and a half Afghans died. Russia and the pro-Russian Afghan government still controlled most of Afghanistan when the Russians left in 1989. The Russians also gave the pro-Russian government some three hundred million dollars a year until the Soviet Union collapsed in 1991. After that, the payments stopped, and the pro-Russian government fell in

1992. The Russians had been supporting the Northern Alliance for the last few years and expected to find another pro-Russian government running Afghanistan if the Northern Alliance won.

Winter helps the Taliban. Afghans prefer not to fight in winter. The winters there are brutal, the roads largely impassable, and Afghans had never developed the equipment or techniques necessary for spending much time outside in this season. With all the Taliban aircraft destroyed, the only way to move troops was by truck. Going cross-country was risky and often impractical because of snow and freezing cold. Many of the roads going through high mountain passes are closed by deep snow during the winter. Meanwhile, American troops do have air transport and regularly practice operating in the winter. American troops can move; Taliban troops cannot. Moreover, the heat sensors on American satellites and aircraft work better during this time of year. For the American forces, winter is an ally. And with the Americans starting to bomb Afghanistan in October, winter was right around the corner.

Afghanistan is a country. Afghanistan has, for most of its history, been a region, not a country. Various nearby empires (Iranian, Indian, Mongol, and others) grabbed portions of Afghanistan for centuries at a time. In the last few centuries, most of the these powers lost interest in Afghanistan, except to go in and punish the Afghan tribes if the raids got out of hand. Sometimes, the local empires found it cheaper just to pay protection money to the stronger tribes to keep the Afghans out of civilized territory. Two centuries ago, the many tribes of Afghanistan worked out a deal in which the leader of one of the stronger Pushtun tribes would be recognized as "king." But the king of Afghanistan's job was mainly to deal with foreigners (keep them out) and arbitrate disputes between the Afghan tribes. The monarchy was overthrown in the 1970s when urban Afghans (a minority) wanted a stronger central government. They wanted Afghanistan to be a modern country. Most Afghans disagreed.

You can see everything that's going on. While the bombs and bombers make great visuals, as do the Northern Alliance military parades and training exercises, the most important parts of the campaign were not seen. The most important military operation was the logistics buildup. While we've called this the "FedEx War," most of the vital supplies were coming in by ship. The material was being landed in the

Persian Gulf, Pakistan, and the island of Diego Garcia, and then flown into Afghanistan. Large ground forces cannot enter the battle until the mountain of supplies reaches a certain point, and that takes weeks or months, depending on how many troops are being sent in. Another, and more vital, part of the campaign was the diplomacy going on with Pushtun leaders in Pakistan and just across the border in Afghanistan. These discussions, more than anything else, determined how quickly the Taliban was defeated.

Afghanistan has never been conquered. Over the centuries, Afghanistan has been conquered many times. Few conquerors bothered to subdue all of what is now Afghanistan. The region is poor, and all great conquerors have a sense of what is worth fighting for and what isn't. The Afghan tribes were always considered formidable warriors, but they were seen as more of a nuisance than anything else. The Afghan tribes liked to raid their wealthier neighbors, and this often brought savage retribution by more numerous, and equally ferocious fighters. The invaders would kill women and children, burn villages and crops, and take herds. With the Afghans more poverty stricken than before, the avenging armies would leave with their loot. Afghans don't like to dwell on this aspect of their military history. They weren't conquered because they weren't worth conquering.

THE AFGHAN WAY OF WAR

More than a hundred years ago, Afghan tribesmen got their hands on modern rifles. These new weapons, many of which are still in use, changed warfare in Central Asia. There were three reasons for this. First, these rifles could quickly load bullets from a magazine (which holds five to ten rounds). Second, smokeless gunpowder (which was, as we've noted, not a powder—but it was smokeless) eliminated all the smoke that previously gave away Afghan positions. The new propellant was cleaner (reducing mechanical failures) and capable of moving the bullets at higher speeds and longer ranges. Third, advances in metalworking allowed more precise parts to be made and assembled faster and more cheaply. Thus the rifles were relatively inexpensive. Even though the war with the Russians in the 1980s brought in many automatic weapons such as the AK-47, the rifle is still a weapon of choice for many Afghans. After September 11, 2001, the Northern

Alliance promptly asked for 7.62mm and .50-caliber sniper rifles and instructors on sniping tactics.

What Afghans already had was self-sufficiency (from farming and herding) and centuries of smuggling, which provided a steady source of extra income for things like weapons. Thus for the last century the Afghans (as well as the related Pushtun tribes in northern Pakistan) have been more dangerous than ever. Whereas in past centuries, the Afghans had to get close with their shorter-range weapons, the new rifles enabled them to snipe at the unwary over long distances. The Russians found this annoying when they invaded in 1979. But the Russians used their traditional terror tactics (offering each tribe "gold or lead"), which left more than a million Afghans dead and many other tainted because they took the Russian gold (payments of cash and goods to stay quiet). The mass murder and getting bought off is nothing new. Afghans have put up with this for thousands of years.

Unlike the Russians, Americans cannot offer "gold or lead." Afghans have long been persuaded by threats of mass murder. But they knew the Americans could not use that weapon. Thus the Talibs saw themselves as unbeatable. The Taliban openly disparaged American ground troops, knowing that if U.S. soldiers came in on the ground they would have a hard time, and that American casualties would weaken American resolve back home. What the Taliban did not expect were the American Perfect Soldiers.

While many Afghans were fed up after two decades of war, there were still enough Taliban members to be a formidable force. They have always had a core group of hard-liners. Several thousand armed Afghan Taliban were joined by thousands more Pushtun tribesmen from both sides of the Pakistan border once the bombing began. These men were angry at the American bombing raids on Afghanistan. Then there were some ten thousand Pakistani "volunteers" (mostly Pushtun religious students) and more than five thousand members of various bin Laden organizations. That added up to some twenty thousand armed men willing to fight stubbornly, often to the death. Most of these men, however, were tied up with Northern Alliance forces near the Tajik-Uzbek border at Mazar-I-Sharif and just outside Kabul.

Afghans are not suicidal. It is an ancient custom to switch sides when it looks like you are going to lose big. The Taliban used this tactic successfully when it took over the country, and then in its war against the Northern Alliance. When America entered the war and the Special Forces began directing smart bombs on Taliban targets, it was the Northern Alliance commanders who got on the radio with the classic "offer you can't refuse." And many Taliban surrendered or switched sides. There was very little "fighting to the death." This was the Afghan Way of War.

COMMANDOS WITH BIG BOMBS

What few people expected was how a few dozen Perfect Soldiers would hit the ground in Afghanistan and turn the war around in weeks. This was a new kind of war.

There had been some CIA people and Army commandos in Afghanistan and Pakistan in September 2001, but the first U.S. Army units hit the ground on October 20, 2001. One operation was announced to the media: a raid by Rangers and Delta Force commandos on a Taliban compound and airfield outside the southern city of Kandahar. This produced nothing useful. The more important operation was the helicopters taking two Special Forces A-Teams into Afghanistan that night. One team went to support Northern Alliance general Dostum outside the northern city of Mazar-I-Sharif; the other went to the Northern Alliance defense minister (who had replaced Masood) in the Panjir Valley. The Special Forces troops brought some language skills and small arms. More important, they brought the ability to direct the use of smart bombs carried by American warplanes overhead.

These U.S. Special Forces troops, with the Northern Alliance forces, were in constant communication with aircraft overhead, ready to bring down bombs when Taliban resistance was encountered. The two thousand-pound bombs were favored, as past experience (going back to World War II) showed that only very thick cement fortifications could withstand such a weapon. The Talibs had neither the resources nor the time to build such fortifications, so they were systematically blown out of their earthen bunkers and trenches. Unlike World War II, in which two thousand–pound bombs dropped by heavy bombers often landed hundreds of yards from their intended target, smart bombs hit within thirty yards of their targets more than 95 percent of the time (and not much farther than thirty yards when they "miss"). Thus during World War II, it took several dozen two thousand–pound bombs to do what one could do now. Moreover, back then you had to keep friendly troops farther away to avoid getting hit by the wayward bombs. During World War II, low-flying fighter-bombers like the P-47 could drop five-hundred- and one-thousand-pound bombs with more accuracy, but those smaller bombs were less likely to take out enemy fortifications, and the aircraft were more likely to be damaged or shot down by ground fire. Smart bombs using Global Positioning System (GPS—a space-satellite-based guidance system), or guided by laser designators on the ground, are a lot more accurate than even the low-flying P-47s or later jet fighter-bombers.

This new technique for using airpower was enormously effective. Because the friendly troops could be as close as a third of a mile from the enemy target, they could quickly move in and take the enemy position before the foe could rush in reinforcements. But it got better. The bombs could be dropped by heavy bombers far overhead, out of range of enemy guns or portable missiles. A B-52 or B-1 can carry two dozen two thousand–pound GPS-guided bombs. The guys on the ground can move up to an enemy position, call in a few bombs to blow away the entrenched enemy, and then go in and finish off the dazed survivors. No more problems with overworked pilots coming in fast, trying to figure out who is where, and getting shot at in the process. A two thousand–pound bomb will also disable (if not outright destroy) tanks and other armored vehicles. This approach cracked ground defenses time after time in Afghanistan; the only countermeasure is to have small groups (perhaps only two or three troops) well dug in and spread over a wide area. The Taliban and al-Qaeda quickly adopted this approach when they faced American troops in the mountains from late 2001 on. While this tactic could slow down advancing American troops and use up a lot of smart bombs, the defenders eventually got blown to bits or killed by U.S. infantry. This shows two important things: The new smart bomb tactics work, and the opposition will quickly find ways to make it work less effectively.

STUMBLING ONTO SUCCESS

Before the Special Forces teams began to use this winning technique, someone had to give the order. While some people in the Special Operations Command (SOCOM) and the Air Force had thought of this form of warfare several years ago, the generals making the decisions were not yet convinced. But after a few days of the bombing campaign, it was clear there weren't many targets left. There were some commandos on the ground, but the prospects of getting ground troops over there to fight the Taliban weren't good. Everything had to be flown in. You could fly in a transport of Rangers, but then every day those troops were there, you had to fly in another air transport with supplies to keep them going. There weren't enough aircraft to move enough troops all the way to Afghanistan and keep them in beans and bullets.

The CIA and SOCOM quickly figured out what might work: Send in Special Forces teams (who have the right political skills to work with Afghans) to advise the Northern Alliance commanders on how to make the most of the new generation of American smart bombs. This was important, for you can much more easily pick out the right target if you're on the ground, especially if you're there with local warriors. The Northern Alliance and Taliban were basically stalemated. If the United States could use its smart bombs to kill enough Taliban troops, the rest of the Taliban warriors would, as Afghans have done for thousands of years, change sides or run away.

On September 11, 2001, SOCOM was one of the outfits that knew what they had to do. Men with language or operational experience in Afghanistan were alerted and put to work getting ready for action. Equipment, like satellite phones, that SOCOM had been talking about getting more of, suddenly became a priority item. Other special types of communications gear needed to talk to aircraft were obtained on a priority basis. Within a few days, the first Special Forces, Delta Force, and SEAL teams were on their way to the Persian Gulf and Pakistan. They went in civilian clothes.

Two Special Forces A-Teams (534 and 595), and their fire-control gear, hooked up with Northern Alliance commanders on October 20. In the next week, they worked with the bombers overhead and perfected their fire-control skills. The impact of this precision bombing impressed the Afghans. The older Northern Alliance men remembered the U.S. gadgets (like the Stinger missile, and satellite photos) provided in the 1980s for the war against the Russians. These experienced warriors were not surprised when the latest American military technology was demonstrated. They were grateful that the Americans were still on their side. On October 27, a major use of smart bombs was laid on. Up until then, most of the smart bombs hit targets picked out by intelligence staffs; some of the decisions were made as far away as Washington, D.C. But on October 27, 2001, the Special Forces teams had dibs on most of the smart bombs. They put on quite a show, blasting dozens of heavily fortified Taliban positions outside of Mazar-I-Sharif and north of Kabul. The Northern Alliance gained some ground. The Taliban was now frantically trying to figure out exactly what it was up against. But the word was spreading that the Northern Alliance now had the use of an almost magical "death from above" weapon. Within a month, Kabul and most of Afghanistan's major cities had been occupied by the Northern Alliance or other anti-Taliban forces.

There was nothing unusual about what the Special Forces and other commandos did in Afghanistan. Going in and hooking up with local forces and then directing American firepower to help your new buddies is nothing new. The Special Forces were doing that forty years ago in Vietnam. It worked then, and it worked in Afghanistan.

What made this tactic work so spectacularly in Afghanistan is attributable to several factors that will not be present in most other situations:

- **Afghanistan was a warrior society.** The Northern Alliance troops were as good as the Taliban, and armed in much the same fashion. In most other wars, the opposition is not as well trained or armed as the government forces.
- **The Taliban had worn out its welcome.** Once more Americans were on the ground, especially in southern Afghanistan, it was pretty obvious that most of the population was either anti-Taliban or neutral. Of course, this was pretty obvious from media and other reports coming out of Afghanistan for the previous two years.
- **Although Afghanistan is a warrior culture, they aren't fanatics when it comes to fighting.** It's customary for an Afghan to switch sides if it's obvious he's going to lose. No shame is attached to this. Once the Special Forces showed what the smart bombs could do, most Taliban fighters had all the reason they needed to switch sides, surrender, or just go home.

TIMELINE FOR THE TALIBAN TAKEDOWN

While most observers saw only the two weeks of smart bombs and Taliban advances, there was more going on during the Afghanistan war. To better understand how a few hundred Perfect Soldiers pulled off this rapid victory, and suffered few casualties while doing it, follow this brief timeline of the key events in the war.

September 13, 2001. Several small (three- to five-man) Special Forces and Delta Force recon teams arrive in Pakistan and cross into Afghanistan. Their mission is to gather information on the political and military situation inside the country.

September 16, 2001. British SAS troops enter Afghanistan. Several four-man teams come south from Tajikistan, pass through Northern Alliance territory, and scout inside and around Kabul. One team is discovered by the Taliban on September 21 but manages to get away safely. The SAS may have actually entered Afghanistan before American operators, but no one is talking.

September 19, 2001. The United States begins moving more military aircraft to the Persian Gulf.

September 22, 2001. A CIA Predator recon drone crashes in northern Afghanistan. The CIA is operating the drones out of Uzbekistan, where U.S. Special Forces has already been helping train Uzbek troops for fighting against local Islamic radicals. Special Forces typically operate near the scene of current hot spots and areas American armed forces might find themselves sent to fight. This gives the Special Forces troops insider knowledge that no one else in the American armed forces has.

September 27, 2001. Ten-man CIA team enters Afghanistan to work with the Northern Alliance.

September 30, 2001. The CIA begins flying Gnat-1 recon drones over Kabul. The numbers of flights increase on October 6 when more drones arrive in Pakistan. The photos provide target information for the upcoming U.S. bombing campaign.

October 1, 2001. U.S. aircraft carrier *Kitty Hawk* leaves its base in

Japan. The carrier is headed for the Indian Ocean, where it will cruise off the Pakistani coast, providing a floating base for Special Forces and commando helicopters.

October 6, 2001. A thousand troops from the U.S. 10th Mountain Division begin arriving in Uzbekistan, which shares a border with Afghanistan to the south.

October 7, 2001. U.S. and British warplanes begin bombing Afghan targets. The first night's attacks hit thirty-one targets using fifty missiles, fifteen Air Force bombers, and twenty-five Navy warplanes. Some Navy EA-6B jammer planes are used, along with several dozen aerial tankers. On the second night, thirteen targets are hit using five bombers and ten carrier-based warplanes.

October 9, 2001. U.S. warplanes begin making daylight bombing raids on Afghanistan.

October 10, 2001. U.S. Air Force EC-130s begin broadcasting the U.S. view of the conflict on radio, drowning out the few local Afghan stations that haven't been bombed, and replacing those that have.

October 11, 2001. The initial target list, compiled from satellite photos, radio and cell phone intercepts, and media reports, is taken care of after four days of bombing. These targets included air defenses and communications. Destroying the few anti-aircraft missiles and jet interceptors allows allied aircraft to operate freely and safely (above ten thousand feet—below that there are heavy machine guns and anti-aircraft guns to worry about). Knocking out the telephone system forces the Taliban to use radio, which can be intercepted, tracked, or jammed. From this day on, targets will be supplied mainly by Special Forces and commando ground patrols. The Taliban will try to hide its supplies, weapons, and troops, and it takes people on the ground to sniff these items out.

October 13, 2001. Relying on three aircraft carriers (with some two hundred warplanes on board) and eighteen bombers (ten B-52Hs and eight B-1Bs) based in Diego Garcia (twenty-five hundred miles to the south), seventeen targets are hit by fifteen Navy warplanes (F-18s and F-14s), ten bombers, and fifteen Tomahawk cruise missiles.

October 14, 2001. Seven targets (mostly around Kandahar) are hit by fifteen Navy warplanes, ten bombers, and some Tomahawk cruise missiles.

October 15, 2001. Twelve targets are hit by ninety Navy warplanes, ten bombers, and five Tomahawks.

October 16, 2001. Twelve targets are hit by eighty-five Navy warplanes, five bombers, and two AC-130 gunships flying in from the Persian Gulf.

October 17, 2001. For the first time, Air Force F-15Es bomb Afghanistan, flying in from the Persian Gulf.

October 18, 2001. The U.S. Navy remains short of land-based tankers, and the Air Force is often unable to provide such support. Air Force bombers are flying up from Diego Garcia and need tanker support. Moreover, some transports and warplanes flying over from the Persian Gulf also need in-flight refueling. Navy planes from the carriers are refueling at Pakistani bases on the way back, when they have no bombs. On the way to the target, they refuel from British aerial tankers.

October 27, 2001. Two Special Forces A-Teams (534 and 595) are operating in northern Afghanistan to assist Northern Alliance forces attacking Taliban forces dug in around Mazar-I-Sharif. Another team (555) arrives to assist the Northern Alliance operating north of Kabul. Two more teams will arrive over the next two weeks. The Special Forces teams immediately work with the Northern Alliance commanders to see how American airpower can best help them defeat the Taliban.

November 6, 2001. Almost all of the Taliban radio communications are now in Arabic, not local languages. It appears that al-Qaeda (most of whom are not Afghans) have taken control of most of the radios. This apparently took place over the last few weeks, because al-Qaeda overheard surrender discussions between Taliban and Northern Alliance fighters (who, in some cases, might be from the same tribe).

November 7, 2001. The bombing intensifies, with up to 120 sorties a day. The increase is made possible by the arrival of more aerial tankers and Marine Harriers, flying from amphibious ships that have joined the carrier task forces. During the 1999 Kosovo campaign, there were seven hundred sorties a day (over a much smaller area), and during the 1991 Gulf War more than two thousand a day.

November 9, 2001. Mazar-I-Sharif falls to the Northern Alliance. Taliban losses in defending Mazar-I-Sharif probably total about 10 percent of its armed forces (that is, four to five thousand defected, dead, deserted, or captured). Northern Alliance losses in the Mazar-I-Sharif campaign are a few hundred (dead and wounded). Many civilians (mostly Pushtuns who moved in after 1998) flee with the Taliban. The Northern Alliance declares amnesty for Mazar-I-Sharif residents who support the Taliban. In typical Afghan fashion, the Taliban defends Mazar-I-Sharif by placing troops on high ground overlooking roads leading to the town. The troops dig trenches, or use caves. There are plenty of both around Afghanistan, and this proves to be a problem for American airpower until the Special Forces get onto the ground. From the air, it's not always possible to know if the trenches and bunkers are occupied, and if they are, by which side. Once the Special Forces arrive, they are able to sort out who is who and promptly bring in accurate smart bomb attacks. The speed of these attacks is important, because if the Taliban knows bombs are coming, it can just move out of the way. Since the Special Forces dress like Afghans, the Taliban can't always tell when the American soldiers are around. That, and all those deadly accurate smart bombs, are why Mazar-I-Sharif falls. Once the Talibs realize that there is only one road left to the south that isn't controlled by the Northern Alliance, they decide to run for it, and ended up having to flee to the east anyway.

November 12, 2001. Northern Alliance troops have begun entering Kabul. Herat, the major city in the west, has fallen, as has Taloquan, a key city in the northeast. Herat is important because it opens the road across the southern plains to the Taliban capital of Kandahar. The Northern Alliance estimates that the defections and battle losses of the last week have reduced the Taliban fighting force to some fifteen thousand troops, mostly foreigners. There is still danger in the south, for if many Pushtun tribes see the Northern Alliance advance as a threat, they might join the Taliban. Kabul falls for the same reason Mazar-I-Sharif did: The Special Forces teams methodically call down smart bombs on Taliban positions. After a few days of this, and news that Mazar-I-Sharif was being abandoned, the Taliban decides to head for their cultural capital, Kandahar.

November 13, 2001. While the Special Forces teams are personally directing smart bombs, the pilots above still have other targets that the Special Forces teams cannot see. The Air Force B-52s and B-1s are flying 10 percent of the sorties but dropping half the bombs. Most of the heavy bombing attacks are done for the Special Forces; the heavy bombers just circle over the Special Forces team for hours and wait for the command to drop a bomb. The Special Forces need this because the ground battles are often confused affairs, and it usually takes time to make sure all the Northern Alliance people are in the right place to take advantage of a bombing attack, or to avoid getting hit by it. But the smaller bombers, especially the Navy F-18s and F-14s, are being assigned targets picked up by Air Force and Navy reconnaissance aircraft. There is Taliban traffic on the road as Mazar-I-Sharif is being abandoned. The smaller warplanes are only able to stay in the air over Afghanistan for a short time (an hour or so), so four-engine E-3 AWACS (whose radar can see and track all aircraft for hundreds of miles around) and JSTARS (whose radar can track vehicles on the ground in a somewhat smaller area) sort out which aircraft will hit which target. For hitting moving targets, the F-14s and F-18s can come in lower and use Maverick missiles.

By November, U.S. AH-64 helicopter gunships are flying in from Pakistan and hitting road traffic with Hellfire missiles. And the CIA is using its armed (with a pair of Hellfire missiles) Predator drones to successfully hit several dozen targets. These attacks on the road add to the sense of helplessness and panic among Taliban members. By now there are about a hundred commandos on the ground as well, and they can call in bombing strikes if they have an important target or are in danger of being overwhelmed by enemy troops. Fighting the Russians in the 1980s was one thing; at least you got to see Russians and kill them. But these Americans and their smart bombs and soldiers who dress like Afghans are quite another matter. The Taliban wasn't prepared for this. And that is exactly the reaction the Special Forces wanted.

November 14, 2001. The Northern Alliance has seized all of Kabul.

There hasn't been much violence between non-Pushtun Northern Alliance troops and Kabul residents. The Northern Alliance soldiers, however, sought out non-Afghan Taliban fighters and killed them. American Special Forces soldiers are operating in southern Afghanistan, including Special Forces Team 574, which today joins with Hamid Karzai, a Pushtun leader who is trying to get the Pushtun tribes to fight against the Taliban. Karzai will later be elected leader of Afghanistan by the Loya Jirga (the great council of tribal chiefs and elders).

November 16, 2001. About a hundred British Royal Marines arrive at Bagram airbase, just north of Kabul. Bagram has the longest runway in the country. The Royal Marines will get the base ready to receive aircraft. America's largest transports can land here, bringing in military equipment and relief supplies. Meanwhile, several hundred more American Special Forces and commandos begin operating in southern Afghanistan, looking for bin Laden and his followers. This increase in manpower has been made possible by the buildup of supplies (food, ammo, equipment, and so on) and transport (helicopters and air transports in Uzbekistan and Pakistan) to support the troops.

November 17, 2001. In the north, U.S. warplanes continue to bomb Taliban positions around Kunduz. Most (more than ten thousand) of the remaining Taliban troops, including many of the foreigners, are trapped in Kunduz. Many of the Taliban troops in the south have fled back to their villages or, if they are Pakistani, back into Pakistan. But there are still thousands of Taliban fighters remaining around Kandahar.

November 23, 2001. The Taliban is getting over its near collapse when its forces fled Mazar-I-Sharif, Kabul, and most of the northern and western Afghanistan. Taliban forces continue to hold out in the northern town of Kunduz, in Kandahar, on a ridge line twelve miles southwest of Kabul and in several other places. The fighting south of Kabul is particularly bitter, as the Taliban commander has a particularly nasty reputation and the Northern Alliance troops are out for blood. Also, the Taliban force contains a number of foreigners.

November 24, 2001. Several hundred commandos (American Delta Force, SEAL, British SAS, and contingents from several other countries) have been roaming around southern Afghanistan, collecting information, spotting targets for bombers, and ambushing Taliban troops. None of these soldiers has been killed, although some are wounded or injured in accidents. The commandos get in and out by helicopter, sometimes moving cross-country on armed dune buggies and other vehicles.

November 25, 2001. Several hundred U.S. Marines land at an abandoned airfield south of Kandahar. Soon there will be a thousand Marines here, blocking retreating Taliban forces and searching for enemy weapons dumps.

November 26, 2001. The Northern Alliance takes Kunduz, the last Taliban-held city in northern Afghanistan. Most of the Taliban troops surrender, while others slip away through the mountains. Some Taliban fighters are making a stand west of Kunduz. Northern Alliance troops negotiate with this group to try to get them to surrender. American commandos help a local Pushtun warlord seize Kandahar airport. The battle for Qala-e-Jangi begins as eight hundred foreign Taliban fighters take over part of the prison near Kunduz.

November 27, 2001. The battle for Qala-e-Jangi causes five U.S. casualties when a smart bomb isn't and comes down in the wrong place. Several Afghans are injured as well. Special Forces there blame a senior Special Forces officer who took over the operation and began calling in bombs without sufficient experience.

November 29, 2001. Two platoons of infantry, from the U.S. 10th Mountain Division troops in Uzbekistan, are sent to guard American repair and support efforts in airfields outside Kabul and Mazar-I-Sharif. A few days earlier, troops from the 10th Mountain Division were sent to help in the fighting at the fortress of Qala-e-Jangi.

December 4, 2001. Al-Qaeda forces make a last stand at Tora Bora (near the Pakistani border) and are defeated in a battle that lasts nearly two weeks. Caves in the area are still being searched at the end of the month.

December 6, 2001. Kandahar falls to anti-Taliban Pushtuns. In two months, U.S. armed forces and their Northern Alliance allies have swept the Taliban from power. About half the Taliban senior leaders escape and will still be at large by the summer of 2002.

December 18, 2001. So far, the United States has dropped some twelve thousand bombs in Afghanistan. Some 40 percent were dumb bombs (usually dropped by B-52s and B-1s). The rest were smart bombs, two-thirds of them GPS-guided JDAM (which are guidance kits strapped onto dumb bombs), the rest laser guided. The Navy has used up most of its JDAM, while the Air Force has used up at least a third of its supply.

January 27, 2002. U.S. naval warplanes have flown fifty-seven hundred bombing sorties and dropped nearly five thousand bombs and missiles.

March 2, 2002. Operation Anaconda begins as U.S. troops attack Taliban and al-Qaeda forces in the Shah-e-Kot region. The operation will last for more than two weeks, with relatively high American casualties—six dead, forty-five wounded.

After Anaconda, the al-Qaeda and Taliban forces scattered. They had learned that you don't want to fight battles with American troops, especially if they are of the Perfect Soldier variety. Although the Taliban and al-Qaeda had loudly proclaimed their desire to fight the Americans up close and teach them a lesson, the reality was quite the opposite. For the rest of the year, American and allied forces swept through former Taliban and al-Qaeda strongholds in southern Afghanistan, looking for weapons and al-Qaeda members.

CASUALTIES

The 1991 Gulf War was noted for its low American casualties: 293 dead, 467 wounded. In the Afghanistan war, at least through June 2002, these were much lower still: 48 dead, 162 wounded. While a little more than half the Gulf War dead were from enemy action, it was just the opposite in Afghanistan. Northern Alliance casualties were heavier, including several hundred dead, plus perhaps as many as four hundred civilians. Taliban and al-Qaeda dead were in the thousands. Since the Afghans didn't keep records of combat losses, we'll probably never know the exact figures. There was a survey of the areas where fighting and bombing took place, to find graves and try to count the war dead. But many of the bodies, it turned out, were of people killed by the Taliban before September 11, 2001. While the Taliban tried to score points in the media about "indiscriminate American bombing of Afghan civilians," the war had the lowest casualty count of any major conflict in Afghan history. As discussed, Afghans will fight, but they aren't stupid and know when to back off and give up. Most were also just fed up with more than two decades of killing.

WHERE HAVE ALL THE SMART BOMBS GONE?

Even though smart bombs have been an outstanding success since the 1991 Gulf War, we keep running out of them. During the Gulf War, 4 percent of the bombs dropped were smart bombs. They took out more than half the targets and were actually cheaper than dumb bombs because the bombers had to fly less. These new weapons cost thirty-two thousand dollars each, compared to twenty-one hundred for the dumb bombs, but the cost of running the bombers to carry all those dumb bombs increases the cost by more than twenty times. Moreover, smart bombs were less risky to use (bombers dropped them farther away from the target), and more targets could be hit in a shorter time (giving the enemy less time to avoid damage). Despite the success of guided bombs during the Gulf War, and the all-weather fighter-bombers that carried them, there was still a reluctance to buy new bombs for a future war. Although it takes twelve to twenty times as many old-fashioned dumb bombs to hit a target as it does guided bombs, there was no rush to buy a lot of new bombs. After the Gulf War, some 95 percent of the U.S. bomb inventory still consisted of dumb bombs. The official explanation given was that there is not enough money to do everything and that, rather than increase the number of smart bombs in the inventory, it was seen as more prudent to spend the money on developing even smarter, and cheaper, bombs. This meant JDAM and JSOW, the "smarter bombs" using GPS for guidance. This makes some sense, but it meant that the older smart bombs just sat there, unused, providing some military spokesman with the ability to lie with a straight face: "We have plenty of munitions."

Eight years later, smart bombs were called on once more to bomb Kosovo. This time, most of the weapons used were smart bombs, and again there was a shortage. Fortunately, the Kosovo bombing campaign was only one-quarter the size of the Gulf War operation. Still, there was a shortage.

Two years later came the war in Afghanistan. This time two-thirds of the bombs dropped were smart bombs. Stocks were still being rebuilt from the Kosovo operation, and the U.S. Navy had to ask the U.S. Air Force for smart bomb kits after the sailors had used up most of theirs. At first, the Air Force refused. And it had good reason to say no, for it was working with an inadequate supply of smart bombs as well. The Navy has had a severe shortage of smart bombs for the last few years. Few smart bombs are used in training, and the Navy also had shortages of spare parts and sailors. The Army was in worse trouble with ammunition shortages, even though it doesn't even use smart bombs. The Army ammo shortfall was $14 billion, with a $3.3 billion shortage of critical items such as missiles and cluster bomb munitions.

Part of the reason was a decision by the Department of Defense, after the Gulf War, to try to maintain smaller "just enough" stocks of munitions rather than stockpile large "just in case" quantities. This approach, which implied that someone in charge could accurately predict what "just enough" would be in a future war, didn't work. And then it got worse, because the decision was made to establish larger supplies of munitions in potential hot spots (the Persian Gulf, Korea, and so on). It was more difficult to move ammo from these places to another where a new war cropped up. Although the Army reduced its combat units by about 40 percent in the 1990s, it cut its total munitions stockpile by 78 percent (from 2.5 million tons to 540,000 tons). This, in turn, caused a reduction in munitions manufacturing capability, because enough new ammo was being used to keep factories going. This meant that, in case of a war, new factories would not get going until after the fighting was over (unless it was a long war).

In September 2000 and 2001, Congress held hearings to ask the brass why they kept running out of ammunition. This was a rather pointless exercise, as the real reason was Congress itself. Congress had long used the peacetime defense budget as a major source of patronage. Military spending went to where congressmen would get the most votes. This is why it's such a political hassle to close unneeded military bases. But it also means that money is spent on what is more likely to get a politician reelected, not to buy what the troops need.

Like the military bases, once you start a major project to build a new weapon, it's political suicide to kill the project (and all the jobs in someone's congressional district). So through the 1990s, the military was stuck with a lot of Cold War–era weapons projects they no longer needed. The new weapons were necessary when there was still an arms race going on with the Soviet Union. But in 1991 the Soviet Union disappeared, along with the arms race. The race to keep pork-barrel projects alive, however, continues in Congress. That's one reason the U.S. defense budget dropped only 30 percent from its Cold War peak (in 1988), and has been rising again since 1997. When you add in a lot of new peacekeeping missions, without any new money to pay for them, the armed forces have to take the money from something else. They can't touch the high-profile patronage projects (mostly aircraft), so money is taken from less visible things like ammo stocks. Shortages here only get noticed when there's a war. But the cuts in ammo were so severe in the late 1990s that there weren't enough bullets for the troops to train with their M-16s, and the complaints of the soldiers even made some waves in the media.

The high usage of the new, very effective, and much-in-demand JDAM (satellite-guided) smart bomb caused the Air Force and Navy to place big new orders. In the first half of 2002, nine thousand new JDAMs were built. The Department of Defense wants to build JDAM stocks up to fifty thousand. But this will take until the end of 2003 to accomplish. The stunning effectiveness of smart bombs in Afghanistan means they will be in even more demand for the next war. And there will probably be another shortage. The Perfect Soldiers demonstrated in Afghanistan that they can be tremendously effective. But they can't win these striking victories using their bare hands. Without the right tools, like smart bombs, the Perfect Soldiers will still fight on bravely and with intelligence, but they will die and the battle will probably be lost. It's happened before, and it can happen again.

WHAT SPEAKS LOUDER THAN BULLETS?

The war in Afghanistan featured two weapons that were most responsible for victory over the Taliban. The most visible weapon was the smart bomb, usually a one-ton, GPS-guided weapon dropped from a B-52. The other widely used weapon was cash. Money. Defeating the enemy with a pile of greenbacks is often looked down on, but in Afghanistan it is often much more effective than bombs. Let's look at that aspect.

When CIA agents went into Afghanistan in late September 2001, they already knew that, as the British had noted more than a century ago, "Afghans can't be bought, but they can be rented." Even the Taliban had used bribes to defeat Northern Alliance warlords. Since there was no price list, and Afghan warlords knew the Americans had a lot more cash, there was a lot of negotiation involved and some $70 million was spent this way. For a few hundred thousand dollars, many warlords were willing to switch loyalty. Moreover, this was an ancient Afghan custom. A warlord became a leader of fighting men by having the resources to take care of them. That takes money, and the Americans had a lot more than the Taliban. Going into November and December, more pro-Taliban forces switched sides. This often happened even before a warlord's troops got hit with smart bombs. A greedy warlord was also sometimes led to lower his asking price after a close encounter with a one-ton bomb.

Money was a very effective way to encourage existing Northern Alliance leaders to become more active on the battlefield as well. The Northern Alliance was also encouraged with the prospect of foreign aid. Before September 11, the United States was only planning $2.9 million in aid to Afghanistan (largely as a bribe to encourage the Taliban to continue its ban on the drug trade). After September 11, authorized aid (for the Northern Alliance and its successors) rose to $278 million. At this point, the major problem became figuring out how to distribute the money as widely as possible. Giving it to the new government, however, would likely see it disappear into a few pockets, and then to foreign bank accounts.

There are many techniques for getting the money to as many Afghans as possible. One of the more popular is to hire lots of Afghans to do public-works-type jobs. Construction and repair of roads and utilities can be supervised with a small number of trusted (often American) engineers and bookkeepers, and a lot of cash. This is the sort of thing the U.S. Army Civil Affairs battalions do. At least you see what you're getting, and on a daily basis. And none of this money ends up in a Swiss bank account.

This kind of aid was spread around—more than a billion dollars by the end of 2001. Early on, Pakistan was promised $673 million (up from $10.9 million). Aid to the other Central Asian nations went from $141 to $263 million. It seemed they could be rented, too.

After all the major cities in Afghanistan fell to the Northern Alliance, there was still the hunt for al-Qaeda members and Taliban leaders. Rather than use American troops for this, it was easier to hire Afghan gunmen to do the deed. "Gifts" of cash, food, medical care, or even guns were given to those who provided information about the fleeing Taliban and al-Qaeda. Warlords weren't the only ones willing to rent their guns. Afghans have served as mercenaries for centuries. But Afghans aren't soldiers. They are difficult to use, consider orders a suggestion, and will often disappear at a vital moment. They do, however, know the backcountry, and they are already there. The alternative—getting American troops into Afghanistan—is still a difficult and time-consuming process.

Another aspect of Afghan warriors is their lust for loot. When the battle is over, Afghans expect to be rewarded with it. This means stripping the enemy dead and grabbing anything portable. This became a problem when Special Forces were searching for al-Qaeda documents and other evidence of their terrorism operations. The Afghans hired to help out would often grab valuable items (like laptop computers or cameras containing valuable data) and sell them in the nearest city. So the Special Forces did what the CIA had been doing for years. They bought the merchandise back by offering more money than the Afghans could get from their usual buyers (merchants in the cities). The CIA, for example, is still buying back Stinger anti-aircraft missiles given to anti-Russian Afghans in the 1980s. Now we are buying back documents and laptop computers looted from al-Qaeda caves and camps. It works.

And then there were the cash rewards for the capture of Taliban and al-Qaeda leaders. Not just the promised total fifty million dollars, but also the bonus items like green cards and a witness protection program, as needed. Reward programs have never been a sure thing, and depend, as this one does, on advertising. In addition to radio broadcasts and leaflet drops by American Psychological Warfare units, advertising is also purchased in Pakistan and elsewhere.

Money also comes in handy when setting up an agent network. When bin Laden became a major target for U.S. intelligence agencies in the late 1990s, the CIA set up a network of agents in Afghanistan. From 1998 until late 2001, more than a million dollars was spent to hire over a dozen agents to try to keep track of him. Since then, more has been spent to set up an even more extensive agent network to track him down. This was done not just in Afghanistan, but throughout the Muslim world and in places such as Europe and Africa, where al-Qaeda is known to have extensive operations.

Money talks in wartime, often with more accuracy and effect than bombs and bullets. But it takes soldiers trained to do the negotiations. This is not to say that Special Forces troops take a course called "Bribery 101," but they are made aware of how these things work, and how to make the most of it.

TASK FORCE 11 AND THE COMMANDO OLYMPICS

One of the most unusual, and daring, intelligence operations of the Afghanistan war was put together quickly and largely operated out of sight of the media. Right after September 11, 2001, Delta Force and Navy SEAL commandos were organized into Task Force 11 for operations in Afghanistan. This unit eventually grew to some four hundred operators, all elite commandos. While Special Forces did most of the direct dealing with Afghans, Task Force 11 kept a low profile, but was in the lead whenever it, Special Forces, or the massive American intelligence effort uncovered anything about where Taliban or al-Qaeda forces might be. Members of Task Force 11 took part in the October 19, 2001, raid on one of Taliban leader Mullah Omar's homes. Credit for that raid was given to U.S. Army Rangers, who did provide most of the manpower. But it was Task Force 11 operators who took the lead and controlled the operation.

Once the Taliban fell from power in November, Task Force 11 was told to find the Taliban and al-Qaeda leaders. To accomplish this, operators used an elaborate communications and electronic surveillance system to listen in on any electronic communications in Afghanistan (and, later, parts of Pakistan) for clues about where the Taliban or al-Qaeda might be hiding. The communications system also allowed the commandos to quickly and easily communicate with aircraft, each other, and other support units.

Much of the Task Force 11 work was done in small units of as few as four men. These patrols spent a lot of time up in the hills, getting to know the territory and often staking out a village for days or weeks, watching and listening to any radio communication for evidence of who might be hiding there. There were some gun battles up in the hills, on those rare occasions when a Task Force 11 patrol was found by local Afghans. There had also been casualties in these clashes, mostly Afghan. The commandos had B-52s and other bombers on call, as well as access to helicopter transports and gunships.

Most of the raids and fights attributed to Special Forces were either solely Task Force 11, or led or instigated by Task Force 11. A success, the operation provided a steady stream of al-Qaeda prisoners being taken and sent to Guantanamo Bay for detention and interrogation.

Task Force 11, however, was not an entirely American operation. On September 11, 2001, the elite commando organizations in the world all realized that this was going to be a commando war. So allies of the United States with commando forces promptly volunteered to join the fight. More SAS soon arrived, along with SBS (Special Boat Squadron, British SEALs) and SAS contingents from Australia (about a hundred men) and New Zealand (about three dozen). Germany sent more than a hundred SKS commandos, while Holland and Canada sent smaller contingents. These troops came with their own special equipment, including helicopters and cross-country vehicles. American headquarters (SOCOM and Central Command, or CENTCOM) had to scramble to see that everyone got the right radio equipment and training on the communications and operating procedures they'd be using. This was not a major problem, because the hundreds of commandos were the elite of their respective armed forces, and many had trained with their counterparts in other nations.

Commandos spend most of their time training; actual combat is obviously rare. So Afghanistan became something of a commando Olympics, a rare opportunity to strut their stuff and see whose training and techniques were most effective. But because of the way commandos operate, it may be a while before we know who did what and how well. Commandos are well known for not saying much about what they are doing, or have done. There's a reason for this: If commando tactics and methods become widely known, potential foes can develop countermeasures. Commandos depend on surprise for success, and anything that makes them less of one makes their work that much more dangerous.

THE DRUG GANGS OF AFGHANISTAN

U.S. troops in eastern Afghanistan have found that local tribesmen are not willing to help search al-Qaeda camps for surviving terrorists and al-Qaeda documents and munitions. The tribes along the eastern border have more pressing financial matters to deal with than picking up a few bucks working for the Americans. The eastern Pushtun tribes control the most lucrative part of the country's drug trade. They not only grow poppies, but also run most of the drug factories that refine the plants into drugs. Some of these facilities were found inside al-Qaeda camps.

Since Pakistan stamped out the drug trade in the late 1990s, the Pushtun tribes there simply moved their operations across the border. In some cases, the nineteenth-century border cuts right through the territory of tribes, leaving related clans on both sides. The tribal cousins in Afghanistan were glad to get into the lucrative drug trade. They had noted how wealthy their Pakistani kinsmen had become growing poppies and refining them into opium, morphine, and heroin. The evidence of this success was obvious. New trucks and SUVs, satellite dishes on newly built walled villas, new clothes and jewelry for the women, and even schools for the kids.

This border region had long prospered from illegal activity. Smuggling had been a major business ever since the British set up and tried to guard the frontier. Gun running and banditry were considered a birthright. Earning a living with your weapons was a Pushtun tradition going back thousands of years. And the fanatically religious Taliban leaders, although they were brutal with banditry, were content to tolerate the drug business as long as they got a cut of the proceeds; they picked up forty to fifty million dollars a year in the process. One reason the Taliban leadership and bin Laden have been so hard to catch is that these guys fled with a lot of their drug profits to pay for escape.

The Taliban banned poppy growing in 2000 in an attempt to gain international recognition of their government. This didn't work, and the drug ban was dropped just before the Talibs were run out of power.

But the Northern Alliance also tolerated and taxed the drug trade in its territory (which was much smaller than the operations in the south).

Many tribes have run lucrative smuggling rackets for generations and consider the drug business a natural addition to traditional trade. It's organized, and everyone in the tribe benefits. In typical Afghan fashion, deals are made with the provincial governor and border guards to get the drugs out of the country. Where the border guards could not be bribed (as on the Iranian and Tajik borders), you went armed and fought your way through. The Iranians have been very hostile to the Afghan drug-smuggling operation. In the first six months of 2001, Iranian troops and border police killed 221 Afghan drug smugglers and arrested another 1,489. Activity dropped after September 11, but picked up again in 2002. There was less action on the Tajik border, guarded by two divisions of Russians, who tend to be pretty trigger happy.

The drug business has spread the money around. The tribes that grow poppies get thirty times more money for their crop than if they grew wheat. With the three years of drought, there was another bonus: Poppies use only a quarter of the water wheat needs. Shipping the drugs through tribal territory earns a fee from the smugglers to guarantee safe passage. Tribes on the Iranian border have taken over the smuggling end of things, and often fight each other over who controls the most lucrative routes.

When U.S. troops moved into the territory of the drug tribes along the Pakistan border, they discovered two things. First, the Special Forces had little or no experience with these tribes, and second, the tribes wanted to keep it that way. The tribes were upset that this war on terrorism was interfering with their business. Foreigners, no matter how well armed, were not welcome. The tribes generally held their fire, but the threat was obvious. Not wanting to see one accidental (or otherwise) firefight escalate into a full-scale tribal war, America decided to put as few troops as possible into the area.

In early 2002, the new government in Kabul restored the Taliban ban on poppy production. But the government had no troops or police to enforce the ban, as the Taliban had. It's important to note that the Taliban outlawed only poppy cultivation, not smuggling. When the poppy ban went into place, there were still several thousand tons of drugs waiting to be smuggled out of the country. So in 2001, the smuggling went on. Some suspect that the Taliban would have lifted the poppy-growing ban after a year anyway. When and if the new government does get its new army and police force organized, it might find that taking on the drug tribes proves to be a losing proposition. This has also been the experience in places like Colombia and Burma. In both places, thriving drug operations survived for decades in the face of government efforts to root them out by force.

Worse yet, when drug gangs manage to set up their own mini governments, they are open to sheltering anyone with money, or other advantages. This includes terrorists. The United States is reluctant to get into battles with the tribes, and no central government in Afghanistan has been very successful at it either.

DRONE FEVER

One of the more successful aircraft in the Afghanistan war didn't even have pilots. This was the drone, which proved an extremely useful tool for Special Forces and commandos. Drones were another example of technology that made Perfect Soldiers a little more perfect. These small, pilotless aircraft gave the Perfect Soldiers their own little air force, always available to do aerial scouting in support of commando operations. Speed is usually essential to the success of whatever a Perfect Soldier does, and not having to wait for the Air Force to run an aerial recon mission for you often makes the difference between failure and success.

Drones (also known as pilotless aircraft, UAVs, RPVs, and Bugs) first showed up before aircraft with pilots in them. In 1887, Douglas Archibald rigged a camera to a large kite in order to take aerial photos. An American, William Eddy, adopted the same technique during the Spanish-American War, successfully taking hundreds of reconnaissance photos. Once piloted aircraft came along, research on drones declined, except to adapt older aircraft as pilotless aerial targets. Why? Well, for one thing, the instrumentation needed for a drone that was as effective as a piloted aircraft took a long time to arrive. Even during the Vietnam War, when the Firefly drone (originally a target drone) was widely used, 16 percent of its sorties ended with a botched landing and a destroyed drone. Still, the Firefly flew 3,435 sorties, mainly over areas where it would be difficult to recover a downed pilot. Even so, by 1972 various types of drones flying in Southeast Asia were coming back 90 percent of the time. Still, that's more than ten times the loss rate for piloted aircraft.

With no war to spur development of drones, the U.S. lost interest once more. But in Israel, work proceeded. And drones figured prominently in a spectacular Israeli aerial victory over the Bekaa Valley in 1982. Using drones in coordination with its warplanes, Israel was able to shut down the Syrian Air Force (and destroy eighty-six aircraft) in a few days. Israel pioneered the use of drones for real-time surveillance, electronic warfare, and decoys. But in the United States, there was either no interest, or some inexplicably botched UAV development projects. Americans wondered how the Israelis did it while the Department of Defense continued to screw up attempts to create useful drones.

Finally, with some urging (and ridicule) from Congress, the Department of Defense began to buy drones from Israel. The Navy bought the Israeli Pioneer UAV (Unpiloted Aerial Vehicle, the current official term), which is still in use. Many of these Israeli drones (plus some newly developed U.S. ones) were used in the 1991 Gulf War. There weren't that many of them, but the Army and Marines noted that the Air Force and Navy were stingy with answering requests for recon missions. This made the ground troops aware that they could create their own air force of drones. All of a sudden, the Army and Marines were back in the drone development business. This time they were serious, and a number of successful UAVs were developed. The Predator entered service in 1995.

When the 1999 Kosovo war came along, various NATO nations had ninety-seven UAVs operating in the area. While twenty-seven crashed (mostly due to accident, although the UAVs were frequently shot at), UAVs were considered a great success. The military began to get UAV fever, except for the Air Forces. The U.S. Air Force had actually developed several highly successful UAVs (cruise missiles) in the 1980s, but these were not considered UAVs. To the Air Force, these weapons were enhanced missiles, and all went on one-way missions. The Air Force had a point—recovering UAVs had always been a major problem. As any pilot can tell you, taking off and flying are easy, but landing is difficult.

The CIA also got into the act, obtaining some Predator UAVs for use in Central Asia (and elsewhere) before September 11, 2001. The CIA had no hang-ups (as the U.S. Air Force did) about arming drones. It figured out how to equip a Predator with two (hundred-pound) Hellfire missiles. If the UAV spotted a likely target, it could launch missiles right away. Now, this was no different from the old tactic of turning warplanes loose against "targets of opportunity." But UAVs could circle over a piece of land for hours, something most modern aircraft could not do. Most enemy troops expect jet fighter-bombers to come by, make a few passes, and depart. But the CIA Predators could snoop around for a while, checking out suspected targets, and then fire on likely targets. Since the Hellfire was a highly accurate missile, drones usually hit what they aimed at. CIA Predators did this successfully several dozen times in Afghanistan.

Then, in the late 1990s, the U.S. Air Force became enthusiastic about UAVs. The long-range Global Hawk UAV was a great success, and was first used in Afghanistan (even before it was finished with all its development tests). The Air Force is also developing air-to-air combat UAVs. This shouldn't be too difficult, because tests with prototypes in the 1970s showed that a drone could outfly the best pilots. The U.S. armed forces now have nearly a thousand UAVs in service or on order, and more than a hundred UAV designs are in various stages of development.

Why the change of mind? Mostly it's about technology. The instrumentation that enables a pilot on the ground to control a UAV, or software that allows a UAV to fly missions successfully on its own, is now a reality. This microcomputer-based equipment is cheaper and more reliable than it was just ten years ago. For many decades, the concept of UAVs was good, but the means were not. Now there is affordable technology to make UAVs work. This is a typical pattern with many items. But for UAVs, it meant that an obviously good idea stayed just out of reach for many decades. There was also a problem in that Air Forces, which are run by pilots, are not being eager to replace pilots with robotic UAVs. But with UAV technology so cheap and widespread, Air Forces have to develop UAVs or see their piloted aircraft blown from the sky by someone else's UAVs.

Special Forces see UAVs as their private air force. Unlike piloted aircraft, there is no arrangement giving the Air Force a monopoly on fixed-wing aircraft. This may change, but for the moment the Special

Forces are eager to get their hands on the new generation of smaller and smarter UAVs that can be controlled by Special Forces teams, or even carried by them. Commandos can't have too much technology, especially the kind that lets them see what's behind the hill in real time.

More ominously, we are likely to see the first robot Perfect Soldier in the form of combat drones. While most drones are meant to be flown by pilots on the ground, it is also necessary to equip the drones with software that will allow the aircraft to fly itself when contact with the human pilot is lost. Moreover, robotic combat aircraft aren't really new. Cruise missiles are basically robot bombers. In the 1990s, there were cruise missiles that could drop bombs on one target and then fly on to crash themselves onto another. Equipping such aircraft to make round-trip missions isn't technically difficult. Such an aircraft already exists—the Global Hawk recon drone. While pilots really like to fly high-performance (and very high-cost) combat aircraft, combat drones are cheaper and potentially more effective. And until the "Robot Rights" movement gets started, losing droids in combat won't have much political downside.

BOMBING AFGHANISTAN WITH INFORMATION

The war in Afghanistan saw much use of psychological warfare—the war of information and ideas. This effort came in many forms, most obviously leaflet drops and radio broadcasts. But the Special Forces troops also were trained to use psychology in dealing with Afghans. So too with the Civil Affairs troops who began operating in the country by the end of 2001. The Special Forces were trained to work in a foreign culture, and were also well-trained soldiers. The Special Forces impressed the Northern Alliance by accurately bringing down bombs from warplanes far above. The Afghans in the Northern Alliance had never seen anything like this before. When they'd fought the Russians in the 1980s, they'd never encountered smart bombs (which the Russians didn't have at the time). Moreover, when the Special Forces got involved in ground fighting, they further impressed the Afghans with their combat skills.

Each Special Forces A-Team also had two medics who were very good at treating wounds and many of the illnesses Afghans might have. To top it off, the Special Forces were humble about all this and just kept saying that they were in Afghanistan to catch the terrorists who had killed so many Americans on September 11, 2001. The Afghans could understand revenge, and they respected capable warriors who could also treat the sick and wounded. The Civil Affairs soldiers who showed up later were just there to help civilians live better. This enhanced the idea among Afghans that, while the Americans might be foreigners, they were basically good and could be trusted and tolerated.

This psychological warfare had several targets.

- Hurting the morale of the enemy by reminding him how deadly American weapons and troops were.
- Winning the support of the Afghan people. This was done in several ways, from supplying food and medical care to warning Afghans to stay away from mines and American bombing targets.
- Destroying terrorist activities in Afghanistan. This meant gaining enough goodwill among Afghans that people would report sightings of al-Qaeda or Taliban fighters and their assets (weapons and munitions caches, in particular).
- Keeping the peace. Once the Taliban was out of power, a lot of psychological warfare efforts went into getting Afghans to stop fighting each other and form a workable new government.

The first overt use of psychological warfare came right after the bombs fell. In fact, it was a bomb: a fiberglass M129 leaflet bomb, which comes apart in midair so as to disperse its load of fifty thousand or more leaflets. The leaflets were produced in the United States, packed in M129s, and shipped by air to Diego Garcia or aircraft carriers off the Pakistan coast.

The United States started dropping bombs on Afghanistan on October 7, 2001. A week later, 385,000 leaflets were dropped on Pushtun areas in eastern Afghanistan. At the same time, Commando Solo aerial radio broadcasting aircraft began providing AM and FM news and music service in parts of southern Afghanistan. The basic message of the leaflet was, as it said in the local language, that "the partnership of nations is here to assist the people of Afghanistan." Another leaflet gave the radio frequencies the Commando Solo aircraft were broadcasting on; as we've noted, American bombing had already taken Taliban radio off the air by blasting the broadcast antennas. For the next two months, eighteen million leaflets were dropped on Afghanistan, particularly in areas where American bombers were operating. One such leaflet said, "On September 11th, the United States was the target of terrorist attacks, leaving no choice but to seek justice for these horrible crimes." This, and other leaflets and the radio broadcasts, sought to explain to Afghans why the bombs were falling on them.

In addition to bombs and leaflets, October also saw packets of food dropped in areas suffering most from the three-year drought. Additional leaflets were dropped showing how to use the MREs (Meals, Ready to Eat, which came with user instructions in English). Radios were dropped, both American battery-powered portables and British hand-operated (powered by a built-in generator) models.

During October, some of the radio broadcasts were directed at the Taliban, warning members of what was in store for them. One broadcast said:

Attention Taliban! You are condemned. Did you know that? The instant the terrorists you support took over our planes, you sentenced yourselves to death . . . our helicopters will rain death down upon your camps before you detect them on your radar. Our bombs are so accurate we can drop them through your windows . . . you have only one choice, surrender now and we will give you a second chance. We will let you live.

This leaflet played upon the stories that were rapidly spreading among Afghans about the astonishing accuracy of the American bombs.

Other broadcasts warned civilians to stay away from the American Special Forces troops or bombing targets:

Attention! People of Afghanistan. United States forces will be moving through your area. We are here for Osama bin Laden, al-Qaeda, and those who protect them. Please, for your own safety, stay off bridges and roadways and do not interfere with our troops or military operations. If you do this you will not be harmed.

On a similar theme, a leaflet said:

We have no wish to hurt you, the innocent people of Afghanistan. Stay away from military installations, government buildings, terrorist camps, roads, factories or bridges. If you are near these places, then you must move away from them. Seek a safe place, and stay well away from anything that might be a target.

The Special Forces reported (as journalists and refugees had been doing for years) that most Afghans were not happy with the Taliban or al-Qaeda, and one leaflet said,

Do you enjoy being ruled by the Taliban? Are you proud to live a life of fear? Are you happy to see the place your family has owned for generations a terrorist training site?

When American Rangers raided a compound near Kandahar on October 20, they left behind leaflets featuring a photo of New York City firemen raising an American flag over the ruins of the World Trade Center. Above the picture was the text (in the local language), "Freedom Endures." The message was, "We can go wherever we want and here's the reason why." The area where this took place was near the home of Taliban leader Mullah Omar. The raid, and the leaflets, were mainly for psychological effect. A different leaflet had pictures of al-Qaeda fighters, who are mostly Arabs, in the crosshairs of a sniper rifle. The text read, "Drive out the foreign terrorists." This leaflet, and several others, played upon the unpopularity of the foreigners who made up nearly all of al-Qaeda, and most of the Taliban themselves—many of whom were Pakistani Pushtuns. To emphasize the point, another leaflet showed a picture of Taliban religious police whipping a woman in a burqa (who may have shown a bit of ankle). The text said, "Is this the future you want for your women and children?"

By November 8, sixteen million leaflets had been dropped, and the Taliban was taking notice. It announced in late October that loyal Afghans were burning the leaflets and radios. Nevertheless, the leaflets and radio broadcasts did have the intended effect, as was discovered by Special Forces units that ran into better-informed Afghan civilians in late 2001.

When the Taliban collapsed at the end of November 2001, the leaflet and broadcasting campaign changed as well. There were more efforts to catch Taliban and al-Qaeda leaders. For example, leaflets mentioned the twenty-five-million-dollar reward for Osama bin Laden (and lesser rewards for his henchmen). Others warned Afghans about the danger of mines and unexploded bombs. Still further ones and broadcasts told of food and other aid arriving now that the Taliban was gone. There were even anti-drug efforts, reminding Afghans of the damage heroin does to neighboring Islamic populations. That didn't work very well; Afghans simply made too much money off the drug trade. Somewhat more successful were the leaflets imploring Afghans to stop fighting each other over local issues and urging unity and the formation of a new national government.

Successful psychological warfare efforts are rarely noticed, much less fully appreciated. There's a tendency to attribute success to something else, such as bigger, or smarter, bombs. But in Afghanistan, the psychological warfare efforts did have a noticeable effect. And that was no accident. Less successful leafleting and broadcast operations during the Gulf War were noted. Back in 1991, a lot of the leaflets and broadcast scripts were written by Americans with little, or no, knowledge of local conditions. The failure of that campaign was noted, and the Afghanistan operations was conducted using people with a better sense of what pitch would succeed.

The Perfect Soldier knows how to use words and ideas as well as weapons.

THE EYES UP THERE

When American troops went into Afghanistan, they had ninety years of experience with aerial reconnaissance. But it was only in the 1990s that recon systems were available to effectively support the kind of war the Special Forces and commandos were going to fight. Billions of dollars were invested in space satellites for reconnaissance, but these systems lacked one very important ability: They could not hang around. The kind of reconnaissance needed for fighting the Taliban had to be persistent. Even reconnaissance aircraft or helicopters were unable to do that. Indeed, your average recon aircraft was outfitted like a low-flying satellite, using cameras and other sensors to record what was down there as it quickly flew over enemy territory. But the recon drones that had been used, off and on, for more than three decades had finally gotten to the point where they were reliable enough to consistently operate for twelve to twenty-four hours over enemy-held territory. Moreover, the drones were quiet and small enough to go unnoticed, especially at night.

Electronics had gotten smaller, cheaper, and more powerful every year for the last half century—a process that it culminated for the military in the kind of powerful and reliable sensors a small drone aircraft could carry. Drones like the Predator were providing real-time video that could be seen in the Pentagon, White House, and anywhere else if you knew what satellite the feed was bounced off and what the decryption codes were. Another useful recon gadget was the E-8 JOINT STARS (or JSTARS). Like the AWACS, this aircraft had a radar, but it was on the bottom of the aircraft rather than a saucer-shaped device on the top. The primary task of JSTARS is tracking ground activity; they were designed to better integrate air and ground operations by quickly locating targets for our aircraft and coordinating those attacks with friendly ground operations. The radar has two modes: wide area (showing a twelve-by-fifteen-mile area) and detailed (four thousand by five thousand yards). The radar could see out to several hundred miles, and each screen full of information could be saved and brought back later to compare to another view. In this manner, operators could track ground unit movement. Operators could also use the detail mode to pick out specifics details (fortifications, buildings, vehicle deployments, and so on). While the JSTARS didn't arrive on the scene until the first week of November 2001 (when the Taliban was on the brink of collapse), the aircraft quickly made it difficult for the Taliban to move its troops around by truck, even at night. Although JSTARS were often unable to see into mountain passes, much of Afghanistan is flat, and JSTARS are very good at picking up trucks moving along highways on such terrain. And JSTARS can stay up there for more than twelve hours at a time; two or more of them can operate in shifts to provide 24/7 coverage.

WHY AFGHANISTAN HAD TO BE A COMMANDO WAR

A familiar headline goes something like "Pentagon Reluctant to Get Involved in [name your favorite overseas hot spot]." Generals are quite wary of sending troops to far-off battlefields. And the reasons are not political, but logistical. Gone are the days when a president would order the troops to some distant nation and everyone would wait for weeks while the troops got on ships and slowly steamed off to war. We expect instant response, and that means flying the troops in. The trouble is that in too many cases we don't have enough aircraft to get there fast with enough troops to do the job. Get there fast without enough and you just get a lot of Americans killed.

On September 11, 2001, however, after American generals and admirals became aware of who was most likely behind the attack, and that Afghanistan was the battleground, transportation became everyone's main priority. Every war is a "come-as-you-are" war, and the United States had to move on Afghanistan with whatever air transports it had. Afghanistan was landlocked and far from friendly air bases. America could only land small numbers of troops in the month or so after September 11, 2001. Given a year or so, a much larger ground force could be moved into the area. But the people of America weren't going to wait that long. Neither were the terrorists America was now at war with. By the end of September, everyone had done the math, and it was obvious this would have to be a commando war. And so it was.

So let's do the math. In September 2001, the United States had 126 C-5s, a hundred C-17s, and 158 C-141s. Think that's a lot of air transport? Think again.

In late 1999, the United States sent a 133-man communications unit (and five hundred tons of equipment) to join the East Timor peacekeeping operation. Six C-17s and one C-5 were required. Moving a Patriot battalion, essential for shooting down enemy ballistic missiles (SCUDs) and aircraft, requires ninety-eight C-17 flights. What the Air Force transports are needed for is moving heavy or bulky military equipment such as missile launchers, missiles, armored vehicles, and trucks. The military has, for many decades, signed up civilian airlines in a program that allows the Air Force to take over many civilian air transports to move troops and whatever equipment can fit in cargo containers (or overhead racks). A simple yardstick for the ability to transport by air is the "ton mile": how many tons can be moved one mile by all the aircraft available. Currently the U.S. Air Force has a capacity of some forty-nine million ton miles per day. The farther you want to move items, the fewer tons can be moved. Simple math. But there's a catch. The Air Force transports only supply twenty-nine million ton miles; the other twenty million come from the civilian passenger transports.

The U.S. Air Force's Air Transport Command controls nearly all the military's freighter aircraft. While the Air Force is supposed to deal fairly with other services' transport needs, it doesn't work out that way. This became especially true after the Cold War ended. Before that, America had built up a network of air bases (stocked with fuel, bombs, and spare parts) near likely battlefields. Europe and Korea were the two big ones, and the Air Force knew all it had to do was fly more warplanes in and go to war. But with the Soviet Union gone, the next battlefield could be in a lot of out-of-the-way places. So the Air Force prepared to fly all the equipment, munitions, fuel, and technicians to anywhere. It organized Air Expeditionary Wings (AEWs) that would, in many cases, tie up 70 percent of the air transports in the first weeks of an overseas wartime emergency.

The Navy and Marines never planned on using the Air Force's heavy lifters much. So it's the Army that's fighting the Air Force for a larger share of the available ton miles. The Army needs a lot of ton miles. Even the new lightweight Army Medium Brigade has 10,500 tons of armored vehicles. Take them eight thousand miles and you've used up eighty-four million ton miles. Add in the other equipment in the brigade and you're way over a hundred million ton miles. Remember, the Air Force can only move twenty-nine million ton miles of heavy equipment a day.

The Army wants to get people to the hot spot fast, feeling that troops on the ground are the best solution to such problems. The Air Forces disagrees, believing that getting airpower there first will work best. The Army says that its approach is tried and true; the Air Force says that times have changed and the AEW approach makes more sense given all the new technology. An AEW is a collection of sixty to one hundred combat and support aircraft organized and trained to fly overseas quickly to any hot spot. The Air Force rests its case on what it did against Iraqi forces in 1991, what it thought it did against the Serbs in 1999, and what bombers did in Afghanistan during 2001.

In the Arabian desert, the Air Force was very effective. But this has been the case with warplanes versus tanks in the desert since the 1920s. It's got nothing to do with better technology and everything to do with the desert being a place where you can't hide. In the Balkans, you can hide, and bombing the Serbs was an exercise in futility that airpower advocates have not yet come to terms with. Then there's the problem of the many peacekeeping situations in which you're faced with lightly armed enemy infantry on the ground. Airpower has a particularly difficult time with this kind of target. And these situations are the ones most likely to require a lot of friendly infantry on the scene in a hurry. Smart bombs have a hard time dealing with irregulars lurking in the bush.

In Afghanistan, when the Talibs tried to stand and fight, the bombs got them. When the Taliban and al-Qaeda dispersed, the United States announced that it might take several years to find them all.

Many Air Force commanders really believe that modern airpower is the most efficient way to deal with emergencies. There was a similar conceit in the 1600s, when nations possessing fleets of cannon-armed ships realized that they had more firepower on those ships than any army. Somebody gives you a hard time, just send in some warships and blast their cities. Before too long, everyone found out that all that firepower had its limitations. While some targets were very vulnerable (port cities, enemy shipping), many others were not. When it comes to warfare, one weapon does not fit all situations.

THE PERFECT
SOLDIERS

Around the world, nations are buying into the idea that highly trained volunteer soldiers are the best way to go. For ground troops, this means "ordinary" soldiers being trained up to standards that would have made them commandos sixty years ago. In a parallel development, a lot of new military gadgets are in the works, as well as some startling new tactics that will only work when used by well-trained troops. The future belongs to the Perfect Soldier, and you saw how that worked in Afghanistan.

But don't forget what a long, torturous past the Perfect Soldier has had. A century ago, generals thought elite troops were passé. Before World War I, it was believed that modern training methods could create millions of soldiers prepared to operate at a high, consistent, and decisive level of effectiveness. Not perfect, but good enough and available in large quantities. Then came 1914, and the Great War. Two years and more than ten million casualties later, it was obvious that something was wrong. In a pattern repeated many times in the next century, Perfect Soldiers came to the rescue. Or at least tried to. The German *Stosstruppen* knocked Russia out of the war in 1917, almost did the same to Italy later that year, and almost won the war for Germany in 1918. Had not a million American troops arrived in 1917 and 1918, the storm troopers would have pulled it off.

The Germans lost the war, but they didn't forget what their well-trained and -equipped storm troopers had almost accomplished. They proceeded to train their entire army up to storm trooper standards. Nothing magic was involved; just intense, well-thought-out training and excellent leadership. Officers and NCOs were carefully selected and given more training than those of any other nation. While most military experts dismissed German efforts after World War II ("after all, they've lost two world wars"), some noted that losing wars and losing battles were two different things. For example, a closer examination of combat records revealed that German troops generally outfought their opponents. Even after adjusting for variables (such as defenses, and who was attacking), German troops inflicted more casualties than the soldiers they fought. Not every combat division was the same in combat capability, and it was revealing to see how combat divisions matched up in effectiveness. It turned out that most generals were unaware of some of these differences in combat effectiveness. If it hadn't been for the research of American historian Trevor Dupuy in the 1970s and 1980s, these critical differences might still sit unnoticed in musty archives. Dupuy's calculations brought forth the reasons why some divisions were better than others—mainly training and leadership. Division commanders had (and still have) discretion in how their troops are trained. During World War II, some divisions set up their own training operations and made sure troops and combat leaders received all the training they needed. This made a major difference on the battlefield. Ironically, the Germans noticed it more than the Allies. They accurately identified the best-trained and -led American and British divisions. After the war, such analyses were generally ignored. After all, the Germans had lost.

But in the early 1970s, with the Vietnam War out of the way, American Army leaders began to concentrate on the future. They did this by more diligently studying the past. What began the reform activity was the 1973 Arab-Israeli war. The Israelis won this one, but not in six days as they had in 1967. It took them sixteen days, and a lot more casualties. Two aspects of this war caught the attention of American generals. One was the speed and violence made possible by the modern weapons each side was using. But more important, the Israelis were using the same attitudes toward training as the Germans had in the two world wars. While many pundits dismissed the Israeli victory as inevitable because they were fighting Arabs, a closer look at the battles revealed that Israeli troops were exceptionally well-trained and -led.

The American generals in the 1970s then looked at their current foe, the mighty Red Army of the Soviet Union. This force was arrayed from East Germany back to Moscow, ready to march to the English Channel by using wave after wave of tanks, infantry, and warplanes. There was no way the United States and its allies were going to match the Red Army in quantity, so it would have to be done with quality.

Veterans of the Vietnam War remembered that about 10 percent of the American infantry were SOG commandos, Special Forces, or LRRPS, and that they did very well against the North Vietnamese— and usually in the North Vietnamese backyard. And now the U.S. armed forces were dealing with the end of conscription. All troops would be volunteers. Maybe the solution to all this was . . . the Perfect Soldier?

While the media talked about the American "high-tech armed forces" in Vietnam, the troops themselves knew that there would have to be a substantial increase in soldier skills before they could expect to fight outnumbered and win. There was also the realization that press releases touting great new weapons would not add any combat power right now. Thus the popularity of the phrase "come-as-you-are war." This outbreak of pragmatism led to a largely unspoken, but very real shift to the idea that every combat soldier should be a Perfect Soldier.

PERFECT SOLDIERS EVERYWHERE

Nobody called the new concept "the Perfect Soldier," but it did incorporate the use of better-trained and -led volunteer troops. The idea was to find a way to consistently produce combat troops who were much better at their job than enemy soldiers. In a way, the Army had men like that all along. Ever since World War II, there were the two airborne divisions. These were all-volunteer units with high standards. This worked. Then in 1974, the all-volunteer Ranger regiment was reformed. That worked. The Special Forces had been around since the early 1950s. That worked. By the end of the 1970s, there was Delta Force. That worked. The generals began to see a pattern. The Perfect Soldier was not only the future, but had been around for much of the past. From now on, everyone was going to be a Perfect Soldier. Well, not quite.

A key component of the Perfect Soldier was training a group of soldiers over weeks and months until they not only knew their jobs, but knew each other very well. While the U.S. Army received more money for training in the 1980s, and did good things with it, there was still a problem with keeping units together. During World War II, the United States had adopted the idea that soldiers were parts of a machine and could be used interchangeably. In the decade after the war, research revealed that this was not the case. Combat-experienced troops were not about to trust unknown newcomers, and they tended to shun them. This was the main reason why rookies became casualties so quickly. Most other armies pulled battered units out of combat for as long as possible to rebuild them with new troops. They knew that it was much better to introduce replacements when the unit was behind the lines. That way, the veterans could get to know the newcomers without immediate risk to life and limb. When the unit went back into action, the rookies stood a much better chance of surviving.

In wartime, units are put together, trained, and sent off after having spent enough time together to know each other's strengths and weaknesses. Units take casualties, but the survivors are people who know each and how to survive in battle. These men become a cadre of experienced veterans that keeps the unit operating. Many foreign nations carry this approach over to peacetime, with units being recruited from the same region and recruits kept together in the same unit for their entire service. Reserve units also tend to follow this approach, and it has been noted that despite being full of older, part-time soldiers, they often perform better in combat than active-duty units.

But the U.S. military became obsessed with "ticket punching"— getting a large number of the "right" assignments to enhance promotion prospects. Despite complaints from the troops and evidence piling up that the practice was counterproductive, troops were not allowed to stay with units long enough to become effective. Except in the commando units. Special Forces, SEALs, Rangers, and Delta Force were assignments where you stayed for years, got very good at your job, and got to know the guys you were working with.

Such was not the case with the other combat units. And it's not that the problem went unrecognized. As early as 1980, Army leaders announced plans to solve it. None of the solutions worked. In 2002, a new round of reforms was proposed, which may, or may not, solve the problem. In the meantime, the rapid turnover of troops in regular combat units prevents them from achieving the higher effectiveness standards of the elite, Special Forces, and commando units.

Meanwhile, it wasn't just the Army trying to create Perfect Soldiers; the U.S. Marine Corps had turned itself into an elite organization from the beginning. And was continuing a long tradition.

MARINES

Marines have always tended to be elite troops, mainly because their original function was to provide security for officers (from often hostile sailors) on warships. In battle, Marines provided an elite combat force that was useful more than a century ago when fighting ships often crashed together and the crews engaged in hand-to-hand combat. A third function, which eventually became their main function, was to provide security troops for those times when some of the crew went ashore in hostile territory.

Over the past century, Marines have repackaged themselves as amphibious commandos. The British Marines quickly made the shift during World War II and have thought of themselves this way ever since—as Royal Marine Commandos. The largest Marine force on the planet, the U.S. Marine Corps, never adopted the *commando* name, but they certainly have the commando attitude.

There was one problem: The last amphibious assault against a defended shore was in 1950, when U.S. Marines invaded at Inchon, Korea. This was arguably the most difficult amphibious operation of all time, but there hasn't been another one since. Noting this, the U.S. Marines again transformed themselves, depending more on helicopters for moving inland from their ships. While the traditional Marine divisions still exist, U.S. Marines are organized for action in miniature armies (expeditionary units) of varying size, depending on shipping and other transport available. The basic expeditionary unit is a Marine infantry battalion with enough support units to allow it to operate by itself in enemy territory—fifteen hundred to two thousand troops altogether.

Marine attitudes were heavily influenced by their World War II experiences, of making dozens of amphibious assaults against well-prepared and determined foes. More so than other military operations, amphibious assaults are very susceptible to things going wrong, with the worst possible results. Speed is imperative, in both planning and execution. A Marine's greatest asset is an ability to improvise. It is not enough to possess uncommon courage in the face of the enemy. Equally important is the ability to make do in the face of your own side's shortcomings. Things will go wrong, often very wrong. The USMC is accustomed to taking heavy losses, heavier than those of normal combat, in order to compensate for the uncertainties of amphibious operations. While it's easier to avoid, or improvise around, the mistakes in the first place, there is often neither the time nor the opportunity.

The Marines also have an advantage in possessing their own Air Force. Marine pilots are noted for their ability to give excellent support for their fellow Marines on the ground. The Marines also have use of a fleet of amphibious ships manned and maintained by the U.S. Navy. Thus the Marines are often on the spot, or at least offshore, when a new crisis develops. The Marines are still able to muster a division-sized amphibious force that, with its air wing and various support troops, adds up to some fifty thousand men, more than three hundred armored vehicles, and over 250 aircraft, all carried by about 1.2 million tons of shipping.

In the early 1980s, the Marines noted how special (commando) operations were becoming a permanent part of the military landscape. Since they'd always had (and really believed in) a "can-do" attitude, they came up with the Special Operations Capable (SOC) program. At first, it was an attempt to train Marines for new kinds of jobs: hostage rescue, civil affairs, peacekeeping, and so on. The Marines soon found that commando operations covered a lot of territory, however, and for most of the 1990s, Marine units were left to use their imagination to come up with appropriate training programs. By 1989, the Marines finally wrote it all down, although it's telling that they called their main SOC training publication a "playbook." But there is still no absolute guide for exactly what SOC training is. Local commanders are left to give their Marines as much as they can for the types of SOC operations they expect to encounter in their part of the world. The SOC missions can range from hostage rescue to commando raids and peacekeeping.

This has not bothered the Marines. If a Marine unit hustles and shows that it has acquired a bunch of new SOC skills, then the world becomes a somewhat safer place for Americans. The Marines won't perform the special operations with quite the skill and polish as the Special Forces, SEALs, SAS, or Delta Force, but they will get the job done. And if the Marines are the only ones nearby when an emergency develops, they can do what has to be done. You can't ask much more of a Perfect Soldier.

The Marines do have about a thousand troops whom they consider to be commandos in the classical sense. These are the Force Recon LRRPs. The idea of Marine special long-range patrol units goes back to World War II, and was reinforced during Vietnam. Each Marine division has a company of them. In addition, there are two Force Recon battalions—one active, one reserve. The Force Recon battalions have three companies. "A" company is for training new LRRP candidates. "B" company is for those who have survived the LRRP training. "C" company contains the most experienced operators, who are used for the most difficult recon tasks. Force Recon is ready to send small patrols anywhere in the world, because the Marines see the entire planet as their beat. Given this worldwide reach, the Marines have been negotiating to put the Force Recon battalions under SOCOM control, something they declined to do when SOCOM was first established.

PARATROOPERS

It was noted, during World War II, that dropping paratroopers behind enemy lines, while effective in weakening the enemy, tended to cause enormous casualties among the paratroopers. After World War II, they came to be seen as elite infantry that, while trained to jump out of airplanes into combat, were more useful as a sort of giant SWAT team—in effect, commandos delivered by air. When there was a military emergency somewhere, you could always depend on the paratroopers to go in and do whatever had to be done. In addition to their parachute training, the paratroopers were given a lot of infantry training. Paratroopers were carefully selected and well led. Well, most of the time. In many nations, paratroopers were selected mainly for their political reliability. These politroopers ended up as paratroopers in name only. But they were often useful when the "president for life" needed some dirty work done. The wealthier nations tended to maintain a brigade or two of real paratroopers and use them for emergencies overseas. Paratroopers are expensive to maintain and get chewed up pretty quickly when fighting mechanized forces. When selected, trained, and led correctly, paratroopers are excellent elite troops. Not quite as good as your classic commandos, but good enough for a lot of the jobs commandos are called on to do.

The United States and Russia, which maintained the largest paratrooper forces in the world after World War II, also learned that paratroopers were more useful if delivered by helicopter, rather than parachute. No one has ever come up with a solution to the "scattering" problem when you drop large numbers of paratroopers at once. Especially at night. Moreover, arriving by parachute can expose the troops to enemy fire. And landing by parachute is itself dangerous, injuring up to (depending on the weather and landing area) several percent of the jumpers. Using helicopters solves most of these problems, as the United States discovered in Vietnam and the Russians in Afghanistan. As a result, most of the world's paratroopers also practice traveling by helicopter.

Paratroopers are increasingly being trained for commando missions. This is not all that difficult, because paratroopers are already carefully selected and trained in basic ground combat techniques.

SOCOM AND SPECIAL OPERATIONS DOCTRINE

During the 1980s, American commandos not only survived peacetime (which is often lethal to commando organizations), but actually thrived in it. In 1986, all American commandos were organized into the Special Operations Command (SOCOM), which meant lots more money and considerably more influence in the Pentagon. The reasons for this development are, like most situations involving commandos, stranger than fiction.

By the late 1970s, the all-volunteer army, plus the realization we would have to "fight outnumbered and win" in any future "come-as-you-are war," suddenly made commandos more acceptable to the brass than at any time since the end of World War II. What changed attitudes was the search for "force multipliers" and the realization that the Soviets were forming commando (Spetsnaz) units. A force multiplier is a tactic, weapon, or training technique that makes your troops a lot more effective on the battlefield. In effect, it multiplies the effectiveness of your military force. The new attitude toward training was fueled in part by the past success of the very well-prepared commandos. It was this success that led the Soviets to create their own commando units in the 1960s. The Soviets (as we later found out after the Cold War ended) were only doing this because they noted that Western nations still had commandos. But in the West, it was assumed that the Soviets were on to something new and threatening and must know something we didn't. This was a common situation throughout the Cold War, with each superpower coming up with new weapons or tactics and the other side promptly copying them just to keep up.

But the key factor that allowed commandos all this attention and money was newly elected president Reagan's preference for commando operations. Part of this was driven by the Russian invasion of Afghanistan in 1979. U.S. Special Forces troops were soon sent to Pakistan to train the Afghans to better use the weapons we were giving them. Reagan also believed there were many other Russian-backed guerrilla wars in which American commandos could make a difference. The 1979 failure to rescue the American hostages in Iran, for example, and coordination problems with commandos in the 1983 Grenada operation indicated not failure of the commando concept but a failure to give the troops the kind of money and leadership they needed. And then there was the continuing threat of terrorism, for which commandos were seen as the only visible protection.

These factors led to reform in the military. What had the biggest impact on U.S. Special Operations troops, however, was the 1986 Goldwater-Nichols Act. This was a complex bit of legislation that reorganized the Department of Defense. One new item was the establishment of the U.S. Special Operations Command (USSOCOM). This was a major step up for the commandos. SOCOM was now a "major command," with a four-star general in charge. The SOCOM commander was put in charge of all commandos in the Department of Defense. This was a unique situation. Normally, troops from different services don't operate in the same major unit ("command") like this. But the commandos didn't mind. Some of the service chiefs did; they saw their men as useful "assets" for their service. But there was another trend in the 1980s Department of Defense: "thinking purple." This meant all the services cooperating more closely and thinking about each other's capabilities and problems. Combine all the colors of each service's uniforms and you get purple, and everyone in the Department of Defense was encouraged to get with this program. Not everyone did, but the commandos were enthusiastic about the proposition. They had long noted that commandos had more in common with other commandos (from different services, or even different nations) than with other people in their own service.

About two-thirds of SOCOM's troops came from the Army, which had its own Special Forces, Rangers, Delta Force, Psyops, and Civil Affairs and special aviation units. The next largest contribution (about 20 percent) comes from the Air Force, which has several different types of airpower-related commandos and special aircraft units. The Navy provided its SEALs and the special boat units needed to land them in hostile environments. The Marine Force Recon LRRPs were the only commando units in the Department of Defense that did not join SOCOM at the beginning.

Even within this elite organization, there is an elite, and this is the twelve hundred or so troops of Delta Force and the Naval Special Warfare Development Group, or Dev Group (formerly SEAL Team Six). These are used for the most dangerous commando and counterterrorism missions. About a third of these troops are actual operators, or commandos; the rest are support troops who train regularly, and operate closely, with the commandos.

At the other end of the scale you have the U.S. Army Civil Affairs (CA), who work with foreign civilians after the fighting has died down, and Psychological Operations (Psyops) battalions. There are thirteen CA battalions (twelve of them in the reserves) and five Psyops battalions (two of them active duty). These men and women are not elite infantry, or even ordinary grunts, but are included in SOCOM partly because of tradition (Special Forces started out as a Psyops outfit) and partly because Special Forces works closely with both groups. The Special Forces consider CA and Psyops units as necessary support troops for most jobs the Special Forces are handed.

What USSOCOM is and what it can do is laid down in Section 167 of Title 10, U.S. Code ("Unified combatant command for special operations forces"). This was an interesting piece of legislation. On the surface, it made sense to unify Special Operations Forces. Just getting everyone to use the same training standards, operational procedures, and vocabulary made all American commandos more effective, and eliminated confusion when Special Operations troops from different services operated together. With all the commandos belonging to SOCOM, it was easy to get SEALs, Special Forces, Delta Force, and Rangers to keep in touch with each other and share information (tricks of the trade, experience with weapons and equipment, and so forth).

But there was a very important, and often overlooked, amendment to Title 10. This was Section 2011, which gave commanders of Special Operations Forces the authority to deploy and pay for training of U.S. and foreign troops if "the primary purpose of the training . . . shall be to train the special operations forces of the combatant command." This meant the Department of Defense could send SOCOM troops overseas to foreign nations quickly (without getting congressional approval) and discreetly (the media doesn't even know about, or notice, most of these missions). This provided flexibility for the military to do something in a situation that wasn't officially (or actually) a war, but was getting a lot of media attention. In these circumstances, sending in Special Forces advisers or trainers will often calm things down, without Congress and the president being pressured to "authorize military action." SEALs and even Delta Force have been sent overseas under the same circumstances. Even before September 11, 2001, Special Forces troops spent about half their time overseas, training or just working with foreign armies in forty to fifty different nations. Section 2011 has proved quite popular with almost everyone—the military, the president, the State Department, and Congress—because it allows the use of a little military muscle in an intelligent and circumspect way. The Special Forces have proved to be capable "soldier-diplomats," being very careful to avoid unpleasant incidents. Because Special Forces troops have language skills and knowledge of the local culture, they can go in and find out what's going on in places that the State Department or CIA has a hard time visiting (military bases and areas where fighting is going on, for example). This was why Special Forces troops were in Uzbekistan (next to Afghanistan) training Uzbek troops during the summer of 2001.

Section 2011 and SOCOM changed how Special Operations troops were used. The SOCOM commander, being a four-star general, could talk with the other senior brass and sell them on the idea of using SOCOM troops. Whenever generals and admirals get together, there is a lot of networking and brainstorming. Since SOCOM is a "specialized organization" that usually supports operations by the more traditional organizations, there is a certain amount of selling involved. Through the 1990s, SOCOM troops worked with regular units more frequently. This was largely due to SOCOM "marketing itself" successfully to the other services. This paid off in the long run. For example, it was no accident that the Navy offered one of its carriers to serve as a floating air base for SOCOM's 160th Aviation Regiment during the Afghanistan war. That sort of thing happens because the SOCOM commander has been hanging out with senior admirals regularly. But even with this new, improved relationship between SOCOM and the rest of the Department of Defense, many generals, particularly in the Army, were still a little leery of the SOCOM warriors and their independent ways. This has been slowly changing over the last two decades, but the attitude is still there.

The Special Forces had a long relationship with the CIA, and this carried over to SOCOM. Relationships were also developed with the State Department, something that the Special Forces had long noted the British SAS doing with its Foreign Ministry. By the end of the 1990s, it was common for at least fifty Special Forces, SEAL, and Delta Force teams to be abroad at any time. In addition to providing first-rate military assistance to foreign nations (usually in the local language), the SOCOM troops established personal relationships with men in these foreign forces, and personally observed exactly what was going on in that part of the world. The CIA and State Department began to depend on these reports. The SOCOM operators were experienced, elite troops and thus able to give accurate and insightful accounts of what they saw.

SOCOM defined its operations ("special operations") as missions undertaken by small numbers of elite troops with military, political, economic, or psychological objectives. SOCOM is expected to use imaginative ("unconventional") means and to operate in hostile, denied ("you aren't supposed to be there"), or politically sensitive ("don't let the media know you're there") areas. SOCOM is expected to be ready for lots of peacetime action, as well as wartime operations. SOCOM is expected to deal with political and diplomatic issues, and cope with missions carrying a lot of physical or political risk. SOCOM is recognized and respected because the United States has proved that it can create these kinds of troops. So far, the only thing that has limited SOCOM is the reluctance of the president to risk its operators in highly dangerous tasks. This is a noticeable change from the past, when American leaders were noted for their boldness when dealing with troublesome foreigners. President Clinton was reluctant to take chances using SOCOM. His successor, George W. Bush, was less reluctant. After September 11, 2001, SOCOM was basically turned loose in any area that smelled of terrorist activity.

A major, but generally unnoticed, SOCOM accomplishment was the establishment of standards for missions SOCOM troops would participate in. The Department of Defense (DoD) put it this way in 1998:

SOF ROLES AND MISSIONS

Special operations forces have a dual heritage. They are one of the nation's key penetration and strike forces, able to respond to specialized contingencies across the conflict spectrum with stealth, speed, and precision. They are also warrior-diplomats capable of influencing, advising, training, and conducting operations with foreign forces, officials, and populations. These two distinct missions are complementary, allowing SOF personnel to gain regional expertise and access that enhances their ability to react to any contingency in any region of the world. One of these two generic SOF roles is at the heart of each of the following special operations core missions:

Counterproliferation. SOF are a principal part of DoD's counterproliferation capabilities. SOF provide DoD a ground force option short of a major theater war scenario to seize, recover, disable, render ineffective, or destroy weapons of mass destruction (WMD) and associated technology. Additionally, SOF skills may be used in support of diplomatic, arms control, and export control efforts.

Combating Terrorism. Provide the DoD offensive (counterterrorism) and defensive (antiterrorism) capabilities and programs to detect, deter, and respond to all forms of terrorism.

Foreign Internal Defense. Organize, train, advise, and assist legitimate host nation military and paramilitary forces to enable these forces to free and protect their societies from subversion, lawlessness, and insurgency.

Special Reconnaissance. Conduct reconnaissance and surveillance actions to obtain or verify information concerning the capabilities, intentions, and activities of an actual or potential enemy or to secure data concerning characteristics of a particular area.

Direct Action. Conduct short-duration strikes and other small-scale offensive actions to seize, destroy, capture, recover, or inflict damage on designated personnel or matériel.

Psychological Operations (PSYOP). Induce or reinforce foreign attitudes and behavior favorable to the U.S. or friendly nation objectives by planning and conducting operations to convey information to foreign audiences to influence their emotions, motives, objective reasoning, and ultimately the behavior of foreign governments, organizations, groups, and individuals.

Civil Affairs (CA). Facilitate commanders in establishing, maintaining, or influencing relations between military forces and civil authorities, both governmental and nongovernmental, and the civilian population in a friendly, neutral, or hostile area of operations.

Unconventional Warfare. Organize, train, equip, advise, and assist indigenous and surrogate forces in military and paramilitary operations, normally of long duration.

Information Operations. Achieve information superiority by affecting adversary information, information-based processes, information systems, and computer-based networks while defending one's own information systems.

Collateral Activities. In the following areas, SOF share responsibility with other forces, as directed by the geographic combatant commanders:

Coalition Support. Integrate coalition units into multinational military operations by training with coalition partners and providing communications.

Humanitarian Assistance. Provide assistance of limited scope and duration to supplement or complement the efforts of host nation civil authorities or agencies to relieve or reduce the results of natural or man-made disasters.

Security Assistance. Provide training assistance in support of legislated programs which provide U.S. defense articles, military training, and other defense-related services.

Combat Search and Rescue. Penetrate air defense systems and conduct joint air, ground, or sea operations deep within hostile or denied territory at night or in adverse weather to recover personnel during wartime or contingency operations.

Humanitarian Demining Operations. Reduce or eliminate the threat to noncombatants posed by mines and other explosive devices by training host nation personnel in their recognition, identification, marking, and safe destruction. Provide instruction in program management, medical, and mine awareness activities.

Counterdrug Activities. Train host nation counterdrug forces to detect, monitor, and counter the production, trafficking, and use of illegal drugs.

Special Activities. Plan and conduct actions abroad in support of national foreign policy objectives, subject to direction imposed by Executive Order and in conjunction with a Presidential finding and congressional oversight, so that the role of the U.S. government is not apparent or acknowledged publicly.

Peace Operations. Assist in peacekeeping operations, peace enforcement operations, and other military operations in support of diplomatic efforts to establish and maintain peace.

One reason for the 1998 announcement was to remind everyone that SOCOM was getting with the peacekeeping and humanitarian assistance programs the government had been pushing throughout the 1990s. The U.S. military was not too happy with this trend, but SOCOM saw it as another opportunity. This attitude is incorporated in a set of guidelines SOCOM adopted early on and called the "Special Operations Imperatives." These were developed for the U.S. Army Special Forces, but were adopted for all of SOCOM. While these imperatives are partly in hard-to-understand milspeak, they are:

- **"Understand the operational environment."** Research the geography, culture, and history of the area you will be operating in, which means paying attention to intelligence and reconnaissance. SOCOM spends a lot of money and effort on this.
- **"Recognize political implications."** The OSS background of the Special Forces and their long association with the CIA ensured that SOCOM would never forget the political aspect of any military operation.
- **"Facilitate interagency activities."** SOCOM saw itself as a special service provider for the other, larger, parts of the Department of Defense. This was common sense, but it was also a matter of self preservation. If SOCOM did not make itself useful, the other services would support getting rid of SOCOM.
- **"Engage the threat discriminately."** Again, being a small operation, SOCOM saw the advantages of just getting the job done, not breaking things and killing people. Even Delta Force and the SEALs will engage in psychological warfare on a foe rather than just trying to kill him. It's no accident that the Department of War changed its name to the Department of Defense in 1947.
- **"Consider long-term effects."** SOCOM sees itself as a fire brigade, called out to take care of brushfires, and these are often temporary fixes to situations that have been going on for decades. So SOCOM's policy is to try to make more allies than enemies when out in the field.
- **"Ensure legitimacy and credibility of Special Operations activities."** Another way of saying, "Don't get caught doing something you're

not supposed to be doing." This is not always possible in the some-times murky world of Special Operations.

- **"Anticipate and control psychological effects."** More wisdom from past experience. SOCOM is largely fighting for "hearts and minds" and uses weapons only as a backup.
- **"Apply capabilities indirectly."** SOCOM sends out as few people as possible, often four or fewer troops, so the direct approach rarely works.
- **"Develop multiple options."** Experience has shown that the best-prepared force, with the largest number of solutions for a problem, has the best chance of winning.
- **"Ensure long-term sustainment."** One reason so many people in SOCOM are there to support the operators is because you want to be able to sustain your operators for as long as it takes. It's good for morale, and many missions will fail if you can't keep your guys supplied for as long as they need it.
- **"Provide sufficient intelligence."** The most valuable weapon a SOCOM operation has is information—thus the importance of in-telligence. SOCOM forces are small and have little room for error. Many proposed SOCOM operations are called off because of inade-quate intelligence.
- **"Balance security and synchronization."** In plain English, this means that if you do too much to protect your operators, they won't be able to do their job. Synchronization is what you do when you work with other American or allied forces. SOCOM operations are dangerous, but usually not suicidal.

Another, less official-sounding and shorter list of "imperatives" has long circulated among the troops. There are generally referred to as the "Special Operations Forces Truths." They speak for themselves.

- Humans are more important than hardware.
- Quality is better than quantity.
- Special Operations Forces cannot be mass-produced.
- Competent Special Operations Forces cannot be created after emer-gencies occur.

SOCOM set training and readiness standards, and defined a list of missions that members of SOCOM could most likely expect to undertake. These are called "Special Operations Principal Missions." (Naturally, SOCOM is always ready to do anything that needs be done—preferably legal.) Letter codes are a shorthand for the type of mission:

- **Direct Action (DA)** operations are small-scale, and usually short-duration, offensive operations. This covers a lot of situations that involve seizing or destroying personnel or matériel. Tactical techniques used to carry out these missions include a raid (a quick attack, followed by a retreat), ambush, or direct assault (a slower and more involved attack). Commandos may also use mines or other explosive devices or call in fire from bombers or artillery. Also available for use are portable rocket or missile launchers. Sabotage is also a possibility. SEALs, for example, are trained to attach explosives to ships.
- **Combating Terrorism (CBT)** is a highly specialized, resource-intensive mission. Some SOF units maintain a high state of readiness to conduct CBT operations. This is what Delta Force was originally formed for (and it costs more than a hundred million dollars a year just to keep Delta in business). CBT activities include anti-terrorism (AT, defending against terrorist attacks) and counterterrorism (CT, going after known terrorists after they have attacked). Terrorism missions include things like recovering hostages or sensitive material from terrorist organizations, attacking of terrorist bases and infrastructure, and coming up with ways to reduce vulnerability to terrorism.
- **Foreign Internal Defense (FID)** is a basic Special Forces job and involves organizing, training, advising, and assisting military and paramilitary forces in a foreign nation. This is why Special Forces tend to specialize in a specific part of the world. To do this kind of work well, you should speak the local language and understand the local customs.
- **Unconventional Warfare (UW)** includes guerrilla warfare, subversion of hostile governments, sabotage, intelligence activities, evasion and escape (rescuing friendly pilots, or agents, from enemy territory), and other "war in the shadows" activities. During peacetime, these operations tend to be more political, while in wartime the emphasis is on supporting military operations. In peacetime, for example,

evasion and escape might involve getting friendly agents out of a place like Iraq. In wartime, the same type of mission might involve going into Iraq to retrieve a downed pilot.

- **Special Reconnaissance (SR)** is information gathering in far-off, and usually dangerous, places. You send commandos to look around when satellites, recon aircraft, or spies are unable to get the job done. There are several different types of SR missions, including Environmental Reconnaissance (checking on terrain and climate in an area where larger military operations are planned), Armed Reconnaissance (locating and attacking targets of opportunity), Coastal Patrol and Interdiction (in an area where you suspect hostile forces, or drug smugglers, are operating), Target and Threat Assessment (confirming where targets are in enemy territory), and Post-strike Reconnaissance (confirming whether targets in enemy territory were destroyed).
- **Psychological Operations (PSYOP)** uses whatever works to make foreign populations more pro-American—basically propaganda and spin control against foreign governments, organizations, groups, and individuals. It's not all dropping leaflets and radio broadcasts. Often it's dealing directly with foreign journalists and planting stories.
- **Civil Affairs (CA)** assists military operations establishing, maintaining, influencing, or exploiting relations between military forces and civil authorities, both governmental and nongovernmental, and the civilian population in a friendly, neutral, or hostile area of operation. A lot of this is basically making sure that foreign aid is distributed efficiently and working to establish good relations with the locals.
- **Information Operations (IO)** are really a spin off from Psyops. Information war became all the rage in the Department of Defense during the 1990s. The only new wrinkle with information war is that it pays closer attention to the Internet and information systems (something that sharp Psyops operators would not have missed). Recognizing this, IO stuff basically becomes something involving DA, SR, PSYOP, and CA missions. All this is laid out in DODD S-3600.1 and JP 3–13 Draft. Now you know.
- **Counterproliferation of Weapons of Mass Destruction (CP)** is doing whatever it takes to seize, destroy, render safe, capture, or recover

weapons of mass destruction (WMD). Commandos are ideal for monitoring and enforcing compliance with arms-control treaties. Commandos can also undertake SR and DA missions to locate and interdict sea, land, and air shipments of dangerous materials or weapons. SOCOM has the main responsibility for organizing, training, equipping, and otherwise preparing to conduct operations in support of American counterproliferation objectives.

In addition to their military value, Special Forces have a substantial psychological one as well. Enemy commanders know that the United States has the capability to put commandos and Special Forces in their rear areas. Depending on whom we're fighting, the possible presence of American commandos would cause some enemy generals to send large numbers of troops to hunt them down. It's happened before. During the Vietnam War, two thousand Special Forces troops ran patrols in North Vietnamese–controlled Laos that tied up more than thirty thousand North Vietnamese troops. American commandos have learned from that experience, and deliberately cultivate their reputation to generate the maximum fear in the minds of potential enemy commanders. And the fear is not entirely misplaced.

HEARTS AND MINDS

Psychological warfare is an ancient military specialty, but it only got recognized as a separate military career field in the twentieth century. Actually, World War II was when psychological warfare became a popular item. At first it was the dramatic impact of mass propaganda by the Nazis and communists that impressed everyone. It wasn't long before propaganda was being used on the battlefield.

Before that, what we now think of as psychological warfare was considered just another form of deception. Deception is largely a mental game. While camouflage, for example, involves a lot of hard work, its effect is dependent on the enemy believing he isn't seeing what is there. Between opposing generals, and to a lesser extent opposing troops, it's a battle of wits. If one general understands the other better, that provides a huge advantage for some effective deception. The classic example is one general knowing what deceptions his opponent is prone to fall for. This is all sort of like a chess game, where this form of deception is widely practiced. It's a mind game; it's psychological warfare.

While it's easier to describe deception techniques, all of these depend on how the commanders involved use psychology. The most common reason for a deception failing is that the putative victim simply doesn't fall for it. As a result, psychological warfare is considered a riskier operation than simply bombing someone because it is so much more unpredictable. But there have been enough successes in the last sixty years to prompt the American military to invest a lot of money and manpower into psychological warfare. This type of military operation rarely wins spectacular victories, but usually provides a lot of little successes. During the 1991 Gulf War, however, psychological warfare did strike gold. Once coalition warplanes had isolated Iraqi troops in the desert, they were hit with radio, loudspeaker, and leaflet appeals to surrender. When the ground forces advanced, eighty-seven thousand Iraqi soldiers did surrender, many clutching the surrender leaflets.

Realizing that most people get their information via electronic media (radio, television, Internet), U.S. Psychological Warfare troops increasingly depend on getting to enemy troops via electronic means. Even the poorest nations have lots of radios, and American Psychological Warfare forces have radio broadcasting capability (with both ground and airborne broadcasting equipment). The airborne equipment is particularly useful, for psychological warfare is more effective if it's applied early on.

Once your troops are on the ground, they have to deal with civilians (who may be friendly, or not). Civil Affairs troops are the folks who deal with any civilians in the combat zone. This has always been a problem, or, as many commanders have noted, a necessary nuisance. Until the nineteenth century, a general would, at most, assign some officers and troops to go talk to the local civilian leadership to establish some ground rules so locals would not interfere with your military operations. This, as any competent general knew, was preferable to just allowing civilians to wander all over the place (often to be abused or looted by the troops, and to sometimes fight back). But in the last century, dealing with civilians has become a specific military skill. Much of Napoleon's success in the nineteenth century was due to the attention he paid to civil affairs. During World War II, soldiers with foreign language or government administration skills were collected and used to work with the local civilians and avoid problems.

Current Civil Affairs operations were developed from experiences U.S. troops had dealing with occupied Germany and Japan after World War II (1945–1955), and "civic action" operations in the Vietnam war (1960–1975). Since then, Civil Affairs troops have also been used to administer foreign aid and peacekeeping programs. U.S. Army Special Forces see the Civil Affairs troops as follow-up troops for the Special Forces teams that first go in and work out deals with the locals. This enables the more experienced Special Forces to spend more time doing what they do best. The Civil Affairs are trained to continue working with the Special Forces that may have established first contact with the civilian population. More important, the Civil Affairs units know how to work with aid organizations, local and American government officials, and the many details you have to cope with to keep a population pro-American. The Civil Affairs troops are armed, but their weapons are only for self-defense.

Although the Army has long had a monopoly on Civil Affairs troops, the Marines have two company-sized reserve Civil Affairs units. These troops are to be used to deal with civilians during the unique kinds of operations Marines engage in. So far, however, the Marine Civil Affairs troops have been doing pretty much the same thing their Army counterparts (who belong to SOCOM) do. Eventually, there will be a turf war between the SOCOM (Army) and Marine Civil Affairs troops on some future combat zone. Taking its lead from the Marines, the U.S. Air Force is also creating some reserve Civil Affairs units.

Civil Affairs troops can be decisive. They are proving to be essential in Afghanistan, and any invasion will need lots of well-prepared Civil Affairs to handle huge numbers of refugees, prisoners of war, and war criminals.

RANGERS

The three battalions of Rangers are commandos in the classic (World War II) sense. They are light infantrymen who are trained to perform many of the missions the Special Forces normally take care of (such as raids or pilot and equipment recovery) plus something the Special

Forces normally avoid: light infantry operations (using several dozen or more troops).

The Rangers are America's largest emergency response military unit (the smaller one is Delta Force), ready to fly off to an overseas trouble spot in less than twenty-four hours. One of the three Ranger battalions is always assigned to this duty, spending one month on (ready go on eighteen hours' notice) and two months off (doing intensive training). The 75th Ranger Regiment headquarters is at Fort Benning, Georgia. The 1st Battalion of the 75th Regiment (1/75) is stationed at Hunter Army Airfield, Georgia, the 2nd Battalion (2/75) is at Fort Lewis, Washington, and the 3rd Battalion (3/75) is at Fort Benning, Georgia.

But "the Rangers" are more than the 75th Ranger Regiment. There is also the Ranger Training Brigade, which consists of three more Ranger battalions (the 4th, 5th, and 6th), who train those who wish to join the ranger regiment as well those who are there just to become qualified as Rangers. This is an important distinction that is often misunderstood. There is a difference between those who are "tabbed Rangers"—authorized to wear the Ranger tab on their uniform—and those who are simply members of the 75th Ranger Regiment. Any physically fit infantryman (and troops in other job categories the Rangers need) can apply to join the 75th Ranger Regiment if he has already gone through parachute training ("jump school"). He will have to pass a physical fitness test first, because the standards at the 75th Ranger Regiment are very high and there's no point sending any volunteers if they aren't up to the minimum requirements. The Rangers encourage promising new recruits to try for Ranger duty from the beginning. That way, the new recruit goes to the two-week jump school right after fourteen weeks of basic and advanced infantry training and is ready to try out for the rangers. This involves the twenty-six-day Ranger Indoctrination Program (RIP). About 60 percent of the volunteers fail. Those who pass are now members of the 75th Ranger Regiment, but they are not "Rangers." How can this be?

Simply put, Ranger training was always meant to identify and train the elite infantry leaders. The purpose of Ranger School, for its first twenty years (until the 1970s), was to try to provide one Ranger NCO per infantry platoon and one Ranger officer per infantry company. That goal proved impossible to attain. There just weren't enough qualified volunteers for the tough training. But young infantry officers, in particular, were encouraged to attend Ranger School. The Ranger tab helped a soldier's promotion prospects enormously. Until the 1990s, Ranger School was open to anyone in the Army who could pass the physical qualification test. In practice, the Army wanted its hotshot infantry officers and NCOs to attend; eventually anyone not working in, or directly with, the infantry, was not allowed to try out for the school. Even so, about 20 percent of attendees are from other services (Marines, SEALs, and Air Force Special Operations) and another 20 percent from foreign nations (many of which have their own equivalents of Ranger School, some of which are even harder to pass than the U.S. version).

The Ranger School is a sixty-two-day course designed to identify and train elite infantry leaders. The training goes on for about nineteen hours a day, seven days a week. The attrition rate is about 60 percent. The school emphasizes mastery of basic infantry skills and the ability to lead troops under stressful conditions. Students for Ranger School arrive wearing uniforms devoid of rank insignia. Everyone is of equal rank during the sixty-one days of training, with everyone taking turns leading squad-sized units of their fellow students in various exercises. The Ranger School program emphasizes resourcefulness, physical toughness, and the ability to think clearly while under extreme stress (and lack of sleep).

Young soldiers who come into the 75th Ranger Regiment via jump school and the RIP are allowed to attend Ranger School after they have served in the 75th Ranger Regiment for six to twelve months. Because of the heavy workload in the Rangers, few are allowed to serve in the 75th Ranger Regiment for more than two or three years. This goes back to the idea of the Rangers as more a training program than a combat unit. It makes sense, for if you see anyone wearing the Ranger tab, you know he has gone through an extremely tough and selective training program. So while the 75th Ranger Regiment is a tough combat unit, its long-term purpose is to produce effective combat leaders for the rest of the Army, as well as a source of qualified recruits for the Special Forces and Delta Force.

The Ranger regiment actually hasn't seen much action since its formation in 1974. But that has a lot to do with American political leaders' reluctance to get involved in overseas military emergencies.

And if such action is needed, using fewer troops (as in Delta Force, SEALs, or Special Forces) is preferred. The Rangers are seen as the ultimate strategic reserve. So when there's something really, really important that can only be taken care of with several hundred very well-trained infantry, the Rangers are ready to go.

SPECIAL FORCES

After the Vietnam War, the Special Forces got tagged as big-time bad guys. There were the usual reasons, the same ones that caused the Special Forces to be so unpopular with the brass. The Special Forces were operators and professionals. They did what they knew had to be done, often while under the command of generals who had an imperfect grasp of the situation. The Special Forces were tough-looking characters who didn't say much to outsiders. That worked better in Vietnam, where the Special Forces got results up in the mountains, and the generals didn't really care how the "snake eaters" did it. But in peacetime, the brass considered the Special Forces a potential source of embarrassment. To the media, these Green Beret guys must have been up to no good. Congress went along with new popular misconception and, after the Vietnam War, cut Special Forces strength by more than 75 percent (to about three thousand troops). Even Special Forces reserve units were destroyed, which was a major loss of talented operators. Most of the World War II OSS veterans also passed from the scene via retirement, time having caught up with them. Only three Special Forces groups remained. Moreover, the Special Forces were still part of the infantry, and many a Special Forces trooper who wanted to advance his career moved on to some other kind of Army job. The 1970s were not a good time for the Special Forces.

But when Ronald Reagan was elected president, that all changed. Like President Kennedy, Reagan believed in what the Special Forces were up to. By 1982, Special Forces strength was raised to 4,000 troops; by 1985 it was 4,800, plus 800 men in Psychological Warfare units, 250 men in Civil Affairs, and 800 troops taking care of specialized helicopters and aircraft.

The Special Forces now had more work to do. The U.S. government saw a lot more communist-inspired guerrilla movements around the world. Many of these rebellions would have cropped up even if the

Soviet Union had not existed, for they were feeding off local conditions—dictatorships, corruption, and the like. But the Soviet Union had gotten better and better at assisting, and sometimes instigating, these movements. Even though the Soviet Union was crumbling (economically and politically) and the Cold War was coming to an end, the KGB was doing just fine. The CIA had had mixed success countering KGB activities, so the Special Forces were seen as a slightly different solution that ought to be given a chance. The theory here was that the Special Forces could train the Army and police in threatened countries and, it was hoped, drive home the fact that the best way to beat guerrillas is the American way. This means using more carrots than sticks with local civilians and getting out in the bush to chase down the armed guerrillas. In most of these threatened nations, the army and police tended to attack civilians suspected of aiding guerrillas. These actions amounted to punitive raids, which were now renamed "human rights violations." They were counterproductive. The troops were neither trained or motivated to chase after the guerrillas themselves, and the abused civilians became more pro-guerrilla.

But success using the Special Forces approach was measured in inches, not miles. As any experienced Special Forces operator will tell you, dealing with a guerrilla movement is a long-term operation. The media was looking for instant results (as were many American politicians), and the Special Forces were accused of "training foreign soldiers in torture techniques." There was never any proof for these accusations, but they made for great headlines. While this was not good for morale, the Special Forces were professionals and just went on with their work.

There were many other forms of official encouragement for the Special Forces during the 1980s. In 1982, the 1st Special Operations Command was activated. This gave the Special Forces their own controlling organization. Before that, the Special Forces were part of the infantry, and the establishment of the 1st Special Operations Command began the process of making the Special Forces a separate branch. This continued in 1983, when U.S. Army Institute for Military Assistance (so named in 1969 to replace the more contentious "U.S. Army Special Warfare School") was renamed the "U.S. Army John F. Kennedy Special Warfare Center and School." In 1984, Special Forces was established as a separate career field for enlisted soldiers, instead of just being another infantry specialty. In 1985, Task Force 160 (which contained the helicopters and crews trained and equipped to support Special Forces operations) was transferred from the 101st Airborne Division to the 1st Special Operations Command. In 1986, special signal and support battalions were activated for the 1st Special Operations Command, meaning that Special Forces now had support troops who were trained to meet their unique needs. In 1987, a Special Forces branch was established for officers. Now all Special Forces troopers could make a career in Special Forces. Before that, they were expected to transfer out to other infantry-type jobs if they wanted to get promoted. In 1989, the transformation was completed when Special Forces was designated an Army command (like the infantry, artillery, armor, signal corps, and so on).

In 1990, a fifth Special Forces Group was established (the 3rd), giving the Special Forces sufficient manpower to cover potential hot spots throughout the world.

The Special Forces groups and their regional orientations are:

- **1st Special Forces Group (Airborne)** is at Fort Lewis, Washington (with one battalion in Okinawa, Japan). It specializes in East Asia and the Pacific. If something happened in Korea or China, the 1st would be involved. Works for the Pacific Command.
- **3rd Special Forces Group (Airborne)** is at Fort Bragg, North Carolina, and specializes in the Caribbean and West Africa. Works for the European Command.
- **5th Special Forces Group (Airborne)** is based at Fort Campbell, Kentucky, and specializes in the Middle East and South Asia (Afghanistan and Pakistan, for example). Works for Central Command.
- **7th Special Forces Group (Airborne)** is at Fort Bragg, North Carolina (with one company in Puerto Rico), and specializes in Latin America. Works for Southern Command.
- **10th Special Forces Group (Airborne)** is at Fort Carson, Colorado (with one battalion in Stuttgart, Germany), and specializes in Europe. Works for European Command.
- **19th Special Forces Group (Airborne)** is a reserve unit based in Salt Lake City, Utah, and covers the same territory as the 1st and 5th Special Forces Groups.
- **20th Special Forces Group (Airborne)** is a reserve unit based in Bir-

mingham, Alabama, and covers the same territory as the 7th Special Forces Group.

Each group has a small headquarters unit and three Special Forces battalions. Each Special Forces battalion has a small headquarters (a C-Detachment), three operational companies, and one support company. Each operational company has six A-Teams (officially Operational Detachment Alphas, or ODAs) of twelve men. The total strength of a Special Forces company is eighty-three men. The company headquarters is called a B-Team. The total strength of a Special Forces group is about twelve hundred troops.

The Special Forces are an expensive force to run. Higher pay, training, equipment, and travel costs make it some five times more expensive, man for man, to run a Special Forces unit than a regular infantry outfit. For example, an A-Team has one officer (a captain), one warrant officer, and ten sergeants. The Army has nine enlisted pay grades (E-1 to E-9). The ten enlisted men in an A-Team include one E-8, five E-7s, and four E-6s. In contrast, your typical infantry squad is led by an E-6, with the help of two E-5s. Everyone else is E-4 or E-3. The Special Forces troops have also been in the military longer than your average infantryman, and in the Army, pay goes up the longer you are in uniform.

The higher ranks in Special Forces units are unavoidable. The men who make it through all the Special Forces training are highly promotable no matter what unit they are in, and it's understandable that the Army simply organized the A-Teams with positions reflecting the rank that these men would soon reach. Moreover, the A-Teams were also designed as training units, so you can think of all the members as experienced instructors (which is what they are) who would normally be of higher rank. The Special Forces situation is not unique; all elite commando organizations have the same problem, and generally apply the same solution. Indeed, some countries have more officer positions for their commando units.

The Special Forces may add more officers to A-Teams, although using warrant officer ranks rather than commissioned ones (the people we normally think of as officers). The naming of warrant officers is an ancient practice that promotes exceptional NCOs to "warrant officer" rank. These positions (warrant officer 1, warrant officer 2, and so forth) parallel the pay of commissioned officers (a warrant officer 1 gets paid about what a second lieutenant does, and so on), but the warrants are technically outranked by all commissioned officers. When a sergeant first class (E-7) with ten years' service gets promoted to warrant officer 1, his base pay goes from $2,250.10 a month to $2,423.10. Not much of a raise, but officers and enlisted men now call him "Mister Jones" (instead of "Warrant Officer Jones") and troops have to salute him. The warrants can also go to the officer's club, although many prefer to continue hanging out at the NCO club. When the A-Teams were first organized, there were two commissioned officers. But it was soon realized that a senior man was needed to be the executive officer of the team. The team leader was, at most, a captain, and often just a lieutenant. The executive officer was always a lieutenant, and most of the enlisted members of the team usually had more experience and leadership ability than the officers. So the executive position was changed to a warrant officer slot, and the most experienced Special Forces NCOs were promoted to fill these jobs. The warrant officers on A-Teams provide adult supervision, as all NCOs do. Even A-Teams sometimes need an old hand to keep things on an even keel.

Through the 1980s, the Special Forces raised their standards for new recruits. Only about 10 percent of those who apply make it through all the training. Special Forces are basically looking for guys with lots of brain and brawn. Until September 11, 2001, about eighteen hundred candidates made it as far as the twenty-four-day Special Forces Assessment and Selection (SFAS) test.

Some 60 percent of those applying for Special Forces jobs are from the combat arms. This gives them an advantage, for while Special Forces troops acquire a lot of technical skills, they are also commando-class combat troops. But the army encourages noncombat arms troops to apply, recognizing that a lot of people with infantry potential end up doing something else once they are in the Army. Overall, about 35 to 40 percent of those who make it to the three-week SFAS pass and go on to the forty-six-day Special Forces Qualification Course (SFQC), which only about half pass. The SFQC is most important for those candidates who are not infantry, for it makes sure everyone learns basic infantry skills and then runs a lot of squad and platoon exercises to see who can do what. Those who make it this far go on to the Special Forces training program, which has a much lower attrition rate. The SFAS and SFQC are both intense, and are mainly looking for those who can function well under intense mental and physical pressure. It's ten weeks of constant activity that no Special Forces member is ever likely to forget.

Total Special Forces training takes one to two years, depending on which technical specialty is trained for. The medics have the longest training, some ten months. The training also includes language school (eighteen to twenty-four weeks). At that point, the Special Forces trooper is assigned to a unit and continues to spend a third or more of his time training for the rest of his career. A "seasoned" Special Forces operator requires five to ten years of service in the Green Berets.

Even before September 11, 2001, the Army was having trouble getting enough qualified candidates. Looking to junior sergeants who were very smart, in excellent physical shape, and willing to make a radical career change provided a small recruiting pool. So the Army reintroduced the policy of allowing civilians to apply directly. This can be tricky (it had been tried earlier, with mixed results). Recruits are taking a risk. If they flunk out (and most candidates do), they will be stuck with a three-year obligation in the Army anyway. This often causes unhappy soldiers. This time, the Army is trying to make candidates more aware of what they are getting into and doing more screening before the civilian candidates sign their enlistment contract. There are a lot of civilians who are Special Forces material, but it's difficult to spot them before getting the applicants through SFAS and SFQC. Since screening for commandos began during World War II, there has been a lot of research into developing better screening procedures, but no one has been able to shorten the process by much or come up with a quick foolproof test.

PEACE COMMANDOS

One remarkable thing about the Special Forces is that they are commandos who have a clearly defined and very useful peacetime mission: training troops in nations friendly to the United States. Even before the Vietnam War, it was understood that the Special Forces were most useful in peacetime for training friendly (or even semifriendly) armies.

A-Teams were originally set up so to train battalion-sized forces, and they still do that. In the last few years, for example, one battalion of the 3rd Special Forces Group has trained more than fifty-five hundred African troops.

The Special Forces definitely have a diplomatic function as well. When a Special Forces team shows up in a foreign country and the locals realize that several of these rough-looking characters speak their language and know some of the customs, this makes a positive impression. The Special Forces are specifically trained to make a good impression and establish long-term relationships with some of the troops they train, advise, or support. The media has never caught on to just how valuable this work is. In fact, most media coverage of Special Forces work overseas tends to interpret it as the Green Berets consorting with foreign death squads and uniformed murderers. The Army and CIA would just as soon not have the media getting into what Special Forces does overseas. It's not that the troops are doing anything illegal, but they are collecting valuable information and contacts in volatile parts of the world. This kind of work is a lot harder if you have a bunch of journalists chasing after you.

Most Americans don't notice this, but around the world, especially in poor countries, the American armed forces are much admired, especially elite units such as the Special Forces. The reasons for this are complex. Some of it has to do with the track records of the U.S. armed forces. That is, the American armed forces have been used mainly for defensive wars (except for Mexico, not many "wars of conquest"). During World War II, the U.S. emerged among the winners, and as a genuine military superpower. But there are two other reasons that are less remarked on. First, a lot of foreigners have received favorable reports about American troops from relatives in the United States. America is a nation of immigrants, and many of their kids joined (either voluntarily or because of the draft) and came back with a favorable opinion: Compared to a lot of foreign forces, the U.S. military comes out way ahead, especially in terms of treatment and living conditions for the troops. And then there's the media angle. All those American movies featuring favorable (or at least scary) images of American troops leave a vivid impression. Finally, Special Forces learned over the years to pay particularly close attention to local customs and not come on like superhuman know-it-alls. A little modesty and genuine eagerness to help go a long way.

In the early 1960s, the Special Forces established the concept of four- to twelve-man Mobile Military Training Teams (MTTs). In 1962, 1,512 Special Forces troops operated in nineteen different countries. This activity, which didn't always use Special Forces personnel, got buried, but never disappeared entirely, during the Vietnam War and the aftermath in the 1970s. But in the 1980s, there was an MTT revival. In 1978, only 53 MTTs were sent overseas; by 1982, this had grown to 260 (in thirty-five countries). In terms of "man-weeks" spent by MTT troops overseas, the number went from 1,161 in 1980 to 5,787 in 1984.

Since the 1980s, the Special Forces proved to be a reliable source of skilled, professional, and seasoned soldiers for tasks that required all of those qualities. They have served successfully as long-range scouts (during the 1991 Gulf War), as very effective combat troops (during the 1989 operations in Panama), and, in dozens of countries, as convincing representatives of the United States and the U.S. military. They are much sought after as trainers. The CIA likes to work with the Special Forces (as it has for half a century), and even the State Department finds them useful. The Special Forces have also made themselves very useful in peacekeeping operations, where they made a favorable impression on many anti-American nongovernmental organizations (NGOs) providing aid for the locals. All this work is unknown partly because the Special Forces like it that way. Special Forces are, after all, commandos, and it's a matter of life and death for a commando to stay out of sight and always able to use the element of surprise. The Special Forces remain a unique commando organization. No other nation has anything like it. The Special Forces are a uniquely American organization: commandos who are as useful in peacetime as they are dangerous in battle.

U.S. AIR FORCE SPECIAL OPERATIONS COMMAND

The most recently created of the American Special Operations units, Air Force Special Ops grew out of pilot rescue units that have always been a part of U.S. Air Force. During the Vietnam War, more special aircraft were added (like the fixed-wing gunships), and in 1987 all these units were combined into the 23rd Air Force. This outfit, in turn, was upgraded in 1990 to become the Air Force Special Operations Command (AFSOC). Total strength is some 12,500 men and women—active and reserve military, plus civilians. The main contribution are more than a hundred customized C-130 transports, and crews trained to use them. These include twenty-one AC-130 Specter gunships and twenty-four MC-130 long-range transports. There are also forty modified MH-53 heavy helicopters and a small number of customized Blackhawks. All the C-130s and MH-53s can be refueled in the air and deliver commandos at night in all kinds of weather. When you have to get some SEALs, Rangers, or Special Forces to some out-of-the-way place like Afghanistan, and do it in a hurry, you move via AFSOC aircraft. Also provided are transports capable of dropping the special fifteen-thousand-pound BLU-82 "Daisy Cutter" bombs and carrying the flying radio and TV broadcasting equipment.

The Air Force also has several hundred men trained to fight on the ground, in addition to their specialized Air Force duties: rescuing injured aircrews, air traffic control, calling in air strikes, or setting up weather monitoring equipment. The Air Force actually has a large force of light infantry. These are the people who guard air bases and actually look like infantry some of the time (when they wear their camouflage uniforms and carry assault rifles). In fact, the Air Force has more of these security personnel than the Army has infantry, but that's another story. Many of the elite Air Force operators go through the U.S. Army Ranger School. Because of the large number of aircraft and helicopters available to assist ground troops, the "air commandos" and their special equipment are a welcome addition to any special operations mission. Army Special Forces troops or SEALs can also direct air strikes, but the air commandos practice that all the time and also practice more complex uses of the aircraft overhead—supply drops, stacking up many aircraft so everyone can unload their bombs, and so on.

The primary function of the Air Force Special Ops people remains the recovery of downed aircrew who end up in hostile territory. This is how the air commandos started in World War II, and none of the current AFSOC operators ever forget it. All the services will cooperate on any mission involving the recovery of lost aircrew. It's always been that way, for all the services have pilots, and knowing someone will come in after you does wonders for crew morale.

Most of the Air Force operators are the crews of the Special Ops aircraft. Training takes place constantly, at night, in bad weather, and at low altitudes. It's dangerous work, and only the competent survive. During the 1990s, largely as a result of Gulf War experience, it was realized that the Special Forces could use qualified (that is, commando-quality) Air Force specialists on the ground with the Army operators. So a training program was created that sent Air Force commando air controllers and other specialists to the Special Forces for evaluations. A six-day evaluation program was developed. The Air Force guys who passed were qualified to operate with the Special Forces in combat. These are the Air Force troops sometimes mentioned in reports on the fighting in Afghanistan. The program worked. There was only one case of friendly fire in Afghanistan involving an Air Force controller, and in that case it was a hardware problem (changing batteries in the ground controller radio changed some data in the radio, causing the bomb to hit where the radio was, not where the target was).

The elite of the ground-based Air Force operators are pararescue teams. These are basically airborne medics who have trained to parachute into any terrain, in any weather, in order to provide medical aid for downed aircrew. In practice, the pararescue teams have been used to support Special Forces and other commando missions. If you have wounded men way out there, the medical personnel most likely to reach them first are the AFSOC pararescue teams. The six or seven men in a pararescue team usually include a doctor. The selection process for pararescue service is about the same as for Special Forces. When Rangers, SEALs, Special Forces, or Delta Force get hurt, it's often Air Force pararescue men who go in to treat and evacuate them.

The main operating bases for AFSOC are in Florida, Britain, and Japan. The AFSOC schools and headquarters are in Florida. AFSOC units practice regularly with Army and Navy Special Operations units; everyone assumes a world crisis could occur at any time. In the special operations business, every war is a come-as-you-are war.

SEALs

The SEALs maintain their status as the largest purely commando operation in the United States, and the world. After the recent reorganization, there are some eight hundred SEAL operators. Each of the eight SEAL teams has six sixteen-man platoons. The total strength of the SEAL Team is about 120 men. That's if the unit is at full strength, and many aren't. Recruiting is getting tougher, and no one wants to lower standards. Each SEAL platoon has two officers and fourteen enlisted men who, like the men in the Special Forces, have fairly high rank. But the constant traveling and intense training routine makes it rough on married SEALs.

To provide more flexibility in deploying SEAL teams, and to reduce the amount of time spent overseas somewhat, two more teams were added in March and April 2002. But manpower was not increased. Instead, each SEAL team now has six platoons instead of eight. There are now eight SEAL teams. Before a SEAL team is deployed, it goes through an eighteen-month training cycle. Six months concentrate on individual training, six months training as a team, and then six months working with the various specialist detachments (special water transportation vehicles, logistics, administration, communications personnel, mine clearing, and so on) that, when added to a SEAL team, make a Naval Special Warfare (NSW) squadron. The NSW is a new concept, which includes the six months of training with all the specialists, rather than just joining the specialist units when the SEAL teams reached the area they were to operate in. Each NSW squadron is commanded by an experienced SEAL officer.

The new units are SEAL Team Seven and SEAL Team Ten.

- Naval Special Warfare Group One is based in San Diego, California. It consists of four 120-man SEAL teams and support units.
- SEAL Team One's area of concentration is Southeast Asia.
- SEAL Team Three's area of concentration is Southwest Asia.
- SEAL Team Five's area of concentration is the Northern Pacific.
- SEAL Team Seven's area of concentration was not announced when the team was formed in early 2002.
- On Guam, there is Naval Special Warfare Unit One. This outfit con-

trols SEAL platoons and special boat unit detachments from Naval Special Warfare Group One, which is stationed on Guam.

- In Kodiak, Alaska, there is Naval Special Warfare Group One Detachment. The unit has only six men, who provide training for SEAL platoons and Special Boat Unit (SBU) detachments learning how to deal with cold-weather operations.
- In Bahrain, there is Naval Special Warfare Unit Three. This is a small headquarters that controls SEAL platoons and Special Boat Unit (SBU) detachments operating in the Persian Gulf.
- Naval Special Warfare Group Two is based in Little Creek, Virginia. It consists of four 130- to 140-man SEAL teams and support units.
- SEAL Team Two's area of concentration is Europe. SEAL Team Two deploys platoons to Naval Special Warfare Unit Two in Germany.
- SEAL Team Four's area of concentration is Central and South America.
- SEAL Team Eight's area of concentration is the Caribbean, Africa, and the Mediterranean.
- SEAL Team Ten's area of concentration was not announced when the team was formed in early 2002.
- Like Group One, Group Two has small detachments in Stuttgart, Germany; Naval Station Roosevelt Roads, Puerto Rico; Rodman, Panama; and Rota in Spain.
- Special boat squadrons have units and SEAL delivery teams in Virginia, Louisiana, and Panama.
- SEAL platoons and smaller units are based on warships. For example, many SEALs are aboard warships searching for terrorists aboard civilian boats operating in the Indian Ocean, the Persian Gulf, and other places.

Like Delta Force, small numbers of SEALs were assigned to top-secret intelligence missions in the 1980s and got into some trouble. The details are still murky (most of the details are still supposed to be classified), but, like the similar problems with Delta Force, some people in the government took their secret agent fantasies too seriously.

SEAL TEAM SIX

Until Delta Force was formed in 1977, the Navy SEALs were the most capable American commando troops. Then Delta Force came along and grabbed the current hot mission: counterterrorism. But after the failed 1979 Iranian hostage rescue mission, the Navy decided that perhaps the SEALs could do counterterrorism better, at least when the mission was near the sea. So in 1980, SEAL Team Six was formed as a counterterrorist unit. What this meant was that the six sixteen-man platoons of SEAL Team Six were trained to do what Delta Force did, but with more concentration on coming in on small boats or underwater. The Navy decision was partially driven by the fact that SEAL Team One was already retraining all of its platoons for counterterrorism missions, and SEAL Team Two had dedicated two platoons to counterterrorism. The Navy recruited heavily from these two units to form SEAL Team Six and was able to get Six ready for action in about six months. In the early 1990s, after several SEAL Team Six officers were caught (and convicted of) stealing government money and the team commander had a book published detailing how the unit operated, SEAL Team Six was disbanded and reconstituted as part of the Naval Special Warfare Development Group (NSWDG, or Dev Group). Despite the name change and added responsibilities for trying out new weapons and tactics (something SEALs have always done anyway), the counterterrorism commandos still remain in this outfit. Currently there are about two hundred combat troops and three hundred support personnel in NSWDG. SEAL Team Six lives, but in reduced circumstances.

DELTA FORCE

As the Vietnam War ended, international terrorism became more common. The United States noted that Britain's SAS was a useful tool in dealing with terrorism, and perhaps a similar American unit would be useful. So in 1977, Delta Force came into existence. Like the SAS, Delta was a small, very selective unit. Delta was initially put together by Special Forces troops who had trained, or worked, with SAS. The initial size of Delta, after two years' preparation, was about a hundred operators. By 1980, Delta had grown to its present size: about three hundred men and a few women.

Delta is officially known as 1st Special Forces Operational Detachment—Delta (SFOD-D). It's located in an isolated part of Fort Bragg, North Carolina. While there are only some three hundred Delta troops, there are another two thousand or so support personnel. Delta is divided into six squadrons along with a smaller unit composed of female Delta troopers. Three of the squadrons are actual fighters, plus support, signal, and aviation squadrons. The basic unit is the sixteen-man platoon, although Delta operations use only as many men as are needed. This number is usually small, often eight, four, or just two men.

Like all commandos, Delta trains constantly. Their base contains mock-ups of typical fighting environments—rooms, hallways, bunkers. Specific structures can be built or reconfigured for training if enough information about the target area is known. The training consists of getting into the target area on cue and making sure the people who are supposed to be shot are, and not someone like, say, the hostages you are rescuing.

Like the SAS, Delta is very selective, with about 90 percent of applicants washing out. Those who are accepted undergo a two-year training course to learn the basics. After that, as long as you are in Delta, you are always learning something new. This is one of the things that draws people to Delta—there's always something new. In addition, you don't have to wear a uniform and bother with most of the usual military bureaucracy hassles. There's lots of travel and, let's face it, this is a close as a human can get to being a real live comic book hero.

Since most of the Delta operators are recruited from Special Forces and the Rangers, they have little problem working with those organizations. They know how the other guys operate, and know a lot of them personally. This is important, especially with the Special Forces, which are often the first U.S. commandos to be sent to a potential hot spot (usually to train local troops to deal with the local problem). When the situation gets hot enough to warrant Delta's services, there are rarely any problems with Delta and Special Forces working closely together.

One issue is that Delta doesn't get a lot of real work. Lots of practice, but little of the real thing. This was bad enough, but Delta's first combat mission ended in embarrassing failure. Delta was the ground force for the failed 1979 attempt to rescue the American diplomats held prisoner in Iran. The failure was not Delta's doing, but it caught some of the backlash. Throughout the 1980s, its operators were called out many times in anticipation of some action, but saw real action only a few times (Grenada in 1983, Panama in 1989). Same situation in the 1990s, with a lot of false alarms and two bouts of action (Iraq in 1991 and Somalia in 1993, where two Delta operators won the Medal of Honor).

Delta Force was seen as something of an insurance policy against those situations where terrorists threatened Americans and nothing else seemed capable of fixing things. But Delta itself has been frustrated by the reluctance of presidents, or military leaders, to use commandos. Delta was all wound up, but no one was willing to pull the trigger. A lot of this had to do with the 1979 Iran debacle. The conventional political wisdom has it that President Carter lost his reelection bid because of the failed Delta mission. Actually, that's not really true at all. Carter was a pretty lame president, and the only way he might have won reelection was if the Iran rescue mission had succeeded. But even as a former naval officer, Carter was unable to untangle the interservice squabbling that caused the 1979 mission to fail. The real problem is that American presidents tend to be risk averse when it comes to using commandos in peacetime. Other nations, such as Britain and France, are much more willing to let the commandos have a go at it. It's not for nothing that the British SAS motto is "Who Dares, Wins."

Throughout the 1980s, Delta operators were upset that they were not given a chance to rescue some of the American hostages held in Lebanon. Likewise in the 1990s, Delta was considered for operations in Iraq and Afghanistan, but the risk of failure and American casualties prevented any action. Since September 11, 2001, this attitude may have changed. At the moment, Delta has all it can handle in Afghanistan.

Delta members weren't just training throughout the 1980s and 1990s. They developed working relationships with the CIA. This should not be surprising, because as noted, most Delta operators come from Special Forces and are familiar with the CIA connection. Delta made itself useful by providing bodyguards in potentially dangerous overseas situations. Members guarded key American commanders in Saudi Arabia during the Gulf War and are often there when the president or senior American officials travel to risky areas.

During the 1980s, there were several ugly, or at least embarrassing, incidents involving Delta Force. The item that got the most attention was the accusation that Delta Force members had embezzled half a million dollars meant for secret operations. Exactly what was going on in several different incidents is still somewhat murky. It appears that Delta Force, and a special unit of SEALs, was seen by the CIA and the White House as an adequate substitute for the secret activities Congress forced the CIA to abandon in the late 1970s. This was also the era of clandestine, and often illegal, U.S. operations in Central America and the Middle East.

Delta Force and the SEALS survived this, but perhaps as an after-effect, Delta and SEAL Team Six were both placed under the control of the Joint Special Operations Command (JSOC). Despite that, the use of Delta Force and SEALs for CIA and other intelligence operations continues. This makes sense, because a string of embarrassing incidents and lots of bad press caused the CIA to shut down much of its overseas agent operations. But there were still situations overseas, often unanticipated ones, where you really, really needed to get an American in there to look around or make contact with local agents. Special Forces and JSOC operators were just the thing. While many of these guys look like pro football players (kinda makes them stand out, even in civilian clothes), many do not. Turning one of these guys into a secret agent is apparently not difficult. And they already have a license to kill.

One thing that may make Delta more likely to be used in the future is the availability of better intelligence capabilities. Some of this is new gadgetry (drones and information-analyzing software), but a lot of it is a new willingness to put people on the ground (CIA or Special Forces) to collect information Delta needs before it can plan and execute a successful mission. And often it's Delta that's going in first to ferret out the information needed to prepare an armed strike.

No one has said much, officially, about the use of American commandos as spies and intelligence agents. But these lads are trained to be flexible, think fast, and operate under any conditions. While they normally train wearing a camouflage uniform and carrying an assault rifle, they have no problem going on a recon mission in a suit, armed with a 9mm pistol, or no weapon at all.

Delta continues to learn from the British SAS, which has long made good use of close working relationships with British diplomats. In this respect, Delta may begin performing secret operations (that stay secret) involving anti-terrorism activities or nastier forms of diplomacy. If the word was ever given to kill Saddam Hussein, Delta operators would be the designated executioners.

LRSU, SON OF LRRP

Radio made possible a unique military unit, the Long Range Reconnaissance Patrol (LRRP). With a radio, a small unit of men could (if skillful enough) sneak deep into enemy territory and report back what they found. Starting in World War II, numerous LRRP units were formed for this kind of dangerous work. In the U.S. Army, LRRPs went in and out of fashion depending on whether or not there was a war on. Some LRRP units were formed during World War II, and then disbanded after the war. Same thing during the Korean War, although two LRRP companies were created in 1958 for wartime missions deep into Russian-controlled territory. LRRPs sprang up spontaneously in Vietnam. All but two of the Vietnam-era LRRP companies were disbanded after the war, and these two companies were used in 1974 to begin forming the Ranger Regiment. But in the early 1980s, as the U.S. Army got serious about troop quality and training, the need for LRRPs was felt once more. This time, the solution developed was a little different. The units were called Long Range Surveillance Units (LRSU) and generally operate in four-man (rather than the eight- to twelve-man LRRP) units. Better equipment and the ability to send the patrols deeper made smaller units more effective. LRSU are expected to stay out there for up to thirty days at a time. LRSUs have been used in every American conflict in the last two decades as well as in anti-drug and anti-terrorist operations. While still trained to fight, the long-range scouts are given even more intensive instruction on staying hidden. Being an LRSU is considered on a par with Rangers or Special Forces, if only because LRSU will often go into an area before any of those other elite troops.

COMMANDOS AROUND THE WORLD

Most nations have some kind of commando unit, usually a hundred or so specially selected and trained troops. Often, the British or American commando units (SAS/SBS, Special Forces) are called in to conduct training and create a commando capability for some countries. As a general rule, the larger the nation's armed forces, the more likely it is to maintain a useful commando force. This is because the commandos are usually recruited from people already in the military. Leaders for commando units are selected from those who have served in the commandos. The smaller commando forces in most nations tend to vary quite a bit in quality, depending on how good the current leadership is. Larger nations have a larger pool of troops to select from and thus are able to maintain quality in their commandos. But in many smaller nations, the local commandos are, at best, a SWAT team with more fancy equipment than capability. Thus the following list is not exhaustive.

Argentina has some anti-terrorist units and special units to deal with criminal gangs. Some of these men are trained to commando standards, but they are primarily intended for police work in Argentina. There are two commando companies.

Australia has its own SAS (Special Air Service) commandos, including a platoon that can operate from the sea (like U.S. Navy SEALs). Australian SAS have a close relationship with U.S. Special Forces and SEALs. The Australian forces consist of the 1st SAS Regiment (500 to 600 active duty and reserve troops), 1st Commando Group (about 250 troops), the 4th Royal Australian Regiment (several hundred commandos), and several companies of LRRPs.

Austria formed the Gendarmerieeinsatzkommando (Police Special Command or GEK) Cobra in 1978 in response to growing numbers of terrorist acts within Austria. This is a very well-trained and -equipped, but small, organization that only operates within Austria.

Belgium came out of World War II with a battalion of commandos who had trained and operated with British commandos. The commando tradition continues, with a Para-Commando regiment and some LRRP units.

Canada formed Joint Task Force Two as an anti-terrorism commando unit in 1993. It has a strength of about two hundred men.

China has formed two "Special Warfare Groups" that are trained for commando-type operations. Little is known about them, but they involve several thousand troops.

Finland has a long tradition of commando-type operations. It currently has four hundred troops in Ranger Warfare Companies. These men perform LRRP duties and commando-type raids. There is also a battalion of paratroopers trained for Special Forces–type work, mainly behind enemy lines (say, in Russia) if there should be another war. There is also a forty-man Bear Force for hostage rescue work.

France has several elite combat units, but only one, the 1st Para-Commando Regiment (about three hundred troops), is of commando quality. These troops are the same quality as the SAS or U.S. Special Forces. The French armed forces also have a number of support units for their commandos—special helicopters and the like.

Germany's KSK (Kommando Spezialkraefte, or "Special Commando Force") was created in 1994 and became operational in 1997; it's getting its first combat experience in Afghanistan. About a hundred KSK troops are in Afghanistan, and more are expected. The KSK were modeled on the British SAS and U.S. Special Forces. The unit was formed after eleven German citizens were trapped in Rwanda in 1994 and it was realized that there was no German military unit available to rescue them from chaos then existing in that nation. By 2000, KSK had about a thousand members. Recruits were drawn from existing airborne units, and British SAS advisers helped devise the training program. Since the unit was officially formed on April 1, 1996, members are nicknamed "the Jokers." It is not known if anyone used the phrase "send in the clowns" when KSK was ordered to Afghanistan. In addition to KSK, there are also three companies of LRRPs and a counterterrorism unit (GSG-9, about 250 troops).

India first formed a commando force, composed largely of Tibetan exiles, after getting the worst of it in a 1962 border war with China. As relations improved with China over the years, the Special Frontier Force (SFF) switched from its original mission of stirring up guerrilla operations inside China to counterterrorism. The size (about ten thousand troops) and organization (six battalions, each of six 123-man companies plus a headquarters) of the units has not changed much in forty years. Training is still rigorous, but there are fewer Tibetans in the unit now. There is also a paracommando battalion, used as a quick-reaction force. A small (about a hundred men) National Security Guards force is organized and trained to deal with hostage situations. A very competent outfit. There are twelve hundred Marine Commandos, who sought assistance from British Royal Marine Commandos and U.S. SEALs to set up their two-year training program.

Israel has a large force of commando troops for a country its size. Two small battalions of Arabic-speaking troops are used for undercover operations and raids into the Occupied (Palestinian) Territories. Sayeret Shimshon (Unit 367) is assigned to the Gaza Strip, while Sayeret Duvdevan (Unit 217) takes care of the West Bank. There are four companies of Ranger-type troops (Palsar) that normally each support one of the four elite infantry brigades of the Army, and two more to support armored brigades. There are also three LRRP companies (Special Command Teams), with one assigned to each of the Army's corps headquarters. Lotar Eilat and Unit Yamam are two hostage rescue units (each with less than one hundred troops). These units can also be used as commandos, such as when there is a lot of violence with the Palestinians. There are also several hundred highly trained LRRP troops assigned directly to intelligence units. The Navy has a SEAL unit (Shayetet 13) of about four hundred men. This unit is more selective than the other commando units, with about 80 percent of its candidates failing the training course, compared to about 50 percent with other units. The Navy also has a company-sized unit of divers (similar to U.S. UDT). And the police force has more than a thousand specially trained men who are a cut above your usual SWAT teams.

Italy experienced some horrific homegrown terrorism in the 1970s. That has passed, but there is an ongoing problem with organized crime (the original Mafia). As a result, officials created two elite counterterrorism units. The GIS is actually a police unit of about a hundred men. The Navy has a SEAL-type unit (COMSUBIN) with about 250 men.

Japan has a two hundred-man Special Assault Team for counterterrorist and hostage rescue missions.

Netherlands has an SAS-type unit, the KCT (Army Commando Troops). This small battalion has one company of commandos and two of LRRPs. There is also a twenty-five-man Special Boat Section that is similar to U.S. SEALs and British SBS. The BBE (Special Intervention Force) has about a hundred troops used for counterterrorist work and hostage rescue.

New Zealand has a small SAS unit (about fifty men) that trains to the same standards as the British SAS.

Norway has a Ranger/LRRP battalion and a smaller unit of SEALs (which regularly trained with U.S. SEALs). Norwegian Rangers are very experienced in mountain and cold-weather operations. A Norwegian Ranger detachment served in Afghanistan in 2002.

Russia has a LRRP company and a parachute (commando) company assigned to each combat division—although not all have them. Beyond that, there are about eight thousand Spetsnaz (in seven brigades). Some of these brigades are trained so that their troops operate in battalion- or company-sized units for reconnaissance duty. Other are trained to operate in smaller nine- to twelve-man teams for classic commando operations.

South Korea has the 707th Special Missions Battalion with about three hundred men (and a few women) trained for counterterrorist and hostage rescue missions. There are seven Special Forces brigades meant for service in North Korea in wartime. These units are actually a cross between U.S. Rangers and Special Forces. The South Korean Special Forces will try to provide information on enemy rear-area operations. North Korea has some twenty-two Special Forces brigades. In the case of both nations, the major problem will be getting Special Forces into the enemy rear area. If either side (most likely the south) gets command of the air and sea, it will have Special Forces in enemy territory. U.S. SEALs and Special Forces provided assistance and trainers when their South Korean counterparts were formed. Many American operators consider some of the South Korean commando training even tougher than that found in American special operations schools. The Koreans have long had a tradition of toughness, and the concept of highly selective commando units that go through brutal training has a lot of appeal in South Korea.

Sweden has a small battalion of Airborne Rangers that operates like the SAS: in five-man units behind enemy lines. There are also several companies of Coastal Rangers, who are trained as commandos to re-take coastal islands and forts captured by the enemy. The SSG is a small unit (less than a hundred men, all officers) that performs hostage rescue missions and provides security for top leaders.

Thailand has a 144-man SEAL unit, which has trained with American SEALs. There are also some LRRPs and elite infantry.

Turkey has three commando brigades (about five thousand troops), but these are more like U.S. Rangers in function. The commandos have a lot of practical experience from the ongoing war with Kurdish separatists.

United Kingdom. The country that invented the modern commando concept has three battalions of Royal Marine Commandos and about two hundred SAS commandos. The 21st SAS is a reserve unit that frequently has members called to active service. The 22nd SAS is an active duty regiment (which, in British parlance, is a battalion-sized unit). There is also the Special Boat Service (SBS), which is similar to the U.S. SEALs but keeps a lower profile. SBS operates up to twelve miles inland, and many of its operations have been mistakenly reported as SAS. SBS has about 120 men and recruits from the Royal Marine Commandos. Since September 11, 2001, Britain has begun hiring retired SAS personnel as "contract workers" to perform some of the intelligence jobs that SAS usually handles.

The United States has the largest array of commando-type troops. All are organized into the Special Operations Command (SOCOM). This organization has some forty-five thousand troops assigned, but only a small proportion are "operators," or gun-carrying commandos. This main operator units are Delta Force: about four hundred elite commandos for counterterrorism, hostage rescue, and any operation requiring the services of a small number of very good operators. The Special Forces is comprised of five Special Forces groups, each with about twelve hundred troops. There is a Ranger regiment of two thousand two hundred troops. The Air Force has several hundred commandos who rescue downed pilots and provide air controllers (to call in bombing strikes) for ground units. The Air Force also has a lot of people operating and supporting special operations aircraft, requiring the services of some twelve thousand personnel. The Navy has its SEALs and supporting units (about two thousand men).

SPECIAL AIR SERVICE

The British Special Air Service is a secretive commando organization, perhaps the best in the world. But since September 11, 2001, wealthy people have become more concerned about security. This has caused frequent attempts to recruit SAS for civilian security jobs. Apparently former SAS members, now working security jobs (and with access to active duty SAS men), began to offer active duty SAS troops civilian jobs. An experienced SAS member makes about fifty thousand dollars a year. They have been offered up to $150,000 a year for civilian work, and several dozen have accepted. This has made a dent in the SAS, which has a total strength of (at most) 240 men. The SAS has to get about ten candidates for every man who can make it through the training. The formidable reputation of the SAS keeps all but the most stouthearted from even applying. To deal with this looming shortage, in early 2002, the SAS began allowing civilians to apply. Previously, only active duty military were allowed.

Another advantage of Britain's MI6 (external intelligence, similar to the CIA) is that it has long had a number of SAS commandos trained to work with MI6 and always available for any MI6 needs. This commando organization is called Increment and is used for assassinations, sabotage, or other dangerous jobs (say, arresting war criminals in the Balkans). In addition, every MI6 station chief overseas has a direct line to SAS headquarters and a good working relationship with the commandos. Given the long and close relationship between SAS and Special Forces, and between MI6 and the CIA, it is likely that the increased use of Special Forces and SEALs by the CIA in the 1980s had something to do with knowledge of SAS Increment.

BLUNTING THE SHARP END

The *Sharp End* is one of the many slang expressions for infantry fighting. These days, there are fewer and fewer people working it. No wonder. It's dangerous up there. The military has long resorted to a number of sneaky maneuvers to get people to volunteer for front-line work. Even if you could conscript grunts, you had to find some way to generate a little enthusiasm; otherwise the term *cannon fodder* becomes a primary consideration, and your ground troops aren't very useful.

Going into the twenty-first century, most nations depend on young men to volunteer for the Sharp End. This isn't working too well. The U.S. has about one hundred thousand infantrymen of all types, and most infantry units are understrength. But it gets worse, for the glamorous Special Operations (commandos or operators) units are also having problems. The Navy SEALs have to train nine hundred new recruits a year to maintain strength. But for the last seven years, no more than 751 candidates have been found. The Army is actually recruiting more Special Forces than ten years ago, for these troops are perfect for peacekeeping and training well-behaved troops for unsettled nations. But recruiting goals are met by lowering standards, and this has become a sore point among Special Forces troops. The Air Force has commandos to go in and set up air control posts or rescue downed pilots and is unable to fill more than 80 percent of the positions.

In the last few years, people in Congress and the media noted that minorities were underrepresented in Special Operations units. Minority representation in these units averaged about half what it "should" be given the proportion of that minority in the armed forces as a whole. Worst was the Navy SEALs, where only 2 percent were black. Naturally, a think tank was commissioned to do a study on why this was so. The results were interesting. A big problem was swimming. All operators are expected to encounter many water obstacles (oceans, rivers, swamps) and thus must have good swimming skills. In America, for whatever reason, minorities are less likely to acquire swimming skills. Then there's the career potential angle. After a tour with special operations, minorities see reduced employment opportunities as civilians. While this is also true for whites, since the volunteer army was introduced in the 1970s, combat units have been disproportionately full of white kids looking for a few thrills before going off to college (or not, no one knows why this is so). Black and Latino kids prefer military jobs where they can get skills usable in civilian occupations. The armed forces hasn't complained, but now that the Sharp End is thinning out, it's a problem.

Minority troops are more likely to be married and also (especially among Latinos) put more emphasis on close family relationships. Operators travel a lot, and everyone knows it. The amount of travel time is a large disincentive. Minority recruits also have more problems with navigation (making your way across unfamiliar terrain). No one knows why. However, navigation is an essential skill for Special Forces. Minorities also have a harder time getting good scores on the written test. A lot of this is cultural; even black educators now openly admit to a long-known phenomenon—the black youth culture has long been violently "anti-nerd." Study and doing well was seen as "acting white" and discouraged. Once the kids were old enough realize that all the "keeping it real" was nonsense, they had already lost many years of good schooling.

The low percentage of black and Latino kids in the Special Operations units led to another problem: Many potential volunteers thought that these outfits full of tough white guys had to be a hotbed of racism and bigotry. This was untrue, as minority operators tell anyone who asks. But the bad rep is hard to shake and makes it harder to attract minority candidates.

There has been some right-wing and racist stuff in regular infantry units. This was largely the result of lower standards for officers and NCOs. The 1990s were not a good time for the military to attract the best and the brightest, and the infantry was hurt pretty bad in the leadership department. This was made worse by the need to crack down on harassment (real or imagined) of homosexual and female soldiers. Leaders had a lot of bad habits to keep an eye on.

The elite units are the first ones to be used in an emergency. Some of these operators are ready to get on an airplane and fly to a distant trouble spot on a few hours' notice. It's telling that there was no public outcry about the recruiting problems until it was framed in racial terms. Everyone insists that there will be no quotas or lowering of standards. If that happened, and word got out, it would be even more difficult to recruit competent operators.

But then, stranger things have happened in the past.

COMMANDO CARRIER

The U.S. Navy has a long tradition of using its ships to support commando operations. It goes back to the founding of the Navy, when it was understood that the Marines carried on each ship were available for commando-type operations ashore. For larger operations, sailors would be armed and sent ashore under the leadership and supervision of the Marines. During World War II, submarines and destroyers were used to move Marine commandos to shore targets and retrieve them after the land combat was complete. After World War II, special small boats were developed for moving SEALs to shore objectives. In 1992, a ballistic missile nuclear submarine (SSBN) was converted to carry as many as two hundred SEALs or Marines to a hostile shores for land missions. Four more older SSBNs may get the same treatment. During the Afghanistan war, the carrier *Kitty Hawk* was provided to the army as a floating base for its Special Operations helicopters. The success of that operation led, in early 2002, to the Navy investigating the possibility of converting the forty-two-year-old carrier *Constellation* to a commando support ship, and giving the Army's Special Operations helicopters a permanent seagoing home. This is an attractive proposition for the Army, because most of its commando operations take place within a few hundred miles of an ocean. The commando carrier would provide a well-equipped and secure base for commando operations. This was proven in Afghanistan, and if the Army and Navy can work out a deal, the commando carrier could become a reality. The carrier would probably belong to the Special Operations Command, which controls Special Operations forces from the Army, Navy, and Air Force.

FINDING NATURAL-BORN KILLERS

The U.S. Marines have a macho reputation. And they like it that way. One member of the Clinton administration described the Marines as "extremists." Privately, many Marines took that as an unintended compliment. Potential recruits see the Marines the same way—as a bunch of tough, lethal, disciplined troops with impressive uniforms. And since most of the potential recruits for any branch of the military are teenagers, the Marines have a natural appeal. If you need any convincing, just take note of the kinds of music and movies teenagers like, and the fact that the Marines have the least trouble meeting their recruiting goals. Further proof can be found by attending the recruiting presentations regularly held in many high schools. Each of the services gets up and makes its pitch. The Army, Air Force, and Navy rattle off all the goodies they offer, like travel to foreign countries, money for college, and career training. Many of the students nod off. Then the Marine sergeant gets up and shows a short video of tough-looking teenage Marines storming beaches, jumping out of armored vehicles and helicopters, and generally behaving like natural-born killers. The sergeant then tells the kids that the Marines can only promise them challenges. Not everyone can be a Marine, and he only wants to recruit those who are up to it. The students are fully awake through all this, and the Marines generally end up with more recruits than anyone else. The other NCOs mutter about how much better they'd do if they had a better-looking uniform.

The Marines have another advantage. Just about all Marines have combat jobs. The Navy provides all the support troops. It's as if the Army Rangers or paratroopers had their own recruiters. Their pitch would be very similar to the Marines, and would get similar results. That idea has been tossed around in the other services, but no one has taken the plunge yet. Yet it's an old idea. For thousands of years, individual military units went out looking for recruits. The idea of one recruiting organization for everyone is relatively new. In the past, each regiment or ship had its own small recruiting staff, and the new guys were generally taken from the same area. This was a big help for unit cohesion, which is today called "team building." Commanders have known for thousands of years that, in the thick of combat, the principal motivation is men fighting for each other, for their friends and teammates. Military and civilian organizations strive to build this unit cohesion. Few military organizations, or companies, pull it off. Except for the Marines.

What the Marines have done is part show biz and part common sense. Everyone notices the snappy dress uniforms and military bearing of marines. There's also that cocky attitude. And career Marines are expected to scowl at the camera when official photos are taken. All that is the show biz. The commonsense angle is the Marines' emphasis, in their training and indoctrination, on their main job: ground combat. Get ready for that and you get fewer Marines killed when you get into a fight. Even though the Navy supplies many of the support functions, many Marines are not in combat jobs. Yet it's a tradition that "every Marine is a rifleman." Noncombat Marines spend part of each year going through infantry drills. The older NCOs repeat the stories of how, in the past, Marine cooks and clerks were thrown into the line when the situation got desperate. And the Marines relish a desperate situation. They have favorite maxims like "There's no such thing as being surrounded, but there are times when you can attack in any direction."

But soldiering has changed for most of the other troops in the world. It's fashionable to play down grim and costly ground combat in favor of precision weapons and push-button warfare. For this reason, the Marines are seen as a bunch of roughneck throwbacks. Yet even today, in any of the two dozen wars being fought around the world, the troops who are the most successful are the ones who operate most like the Marines. What the Marines are may not be fashionable, but when you have to get close to the enemy, what they do works.

SURVIVAL OF THE DEADLIEST

Recruiting commando-quality troops is a difficult process. But over the last sixty years, a particularly effective method has been developed. It all has to do with training that takes men to the edge, and a little beyond. One of the unheralded military developments during World War II was training methods that can detect, and enhance, those soldiers who can reliably operate in extreme situations. These initial commando training courses can last from a few weeks to a few months and are meant to evaluate a candidate's psychological, as well as physical, stamina. The training method consists of many of the usual military tasks, but performed to a higher standard and much greater intensity. Typical activities would be frequent long marches with heavy loads, lots of physical training, and lots of running. Added to this is decreasing time for sleep.

At the end of particularly long and arduous marches, the trainees will be set to performing more military chores, like planning an attack or stalking another group of troops, trying to get close enough so that they could, if this were the real thing, kill them with a knife, bare hands, or silencer-equipped pistol. At every stage of this increasingly grueling training, some trainees are expected to drop out from exhaustion or because they decide this is a bit more than they are ready for. The training also involves use of weapons and live ammunition. This can get particularly scary, because the trainees out there using real bullets may have had only a few hours of sleep in the last few days and just completed a high-speed forty-mile march. The danger is intentionally real, and meant to determine who has the ability to perform effectively under extreme conditions. Most final tests are administered after the trainees have been exhausted in one way or another. This is realistic, because combat often involves staying awake for long periods, and then carrying out a difficult mission.

A final exam will often consist of things like being sent off into the wilderness for a week or so with only a knife and some matches. This will sometimes be enhanced by sending training staff out to try to find the trainees. Anyone who's found fails the course. You can tell a lot about how elite a force is by how high its washout rate is. This usually varies from 20 to 80 (or more) percent. A higher washout rate rejects a lot of excellent warriors, but leaves you with a truly elite group.

Usually, elite forces recruit from existing military units. This provides a form of prescreening, making sure that the trainees already have some level of familiarity with military matters. When volunteers are sometimes accepted directly from civilian life, you don't have the ability to see how the trainee will deal with being in the military for an extended period (such as a year or more). The stress testing for these men has to be different, because they lack many basic military skills. Still, it can work, and sometimes it's necessary if there aren't enough suitable candidates in the military. The U.S. Special Forces began doing this after September 11, 2001, because they wanted to expand and they needed a larger pool of talents to choose from.

One of the advantages of commando training is that it forces every man to be a leader. All commandos must be prepared to think for themselves and take over in stressful situations where the usual leaders are out of action or elsewhere. This has provided a bonus for nations with commando units: Those men who do not make a career of it go off to noncommando units with excellent leadership training. Even those who wash out of commando training retain a more accurate appreciation of their capabilities under high-stress situations. Those who serve as career commandos often get injured, or become too old to keep up, and leave commando units. Such men have leadership skills that are valued in any unit they end up in.

During World War II, these training methods were somewhat theoretical. Many senior commanders feared that commando units would drain other units of their best men and leaders. This did not prove to be the case. Many of the men who made the grade as commandos needed that kind of extreme challenge to really get motivated. These guys were often tagged as "troublemakers" in their mainline combat units. Moreover, the most elite commandos work in small groups, and this also attracts a certain type of individual who prefers to work alone or in small groups. The generals, while impressed with what commandos could do, took several decades before they realized what the other benefits were. After half a century, the unique commando training methods have proved to be something that works.

TRAIN AS YOU FIGHT, FIGHT AS YOU TRAIN

Another World War II innovation adopted by commandos is the intensive use of very realistic, and dangerous, training. In wartime, you can justify the heavy use of live ammunition during night exercises because you know the trainees are soon going to be under fire for real. No matter how dangerous the training, it will impart skills that will save the lives of trainees and do so very soon. In peacetime, training casualties are less acceptable, and most armies avoid dangerous live-fire exercises. This was particularly the case with draftees.

But commando units were always a different story. The commandos' motto has long been, "Train as you fight, fight as you train." That has meant using live ammunition in training. Being elite volunteers, commandos have continued to practice these dangerous, but very useful, training methods. Moreover, commandos developed the idea of the "Kill House," a building used for live-fire exercises. After the Vietnam War, when counterterrorism operations became more popular with politicians, money was available to build more elaborate Kill Houses. Some of these had walls capable of absorbing bullets (using plywood and steel with an air space between). Some Kill Houses were wired to record sound and moving images of how the trainees performed. Remote-control pop-up targets were available, as well as walls that could be reconfigured. In the last ten years, technology has provided more elaborate Kill House technology, with running man targets, and targets that indicate you were not quick enough and that the bad guys are now shooting back.

The Kill House recognized that terrorists would be more likely encountered inside than outside. But the Kill House technology has been brought outside, with outdoor live-fire exercises using the same realistic pop-ups, running man targets (of enemy shooters or innocent civilians), and recording technology. While a lot of the Kill House training is generic, some of it is specific. If details of an upcoming mission are known, especially the layout of a particular building, key parts of the target area can be mocked up and live-fire drills run.

Most major commando organizations have one or more Kill Houses for training. The concept was pioneered during World War II and has grown in popularity since then. The U.S. Army and U.S. Marines have several Kill House complexes for training their troops. The U.S. Navy SEALs have a Kill House that cost twenty-five million dollars to build. No one who has trained regularly in a Kill House doubts their effectiveness. In nearly all cases where commandos had to go inside quickly against an armed enemy, the speed and precision they obtained from Kill House training saved lots of lives (except for the terrorists, who died in greater numbers because of this training).

Less well-trained soldiers use electronic bullets in training to prevent friendly fire accidents in combat and improve their shooting skills. Good, but not as good as live ammunition. Everyone, however, gets to experience the risks of just getting into a Kill House. You must practice the techniques of coming in through second-story windows or the roof (via a helicopter or adjacent building). Lots of broken bones, bruises, sprains, and even a few deaths happen here. But it's the live-fire training that requires constant practice, and the best commandos fire their weapons weekly. If you don't constantly practice these skills, you lose them. Commandos don't get much real action but must always be ready for intense and dangerous situations. Counterterrorism or hostage rescue incidents can occur at any time, and outfits like SEALs, Delta Force, and SAS must be ready to be on their way within hours. At that point, there's no time for weapons practice. You have to be ready all the time. Regular visits to the Kill House are the best way to save your life.

WHERE THE OPERATORS ARE

You don't hear much about American commandos in the news, even with the fighting going on in Afghanistan. You don't hear much about wartime operations at all, because success depends on new and innovative tactics, techniques, and equipment. Eventually the surviving enemy troops get the word out, and new approaches have to be developed. This kind of "technical surprise" is important, because it gives often outnumbered commandos an edge. For the troops who can use it, surprise is a lifesaver.

Even in peacetime, most American commandos spend about half their time outside the country, either training with foreign armed forces, scouting potential operations, or actually doing something that is not likely to get reported. The United States has some eight thousand commando-type troops. The two thousand Rangers operate in large units for raids and reconnaissance and spend most of their time in the United States. Most of the Rangers are young, noncareer troops and spend most of their time training at their U.S. bases. The five thousand Special Forces are career soldiers who spend a lot of their time studying foreign languages, cultures, and politics. In addition, they study military specialties (weapons, explosives, engineering, medicine) and what we would consider commando operations. Special Forces troops spend about half their time overseas, either on training missions to assist foreign armies or on reconnaissance operations. Some of the snooping jobs are done in cooperation with the CIA. It's important to remember that Special Forces are a unique form of commando who rely more on negotiating than fighting, but can shoot it out with the best of them if need be.

The Navy has most of the top-line commandos (about seven hundred SEALs, versus some three hundred Army Delta Force) as well as a number of support units (with various types of small boats for getting SEALs ashore from submarines or surface ships). Many SEALs operate out of half a dozen overseas bases. In addition, many SEALs are on warships and submarines, either for missions or training.

All this traveling is expensive, and puts a strain on the operators and their families. Few men spend an entire twenty-year career in an active duty commando unit. The stress catches up with you after a few years. Many commandos move on to support or training units for commandos, or some related part of their service. One reason there are two Special Forces groups in the reserves is because many Special Forces troopers who leave the Army—to save their marriages, make more money, or both—like to keep a hand in the job they worked so hard to get. Increasingly, commandos are sought by civilian firms for security or intelligence work. This is causing an increasing number of them to leave before they are eligible for retirement (after twenty years' service).

PERFECT SOLDIERS OF THE TWENTY-FIRST CENTURY

The twenty-first century is going to see a lot more carefully selected, intensively trained, and lavishly equipped troops. While Perfect Soldiers aren't cheap, they are effective, and they have been a long time coming. Industrialized countries have, over the last century, invested more and more money and technology in individual soldiers. This was done because the money was there, and because most of these nations were democracies—which encouraged generals to find ways to reduce casualties. Killing off too many voters needlessly in battle just doesn't work in a democracy.

It's taken most of the last century to figure out just what a Perfect Soldier is, and now everyone believes. This includes those who really can't afford too many Perfect Soldiers. Large but relatively poor nations such as China and India (which together contain 35 percent of the planet's population) are scraping together the resources to create some units of Perfect Soldiers. Not just commandos, but also elite Air Force, Navy, and information warfare units. They realize that without some Perfect Soldiers, their larger units full of average soldiers will just get chopped to bits.

The Perfect Soldiers are not just another type of well-equipped and -trained supersoldier. We have seen those before, particularly the armored horsemen who dominated warfare for two thousand years. Technology also makes it possible for the Perfect Soldier to train more realistically and more often. This provides an edge Perfect Soldiers of the past rarely had. Simulation technology used in computer games has long been adopted for military training. This is not only for practicing, but also for planning. Experienced soldiers expect things to go wrong once the shooting starts. But things go less wrong for the side that has spent some time working out the details of the mission on a combat simulator. The U.S. Air Force was the first to use this approach two decades ago. The Navy then adopted it for warships, and eventually the Army and commandos did as well. Smart training, smart weapons, smarter warriors, and smaller numbers of troops are the future. This means combat robots as well, which are actually not all that bright, but are useful if deployed by very capable troops.

The twentieth century was noted for mass armies composed of average people. Everyone who was physically capable of serving was conscripted. That has changed over the last few decades. Now the trend is toward smaller armies of very bright volunteers. The conventional wisdom has a hard time keeping up with this. It will be a few more years before journalists stop being startled at how bright and articulate the troops are. But as any recruiting sergeant will tell you, he can't meet his quota with just average people. The armed forces increasingly want only very bright, physically fit, and openly enthusiastic recruits. That's the raw material for the Perfect Soldiers who will dominate twenty-first-century battlefields.

INDEX